F[illegible] NO
MORE

To Anne

Acknowledgement

The author's accounts of the deck accident aboard *HMS Centaur* in Chapter 6 and the collision between the Gannet and the Vulcan in Chapter 13 were previously published in *Fly Navy* by Charles Manning. Airlife wish to thank the publishers of that book, Pen and Sword, for permission to include the works here.

Foreword

The book covers learning to fly and fight an aircraft, squadron operations in the Fleet Air Arm and seven years as a Naval Test Pilot. I established a new World Airspeed Record from New York to London during the Daily Mail Trans-Atlantic Air Race of 1969 when I was the Commanding Officer of 892 Squadron operating the Phantom FG1.

I joined the RN on an eight-year commission as an aviation cadet in February 1952, and eventually left the RN in February 1972 as a result of the defence cuts of the late 1960s.

During that twenty-year period I flew some fifty types of fixed-wing aircraft and helicopters in the UK and USA. I flew all the RN fixed-wing aircraft, and most of the aircraft in the RAF and USN inventories. My personal flight envelope extends to 2.1 Mach number and 75,000 feet.

Why call the book 'Fly No More'? Well, the range and quantity of aircraft in the present Fleet Air Arm no longer exists, nor do the ships from which they were operated. The book relates to the days of fixed-wing, multi-role aircraft carriers. The current 'aircraft carriers' in the RN were not intended to replace the concept of the multi-role aircraft carrier, but rather to retain an aviation 'element' in the form of the Sea Harrier and the helicopter.

The balance of the book relates to how important were the events. At times weeks went by without anything specific happening. At other times memories are dominated by one particular flight, series of flights, or personal incidents in my life.

I have written the book to give an impression of life and aviation events with which I was connected during the post-WW2 period of the early fifties to the late sixties. It is a book about flying and you will enjoy it more if you are conversant with flying.

Storrington, West Sussex

Contents

Chapter 1

Naval Training

February to November 1952

On 6 February 1952, the first day of the reign of Queen Elizabeth II, I joined the Royal Navy as an aviation cadet. Eighteen years old and fresh out of grammar school, I was to be trained as a pilot. I had more or less joined the RN by accident. Only six months previously I had managed to fail the interview at the Royal Naval College, Dartmouth, to become a career engineer officer. With the letter from 'Their Lordships of the Admiralty' to inform me of my failure came one of the earliest mail shots of the era. Enclosed with the letter was a coloured brochure inviting me to become a 'Naval Aviator', as either a Pilot or an Observer. Luckily I had managed to pass all the tests and the interview to become a pilot.

My failure to join the RN as an engineer officer didn't hit me particularly hard. To be honest, I didn't really want to become a marine engineer, much preferring the idea of becoming a pilot flying off of aircraft carriers.

I had grown up as an aviation enthusiast, and during WW2 I had been very much involved on the receiving end of the Luftwaffe's 'Blitz' on Portsmouth. As a result of the Blitz the family moved to Bognor Regis in 1942 to get out of harm's way. Aircraft recognition in boys of my age became a way of life. We knew every type and model of aircraft. All our own and all of the Germans'.

I had been sent my cadet's uniform, with instructions to join HMS *Indefatigable*, an aircraft carrier that had been converted to a training ship, along with the train times and a service travel warrant to enable me to get to Plymouth. I was directed to wear the uniform on the day of joining.

On 6 February I dressed in my uniform, feeling somewhat embarrassed. I felt I was sticking out like a sore thumb. Once I got to Paddington I could see all the other sore thumbs on their way to join the RN. In my compartment were identical twins Brian and

Alan Giffin and Derek Evans. There were a few others as well, but the four of us hit it off straight away, since it turned out that we had all tried for Dartmouth entry at the same time and we had all failed. It was dark on our arrival at Plymouth. We were met off the train by Chief Petty Officer Taylor, our course CPO. We were bundled into a service bus, having heaved our baggage into an attendant truck, and driven down to a landing stage on the shoreline. A motor cutter belonging to HMS *Indefatigable* was waiting for us. We unloaded the baggage into the cutter, boarded and set off for the ship anchored in Plymouth Sound. The ship towered above us as we pulled alongside one of the accommodation ladders. We leapt from cutter to ladder, made our way to the top and were then led through what seemed a myriad of doors, ladders and passageways to the gunroom mess.

The gunroom is the traditional name given to accommodation provided for junior non-commissioned officers in a capital ship. In HMS *Indefatigable* the public area consisted of a room about 50 by 30 feet. The gunroom was to be home for the 20 or so members of '31 Pilots' Course' for the next six months of our basic naval training. We were quite a mixed bunch and not all straight out of school. The age limits for the aircrew courses were 17 to 24 years of age, so our backgrounds were very varied. Two of the older members had held commissions in the Army during their recent national service.

The first thing that happened after our arrival was the issue of our immediate clothing requirements – bedding, pyjamas, hammocks and working dress (Number 8s in naval parlance) – followed by an evening meal. During this process there was a gentle shudder through the ship as we weighed anchor and set sail for Gibraltar. I have always thought that few recruits to the RN have joined a ship straight from civilian life and set sail for foreign parts about an hour later.

No. 31 Pilots' Flying Course, February 1952 *(Crown copyright)*

HMS *Indefatigable*, 1952
(Crown copyright)

We were instructed on how to set up and sling a hammock, issued with keys to our individual storage lockers and wished 'good night'. 'Lights out' was at 10 p.m. – sorry, 22:00. By then we had slung our hammocks from bars across the deck head (ceiling) in ranks throughout the Gunroom.

'Wakey, wakey' was at six in the morning. Chief Taylor, or one of his henchmen, arrived with shouts of 'show a leg' and other less refined expressions. For those oblivious to noise a sharp rap with a hammock baton on the backside was more effective. We washed, dressed in our newly issued working uniforms and fell in to be allocated with our cleaning station. This was to become the daily routine on the training carrier. Parts of the deck in the Gunroom and passageways, the washrooms and the heads (toilets) were allocated to teams of cadets to clean. This normally took an hour or so, after which we cleaned ourselves up and had breakfast.

By the time we arrived in Gibraltar we had just about established a domestic routine and we were getting used to naval terminology. The entry into Gibraltar harbour was timed for 08:00. Unlike the Army and the RAF the RN never added the word 'hours' when expressing time. So our harbour entry was to be at 'O-eight hundred'. The ship tied up on the South Mole.

To me, Gibraltar was a magical place in those days. Having only ever known the austerity of the war and post-war period in the UK, I found the shops in Gibraltar Main Street a revelation. Luxury goods

Cadet Brian Davies on board HMS *Indefatigable* in 1952

abounded everywhere. I bought the odd gift to take home, but none of us was very well off at the time. Cadet's pay ran to 10 shillings (50p) one week, £1 the next. Mind you, with all the accommodation and food provided, the money didn't seem bad. If you wanted a steak dinner it would only set you back 20p in one of the local restaurants. Yes, in 1952 Gibraltar was some place and would always be a favourite port of call over the years to come. But in 1952 its entire *raison d'être* was as an outpost of the British Empire to support the fleet, the RAF and the Army garrisons.

After a few days the ship returned to the UK to anchor in Portland Harbour. By now we had established that the ship was crammed full of naval personnel under training: national service, regular navy and 'Upper Yardmen'. These latter consisted of national servicemen who were currently ratings but would be commissioned as officers on completion of their basic training. There were also 'Senior Rating Upper Yardmen'. These were young CPOs and POs, under the age of 24, who had been selected for aircrew duties. They would be commissioned on completion of their six months' training. Not only was the 'Indefat' full of trainees, but HMS *Implacable*, 'Implac', a sister ship of 'Indefat', anchored alongside us shortly after our arrival with a similar complement. I might mention here that there was a senior course of aircrew cadets three months ahead of us sharing the gunroom. They were of a similar number to our course but were destined to become observers.

The six months we were to do in 'Indefat' was intended as basic naval training. The days were long and we were kept on the go all the time. As summer approached we learned that 'Indefat' and 'Implac' would set off on a cruise. We were to spend a month away from Portland visiting Invergordon in Scotland – very briefly, thank goodness, because there was not much there except for a temperance hotel and lots of sheep. Then to cross the North Sea to Denmark where 'Implac' would visit Copenhagen and 'Indefat' Aarhus on the eastern coast of Jutland, famous at the time for trotting races and topless bathing. On our return to Portland we sat our final examinations and I think all passed.

It was at this time I could have elected to go to the USA to do my flying training. We were asked to volunteer if we wanted to go, but to be aware that if the USN trained us it would take an extra three or four months to get our wings. Like the keen, budding aviator I was I decided to opt for the flying training in UK since I would qualify earlier. What a fool!

The training in England would take the form of a pre-flight training course at HMS *Siskin*, a shore establishment just outside

Lee-on-Solent in Hampshire, followed by nine months' flying training to wings standard with the RAF. A little explanation might be appropriate at this time.

Firstly, all RN shore establishments are geographical locations and ships. For instance RNAS, which stands for Royal Naval Air Station, Lee-on-Solent, was the headquarters of Naval Aviation in 1952. It was an airfield on the shore of the Solent in Hampshire. But it was also known as HMS *Daedalus*, a shore establishment with its own management structure and complement of personnel. Nearby was HMS *Siskin*, which had a small grass airfield. In 1952 it was a training establishment. Secondly, RN pilots had to do their basic training at an RAF flying training school (FTS). The FTS that the RAF had allocated was 22 FTS, RAF Syerston, just south of Newark-on-Trent in Nottinghamshire.

At the end of July 1952 we left 'Indefat' for good and I took a spot of leave before joining HMS *Siskin*. Back in Bognor I met up with all my old friends. One of my contemporaries, who had joined the Dartmouth Naval College as a cadet some six months before I joined the RN, was also home on leave. Harry Bond was in the permanent career Naval Officer stream, but was interested in becoming a pilot in the future.

Another explanation would be appropriate here. Harry was on the General List, which meant he was a full career officer. He would complete extensive naval training in all aspects of the Service and would be promoted through the ranks of Midshipman, Sub-Lieutenant and Lieutenant over a period of four years or so. He would serve as a seaman officer in ships at sea and also complete courses in the various specialities available to him. Once fully qualified as a seaman officer, he would sub-specialise in one particular aspect of the Navy, such as Gunnery, Communications, Submarines, Anti-Submarine Warfare or Aviation, as a pilot or observer. But he would be about 24 years old before he started his flying training.

I, on the other hand, had joined the RN on an eight-year short-service commission as direct entry aircrew, would spend my time in Aviation alone, but complete my service at the age of 26 after eight years. The reason that these short-service commissions were being offered was the aircrew build-up for the Korean War.

Anyway, Harry had arranged a visit to RNAS Ford, a naval air station a few miles from Bognor, to obtain some air experience. Why didn't I come with him and try to get a flight as well? We turned up on the appointed day and were allocated to a trials squadron that operated a number of different aircraft types. Our pilot for the day was to be a commissioned pilot (yet another aircrew category), John Nielson, who would take us up in a Fairey Firefly Mk 6 anti-submarine aircraft. This was a single engined aircraft that normally operated with a crew of pilot and observer. We would be flying in the observer's cockpit.

John briefed us on the flight and kitted us out with some flying clothing, a leather helmet and an oxygen mask. The oxygen mask was not required to use oxygen, but was fitted with a microphone that enabled us to talk to John over the intercom.

Since Harry had arranged all this he would be the first to have a go. The flights would take about half an hour each, and would be the very first time airborne for both of us. I watched as Harry was strapped into the rear observer's cockpit and briefed on what to do by John, who then climbed into the pilot's cockpit and fired the Rolls-Royce Griffon engine into life with a crackling roar and a cloud of blue smoke. The wheel chocks were waved away and with a burst of power the Firefly started its taxi out to the end of the westerly runway and lined up. I sat on the grass outside the squadron crew room and watched as the Firefly roared down the runway, lifted into the air and retracted the undercarriage. It climbed out and disappeared to the west.

For the next half-hour I just wandered around the dispersal and looked in various aircraft. One was a Sea Vampire F-20, a navalised version of the small single-seat twin-boomed jet fighter made by de Havilland, mainly for the RAF. This model had been produced for the RN as a trials aircraft with a hook on the rear central fuselage to enable it to land on a carrier. There were just one or two of them in service with the RN at the time.

The Firefly returned to the airfield and landed. It taxied into the dispersal, the engine remained running and the ground crew

Fairey Firefly Mk 6 *(Crown copyright)*

escorted me out to it. The rear cockpit hatch opened and Harry clambered down the side of the fuselage, took off his helmet and handed it to me.

I climbed into the observer's cockpit, struggling a little through what seemed like a howling gale of smelly fumes streaming back from the engine's exhaust and strapped myself in. I plugged in the radio and intercom lead so that I could hear John and checked that he could hear me. We started the taxi out to the take-off point.

The observer's cockpit in the Firefly gave an excellent view on either side of the aircraft, but didn't stand proud of the fuselage, so you couldn't see ahead or to the rear. I watched the ground go by on either side of the aircraft as we snaked our way out to the end of the runway. We lined up, John let off the brakes and slowly opened up the engine to a deafening roar on the take-off run. I felt the acceleration hitting me in the back and then we were airborne. Weather-wise it was not the best of days. It was pretty hazy and we were soon climbing through a broken cloud layer. I was not really aware of flying since the view outside the aircraft was so restricted and I couldn't see the ground. What I was aware of was the smell. The fumes from the engine pervaded the cockpit. So there I was, sitting in the back of this vibrating, stinking machine without a lot to look at.

'I'm afraid the weather isn't good enough for me to show you some aerobatics', I heard John say from the front.

'What a shame!' I said thankfully from the back. I was beginning to feel ill. We arrived back in the circuit at Ford, turned onto final approach and landed. We taxied into the dispersal, stopped and John shut the engine down. I was left with the hum of the intercom. in my earphones until the electrics were switched off – then absolute silence. The ground crew opened the canopy and in rushed the freshest of fresh air. I took a number of deep, deep breaths, climbed down from the cockpit feeling better with every step, but found my legs shaking a little as I stood on terra firma.

We talked about our flights on the drive back to Bognor, and Harry agreed with me that it hadn't been quite what we'd expected. Probably the lack of view, the smell and the lack of involvement hadn't helped. Anyway, we decided that flying was probably going to be all right, but I was glad I was to be a pilot and not an observer.

The summer leave came to an end and I joined HMS *Siskin* for the two months' pre-flight training course. On completion of our six months' basic naval training in 'Indefat', we had all been promoted. Those of us below the age of 21 became Midshipmen, the rest Acting Sub-Lieutenants. We also joined up with the aviation cadets who had been on 'Implac' and the Upper Yardmen and

RNVR aviation national service officers from both training carriers. There were to be 31 of us on No. 31 Pilots' Flying Training Course. Although we were now land based, the terminology in the RN assumed we were still at sea. Anything that had a connotation relating to a ship retained it. Toilets were still heads, we still referred to bulkheads and decks instead of walls and floors, if you left the environs of the establishment you were going ashore and if there was a bus provided by the RN to take you ashore it was called a liberty boat.

The course was to take two months to prepare us for flying. The subjects we took were Navigation, Aerodynamics, Meteorology and Engines. We also had the odd lecture on the history of the Fleet Air Arm and how it was organised.

The history lessons were quite interesting. The Royal Flying Corps (RFC) was formed in 1912 and consisted of two Wings, the Army Wing and the Naval Wing. In fact the two ranks of Wing Commander and Flight Lieutenant were both originally RFC Naval Wing ranks. When the RAF was formed in 1918 it took over the RFC, that now consisted of the Army Wing only, and the Royal Naval Air Service (RNAS) that had been formed in 1914. At the time the RNAS was the largest air force in the world. The inter-war years produced a peculiar situation. The RN was funded and was responsible for producing aircraft carriers, but the responsibility for putting aircraft on those carriers was the RAF's. Thus the Fleet Air Arm was the term used by the RAF to denote its branch of aviation associated with the RN. However, since the RAF had been formed from an amalgamation of the RFC and the RNAS, Fleet Air Arm pilots were largely ex-RNAS to begin with, and subsequently the majority of pilots were selected from RN personnel. These pilots must have been enthusiastic aviators since, as a career move, becoming a pilot in the RN meant that they were unlikely to be promoted to high rank. In those days and for some time afterwards the RN had a battleship mentality. The RN envisaged using aircraft for patrol, gunnery spotting and providing information from on high.

From a naval viewpoint the use of the aircraft as an offensive weapon would largely be left to the USN to develop between the wars. During the inter-war years the aircraft provided for the RN were few and not of the best. The RN had fought for control of its own aviation branch since the formation of the RAF and had been successful just before the outbreak of WW2. So the FAA went to war with few aircraft and pilots and even fewer maintenance personnel, since the RAF withdrew all of its personnel from the RN. During WW2 it was still known as the Fleet Air Arm, but after the war 'Their

Lordships' decided to use the term 'Naval Aviation'. As a matter of interest, it was officially to be re-named the Fleet Air Arm in the early 1960s, since Naval Aviation seemed such a general term, and by now most people identified the name Fleet Air Arm with the RN.

The navigation lectures covered the use of the Dalton computer. The computer itself bears little relation to a modern-day computer. It consists of a circular slide rule calibrated in functions required for operating an aircraft, weight and capacity conversions and of course the normal arithmetic scales. Additionally it has a geometric screen on which is superimposed a compass rose on which you use the functions calculated from the circular slide rule to geometrically obtain your compass heading to steer and the speed over the ground. If you already fly you will know how it works. If you don't fly it would take another book to explain it all. Suffice it to say that if you fly by using just the map and no other means of navigation, you can't get from A to B without preplanning the flight on a Dalton computer.

We completed the course at the end of October 1952 and went off for a long weekend before joining RAF Syerston for our flying training to 'wings' standard.

Chapter 2

Learning to Fly

November 1952 to July 1953

I arrived at RAF Syerston on 4 November 1952. Service transport was at Newark railway station to meet us and drive us straight out to the air station The bus dropped us off at our own officers' mess and we checked in with the hall porter. This time we were allocated single rooms (which we still called cabins), and during the evening settled ourselves in, reading the briefings provided on the routine we would be working and on the air station and its surrounds. I remember that the introduction to all this paperwork started by telling us that 'Within two miles of the centre of Newark are 69 pubs . . .' and that we were not expected to visit all of them every night. We were to commence our flying training with No. 1 Squadron on the Percival Prentice for three months, and those that passed this *ab initio* stage would then progress to No. 3 Squadron, operating the North American Harvard 2B for six months. Incidentally, No. 2 Squadron also operated the Harvard 2B, but the course ahead of us, who had just finished their time in No. 1 Squadron, were about to start flying with No. 2 Squadron.

Percival Prentice *(Crown copyright)*

Learning To Fly

Our introduction to flying started the very next day. Our course officer was a Lieutenant 'Frosty' Winterbottom RN, a QFI with No. 1 Squadron. He briefed us as to what to expect over the next three months. We were to be split into two groups and would fly in the morning and attend ground school in the afternoon one day, and the next day have ground school in the morning and fly in the afternoon.

My group was scheduled to fly the next morning. We had been told to attend met. briefing at the control tower before continuing on to the squadron crew room. Met. briefing was the first thing to happen every flying day in the Services. It was rather like having morning assembly at school. Something that must be done within the organisation or else things didn't seem right. Apart from that, it was a good idea to know what the weather forecast was anyway. Then we all set off for the squadron crew room with some excitement.

The first flight was to be very short. Just a circuit and landing, as far as I remember. After introduction to our individual instructors and donning our new flying gear, we were led out to the aircraft. Flight Lieutenant Johnny Walker was my permanent instructor. Nearly all military training aircraft until the introduction of the Prentice had tandem cockpit layouts. The Percival Prentice was one of the first trainers to have side-by-side seating arrangements so that the instructor could visually supervise the pupil. The Prentice was not the most beautiful aircraft in the world. It had a short narrow engine cowling housing the ubiquitous Gypsy Queen engine at the front, with the fuselage rapidly expanding to a large 'greenhouse' of a cockpit canopy, followed by a thick rear fuselage and large fin and rudder. The undercarriage layout was conventional – an expression used to indicate that the main wheels were mounted forward under the wing, with a tail-wheel mounted under the rear fuselage. Nowadays, this layout is unusual in that most aircraft have main wheels located in the same place, but the centre of gravity is arranged to accommodate a nose-wheel configuration. Apart from improving the forward view, this latter layout makes the aircraft directionally stable on the ground. With the conventional layout the centre of gravity is behind the main wheels and makes the forward view more restricted and the aircraft directionally unstable on the ground. In the Prentice the undercarriage was fixed and could not be retracted.

We were all issued with Pilot's Notes. This was a slim paperback booklet, designed to fit nicely in the pocket of the flying overalls, which told us all we needed to know about the Prentice. At the back was a pull-out picture of the cockpit surrounded by little name boxes with arrows pointing to various features and controls to indicate what was what. We students went and sat in the cockpit to sort out as well as we could what it all meant. Over the next two weeks I was to fly eight hours of dual instruction before going solo.

It would be easy to go into great depths on what it was like for me to learn to fly, but since this book will probably be read by people who themselves fly or know how to, I shall restrict myself to the milestones and problems I remember, some of which I thought might kill me at the time.

The first eight hours of flying instruction concentrated on stall recovery, circuit and forced landing training. All of our flying was visual below cloud in these first few hours, and it became second nature to scan the ground continuously and always have a suitable forced landing field in mind. Stall recovery practice was essential since the approach speed for the landing circuit required you to fly the aircraft slowly near the stalling speed, and there was always the possibility that you might fly that little bit too slowly, lose control and end up hitting the ground unintentionally! Stalling practice was always conducted at a safe height and never below the circuit height of 1,000 feet above the ground.

Having ensured that you were proficient in these techniques, your instructor launched you on your first solo. Mine came after one or two circuits at a small satellite airfield at Tollerton near Nottingham. Since so many of us were at the same phase, Syerston circuit would have been too full of aircraft and we all used satellite airfields at which to practise circuits and bumps. Suddenly my instructor said 'We'll make this a full stop landing', and as we came to a stop, he wished me luck on my first solo, unstrapped and got out. It was a lovely day and I still remember flying that circuit, making sure I got everything right. There is a saying that the first solo landing is one of your best. Well, mine wasn't to begin with, but I got it sorted out on the second bounce. I picked up Johnny and we flew back to Syerston.

Flying expanded from then on into aerobatics, spinning, navigation, instrument flying and formation flying.

Meanwhile, during the ground school part of the course we learnt more about aerodynamics, engines, meteorology, navigation and the Rules of the Air.

Aerobatics proved very interesting, although the Prentice was not the most agile of aircraft. It did most things at 90 knots in level flight and it took a power dive to get it up to 150. Coping with the 'g', which actually didn't much exceed four, proved the initial learning curve. I was to learn that the best way to combat 'g' was to tense your stomach muscles. Just holding your breath and straining was the best way to prevent the blood rushing from the brain and staying conscious. I expect that is why most fighter pilots are constipated!

Spinning was probably the most disconcerting manoeuvre. The first one or two turns are called the incipient spin. At this stage if you push the stick forward and apply opposite rudder deflection to the spin rotation, the nose will drop, the rotation of the aircraft will stop immediately and the aircraft ends up in a dive above the stalling speed from which you recover. Beyond these initial turns the spin becomes established and the recovery is not quite so straightforward. However, the adrenaline starts to pump at this point. The aircraft is now in an 'auto-rotation' stage of flight. The airflow over the majority of the wing and fuselage is not smooth and the controls do not now have an immediate effect. It can take up to two or three turns of the spin to stop the rotation, having applied the forward stick and opposite rudder. It is then very important for you to centralise the rudder control as soon as the rotation stops, since the direction of rotation could reverse and you will find yourself still in a spin, but in the opposite direction!

Anyway, all these techniques had to be mastered fairly quickly to be able to fly the aircraft with some degree of competence and safety. Some of the students didn't make the grade and were taken off the course in the first couple of weeks.

Navigation was the beginning of the applied flying stage, having mastered the basic handling of the aircraft, which would become second nature. The course progressed into using the aircraft for a purpose, and the first discipline to master was the ability to get from A to B. There was no navigation equipment in the Prentice other than a compass, and your ability to know exactly where you were relied entirely on map reading. As a last resort you could call certain air stations on the radio for them to give you a bearing using the CRDF (Cathode Ray Direction Finding) equipment, which would at least steer you to an airfield where you could land, but this would be the ultimate loss of face. I had become used to flying in the local exercise area, which I knew like the back of my hand, but I had not flown much outside the environs of the airfield prior to flying the navigation exercises.

The first navigation exercise was an out and back flown with an instructor. It was quite an adventure. The instructor didn't say anything unless you asked him a question or it became apparent that you were lost. The planning for the flight had been done using the Dalton computer, but you soon found out that you probably weren't going in the right direction or at the planned speed. Forecasts of wind speed and direction weren't that good in 1952, and with an aircraft that cruised at 80 knots, five knots of windspeed and a 20 degree difference in wind direction introduced a considerable error. The dual navigation exercises were planned to cover triangular courses, and finally a land away, where the triangular courses were aimed to include another training airfield at which we would land.

However, the flight that I distinctly remember was my first solo out and back. November in Nottinghamshire can be pretty bleak, but on the morning of my first solo navigation exercise it was bright and clear with a forecast of isolated snow showers developing during the day. I took off in the late morning. My turning point was a small town called Thorne some way to the north of Syerston. I was flying at 3,000 feet, the correct quadrantal height for the heading I was steering. I kept a tight check on where I was for the first six minutes or so. All seemed well as I picked up the town of East Retford on time and on track. The visibility was excellent, but the weather ahead looked a bit black – literally. At the boundary of my view ahead was a wall of black cloud stretching upwards for what seemed for ever. I decided it would be prudent to turn back to Syerston.

Nowadays in the aviation profession, both civil and military, you are very conscious of flight safety, but in those days in the military, flight safety didn't have such a high profile. The best flight safety programme around at the time, which was also used by the RN and RAF, was provided by the United States Navy, which had in service more aircraft than the RN and RAF combined – and most certainly still does at the present day. This programme related to a fictitious cartoon character called Dilbert, typifying the gung-ho but slightly stupid USN trainee pilot, who would conquer all to win through to achieve the objects set out by the training programme. If he was going to set off on a cross-country navigation exercise, he was going to get there through hell and high water – and probably did. Just about all of the Dilbert situations resulted in his being scared witless during the process without actually being killed. The idea appeared to be to retain the gung-ho attitude but to temper it with prudence when faced with an adverse situation.

I must admit that when I appeared to be approaching a situation that could involve exploring an area of aviation that I had yet to learn about, I was an absolute chicken. Since I had yet to fly in cloud using the flight instruments, I decided to turn around and fly back to Syerston. I turned round, and even climbed to my correct quadrantal height of 4,000 feet, but it became apparent that an even blacker cloud had moved in behind me and cut off my retreat. What to do? Well, I knew the terrain was low enough for me to descend safely to 2,000 feet, and I would feel a little better being closer to the ground. There was a distinct feeling of what is called 'get homeitis'. I hadn't been told what to do in this situation, so the only possible course of action was to try to get back to Syerston.

I ploughed into the bottom of the cloud and tried to keep visual with the ground. The two became incompatible. Looking out through the windscreen, the only thing I could see were myriads of snowflakes hurtling towards me and nothing else – just a grey background of cloud and snow. I decided there was no option but to try and fly the aircraft using the flight instruments. I had obviously used the flight instruments when flying the aircraft until now. The one difference was that until now I had been able to have a quick check on where the horizon was to verify that the instruments more or less represented the attitude of the aircraft. Flying an aircraft in cloud was not the easiest thing to do. What your backside and natural balancing systems told you of the aircraft's attitude did not in general tie up with what the instruments were telling you. You became convinced the aircraft was leaning over to one side when the flight instruments were telling you it wasn't. The conflict between what you saw and what you felt became overpowering and would become one of the reactions I would learn to ignore. The reaction was to rely on what you felt and not what the instruments were telling you. If you followed your natural instincts you still didn't feel as if the aircraft was flying correctly, and the flight instruments were definitely telling you that it wasn't. My saviour was that I suddenly broke out into clear weather and I was in a descending right turn as the instruments had told me!

The problem now was that the ground looked completely different. There was a brilliant white covering of snow that just about obliterated all the normal navigation features I had become used to identifying. Main towns stood out well enough but roads and railway lines seemed to have disappeared. I was lucky that I came across Newark and the river Trent, followed the river towards Nottingham and identified three power station cooling towers that were just across the river from the airfield. I located the airfield, but the triangle of the three runways was obliterated by snow. I made a low pass and located the grass strip relative to the airfield buildings. On final approach I picked up the marker boards delineating the grass strip, checked the rate of descent as I approached what seemed to be the correct height (the snow had made the judgement of height near impossible), started my final flare and eventually made a very smooth landing. The snow slowed me very quickly, and with a great deal of engine power I was able to make my way back to the dispersal. I was very grateful to be back on terra firma.

Night flying was quite interesting in that you couldn't see much of what was going on, and formation flying required you to ignore your own space and fly the aircraft purely relative to the leader on whom you were formating.

The next memorable milestone was the final handling check on completion of the *ab initio* flying on the Prentice. This was the flight where, having shown that you could basically navigate, fly on instruments and formate in safety, the squadron commanding officer took you up and allowed you to demonstrate your skills. I had not flown with him before, and although a little nervous of the occasion, I felt confident I would pass.

The flight went well. I can't say that the CO had any sort of reputation for being other than normal. He had seemed a quiet sort to me. However, after completion of all the facets of the test he took control. Whether he had been a little frustrated that day, or whether he just wanted to show off I don't know, but under the guise of 'I don't ever want to see you doing this sort of thing' he frightened me, as we say in the aviation world, fartless! We beat the hell out of the local countryside and broke every rule in the book. On the way back to base I assured him that I had never flown that way before, nor with his demonstration would I contemplate it in the future.

One thing I had learnt during the initial flying course was that you really had no idea how you were doing. There was no way to compare yourself with your peers. All instruction was on a one-to-one basis, and the only standard of flying you were aware of was your instructor's. However, the social life almost completely revolved around the bar in the mess. All the conversation was about flying, and a sort of pecking order of flying ability had been established, based mainly on the daredevil nature of the stories told. Bravado seemed to be a prerequisite for those who had established themselves at the top of the list, and you never admitted to being chicken. At that time I was a quiet lad, didn't drink to any great extent and so did not feature too high on the list, since the ability to hold your beer and be voluble was a prime necessity. It was something of a shock to be told by my instructor at the end of the Prentice course that I was considered to be a well-above-average pilot.

The second phase of the course was to move on to the Harvard. To all of us it was the 'hot ship'. It looked more like a military aircraft than the Prentice, and could be mistaken for a fighter. The Harvard's main improvements over the Prentice were a superior performance and the single seat environment. It was harder to fly, in that it was less stable, and the forward visibility from the cockpit

North American Harvard 2B *(Crown copyright)*

was very much reduced because of the larger engine cowling. It had a powerful enough engine to produce directional control problems as soon as you increased power for the take-off run. A combination of this and the undercarriage geometry also required a high degree of concentration to keep the aircraft straight after landing. To assist in the control of the aircraft under these conditions the tail-wheel could be locked in the fore-and-aft position.

The crew room in our new squadron's office block had an excellent view of the main runway, and one of our early entertainments was to watch the take-offs and landings of our contemporaries. Whatever reputation had been established at the bar was modified by the ability to perform well in full view of the crew room pundits.

I won't go into any detail about the advanced course in the Harvard. It amounted to more of the same experienced on the Prentice, but in greater depth and for six months instead of three.

Personally it was noteworthy for three flights. The first was when practising solo aerobatics. I had been doing a number of different manoeuvres before starting on the slow rolls. The first slow roll was most encouraging. I maintained the heading and height throughout the roll, but as the wings approached the horizontal and I started to ease off the aileron control, I found it stuck over to the right. I gave it a bit of a heave, but to no effect and the aircraft started into a second, unplanned, slow roll followed by a third. I got two hands on the stick and gave it a heave to the left and nearly got the stick back in the middle. But I still had a fair amount of rudder on to keep the aircraft straight. I set course for the airfield and called the airfield ATC to tell them of the problem. No advice was given. They cleared the circuit whilst I made my approach and landing. This time I came in at a higher than normal speed without using the flaps. I managed to get the aircraft safely on the ground. I taxied in and got out with some relief. The subsequent inspection revealed that a spanner had been left in one of the wings after maintenance and had jammed in the aileron control run.

The second instance occurred in the airfield circuit whilst practising circuits and landings. Looking into the engine cowling in front of the windscreen, I could see flames around the top of the engine. I throttled back, telling ATC that I had a problem and was landing immediately. By the time I was on final approach the engine seemed well and truly alight. I landed, ran the aircraft off the runway onto the grass, shut down the engine and hopped out. This time a fuel lead had partially fractured and had sprayed the engine with aviation gasoline, which had ignited.

The third flight was rather strange in a way. If it was intended to practise instrument flying, the student flew in the rear cockpit 'under the hood' (a pull-over hood that prevented you seeing out and cheating), with the instructor in the front cockpit acting as safety pilot. However, the instructor's wife was in the local hospital having a baby, and he decided to do a bit of pacing up and down in the air over the hospital. The planned instrument practice was obviously abandoned at this stage. Half way through the pacing he decided we would do something else. By this time I had removed the hood. 'Let's see how high this thing will go, Brian', he said, and we set up climb power and airspeed.

Under normal conditions you didn't take the Harvard much above 8,000 feet. Ten thousand feet was the normal limit, since flights above this height required oxygen, with which the Harvard was not equipped. Well, in those days the instructor knew best. Although I was a little apprehensive, if he said we were going to climb, we were going to climb. It was a nice sunny day, the visibility was good and it would be interesting to view the earth from a higher altitude than normal. I was flying the aircraft from the rear cockpit and enjoying the view as we climbed through 15,000 feet. Up front the instructor was breathing rather deeply and had leaned forward with his arms draped over the front cockpit coaming. It didn't seem to concern me at all and it was only when he suggested we go down that I closed the throttle and started to glide down towards the airfield. I remember the altimeter indicating 17,000 feet at one stage on the way down. I started to feel a little sick, but it soon passed. What we had done had been incredibly stupid. We would have passed out through lack of oxygen had we stayed at altitude much longer, and from the symptoms were close to doing just that. However, this particular experience was to save my bacon about a year later.

At the end of the Harvard course the top three students were selected to compete for the 22 FTS Aerobatic Trophy. I was one of the three selected, and we were all given a few days to practise a set routine that would demonstrate all the manoeuvres we had learned. The day of the competition dawned fine and clear and the three of us got airborne with instructors in the rear seat acting as safety pilots. They were really there to make sure we didn't overdo it. We all got airborne, cleared the circuit and were called in one at a time. Luckily, I would be the last to perform, so wouldn't have to stand around and watch the other two.

I was called in to do my stuff. The aerobatic routine went very well. I was judged to have given the best performance and won the trophy.

Brian Davies receiving the No. 22 FTS Aerobatic Trophy from Sir 'Roddy' MacGrigor. The OC of Syerston is on the far right *(Crown copyright)*

My first reaction was one of disbelief. There was now a certain amount of celebrating to do, which culminated in the 'Wings' parade on our final day at Syerston. Admiral of the Fleet Sir 'Roddy' MacGrigor presented me with the trophy and all of us with our wings.

Under normal circumstances the next progression was to return to Naval Aviation to train as a fighter pilot, anti-submarine pilot or torpedo bomber pilot. Unless you stated any preference, the course would be proportioned off to these three specialisations based on service requirements and your flying ability. The top guys would go on to fly Seafires (navalised Spitfires) and then convert to the Hawker Sea Fury, the next in line to train on the Firefly in the anti-submarine world and the next to fly the newly introduced Westland Wyvern torpedo bomber. This time they added another option. The top ten pilots were to be given a jet conversion on the Gloster Meteor at RNAS Culdrose, the RN Fighter School in Cornwall. The Meteor Mk 7 was the training version of this aircraft, and after successfully completing the Meteor course we would be given another conversion onto the Supermarine Attacker, the first jet ever to enter operational service in an aircraft carrier in the RN.

Chapter 3

Jet Conversion

September to November 1953

I attended a short course at Seafield Park before travelling down to Culdrose. Seafield Park was a small country house and estate just along the coast from Lee-on-Solent. In 1953 it was the headquarters of the Air Medical section of Naval Aviation.

Those of us who had been selected for jet training had to jump a little hurdle beforehand, since it was necessary to find out if we were physiologically suited to operating at altitudes attained in the jet era.

Meteor Mk 7 *(Crown copyright)*

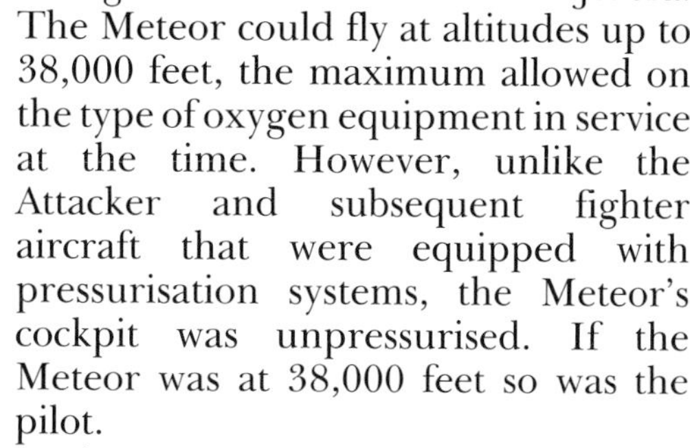

The Meteor could fly at altitudes up to 38,000 feet, the maximum allowed on the type of oxygen equipment in service at the time. However, unlike the Attacker and subsequent fighter aircraft that were equipped with pressurisation systems, the Meteor's cockpit was unpressurised. If the Meteor was at 38,000 feet so was the pilot.

Divers can suffer from the bends if they have been at depth in the sea and are subsequently raised to the surface too quickly. In mild cases they cause pain in the elbow and knee joints and sickness; in more serious cases, death. The equivalent phenomenon in aviation is that we are all at depth in the atmosphere and that the same effect could cause bends or sickness as a result of climbing to high altitude very quickly in an unpressurised aircraft.

We had to find out if we were susceptible to these effects, and to this end were to conduct a series of runs in a decompression tank, which would simulate an aircraft climbing quickly to 38,000 feet. We would remain at this altitude for an hour and then descend again. We would use oxygen equipment similar to that installed in the Meteor. Only one run would be made each day over a three-day period to allow the body to adjust to sea level conditions each time. Those of us who completed the runs without any adverse effects would be given an 'A' Category, those who experienced mild effects a 'B' Category and those who succumbed to anything more severe would receive a 'C' Category. 'A' and 'B' would suffice for jet training. 'C' would mean that you would be limited to flying at low level.

The chamber itself consisted of a cylindrical tank about ten feet in diameter and 20 feet long, made of thick metal with reinforced round glass windows down one side to allow external observers a view inside. At one end was an air lock that allowed rapid exit or entry to the tank if necessary. The whole set-up gave the impression of experimental conditions and that we were going to be the guinea pigs! However, they did help us to relax by suggesting we take plenty of reading material to overcome the boredom.

For the first run we sat in the tank reading magazines whilst the pressure altitude was taken up to 38,000 feet. We were wearing leather flying helmets with masks now attached to the oxygen system and plugged into the intercom. system so that we could talk to each other and to the doctors supervising the run outside the tank. We also had one of the doctors with us in the tank in case of any problem that might arise. No one experienced any adverse effects that would put him into a 'C' category. About half had no adverse effects at all and the rest, including myself, experienced mild pains in the elbows or knees after 30 to 40 minutes. The only real adverse effect related to most of us eating a full breakfast. The rate of passing wind was phenomenal! We were actually breathing an oxygen/air mixture, so became very much aware of what was going on.

The next day the run was the same as the first except that it included a rapid decompression. This was to simulate what we might experience in the future when flying pressurised aircraft, which might have a cockpit pressurisation failure. The tank was taken up to 20,000 feet and then rapidly decompressed to 38,000 feet. This took literally two seconds. The physical symptoms were a sudden fogging of the atmosphere inside the chamber as the water vapour condensed out, popping of the ears and another round of farting! The rest of the run was similar to the first, only this time some of us who had not had the bends the first time did and others, who had, didn't.

The third run was to be the most interesting. To demonstrate to us the effects of no oxygen at 38,000 feet, each of us would in turn take off his oxygen mask, under the supervision of the doctor in the chamber, and carry out a few simple mental tasks. The lectures we had been given during the rest of the working day when not in the tank had covered the fact that if the oxygen system failed at high altitude we would only have a matter of seconds before lapsing into unconsciousness and subsequent death.

The tank was taken up to 38,000 feet and the fun commenced! We had not been told in detail what would happen, except that we would come to no harm. The first victim unstrapped his oxygen mask. Having settled down to breathe normally, the subject was asked simple questions by the doctor and required to write the answers on a sheet of paper. All went well for 30 seconds or so. Then he suddenly seemed to ignore the doctor and switch from writing normally to involuntarily scribbling across the page. When it became apparent that he was getting close to collapse, the doctor reinstated his oxygen supply. Within a few seconds he was back to normal; the doctor still asking questions, he still writing down the answers. At the end of the run he had not realised what had happened, and the only proof that he had acted in any way abnormally was to show him the scribbled notes. It was the same for all of us. When it came to my turn I had absolutely no recollection of the period when I was on my way to oblivion. It had seemed as if the question period was uninterrupted.

It was a little inconclusive what you could learn from the anoxic run as it was called. There was not the euphoric feeling or the sickness I had experienced during the climb in the Harvard. You just 'went'. Perhaps it did show that if you became obviously disconnected from the oxygen system, you didn't have long to sort it out. On the other hand, if you were contemplating suicide, there couldn't be a nicer way to go!

The last part of this short course related to learning about ejector seats. With the introduction of jet engines aircraft shapes had changed. Engines mounted on the wings such as the Meteor didn't require much of a change, but single-engined aircraft, with the engine mounted in the fuselage, did. With the jet aircraft the engine was mounted further back. Because the centre of gravity of the whole aircraft would be further back, the wings would have to be further back as well, with the cockpit much further forward. Thus, unlike aircraft with a single piston engine, the engine would be behind the pilot and not in front. This had the advantage of providing the pilot with a much better forward view. It had the disadvantage of having most of the aircraft structure behind him when it came to baling out. It also placed him in a highly vulnerable position, with no frontal protection when attempting a forced landing.

To overcome this dual problem, Martin Baker, a firm that had produced aircraft on a small scale in the past, had cornered the market in the British military aviation field with their ejection seat. The idea was that the pilot's seat would not now be an integral part of the aircraft, but a separate entity, slid vertically into the cockpit on a set of rails and locked in place. It was integral with a 'gun' that the pilot could fire. This gun would propel the seat up the rails with sufficient velocity to clear the aircraft's structure, and would then separate from the pilot and deploy his parachute for him. If he ejected above 10,000 feet the seat would be stabilised by a drogue until down to 10,000 feet, when a barometric pressure unit would fire, separate the seat and deploy the parachute. The limit for the operation of the seat was a height exceeding 400 feet with a minimum forward speed of 200 knots. Although the Meteor trainer wasn't fitted with ejection seats, since it had two-engine reliability, the Attacker was, and it was considered necessary for us to have instruction on its workings. The culmination of this instruction was a ride up a ground-based ejection seat ramp to make sure we knew the correct techniques to use.

The training ramp consisted of a base with an extended track going up 25 to 30 feet in the air. The seat was mounted at the bottom of this ramp. The idea was that we would strap ourselves into the seat as we would in the aircraft, set our bodies and necks up at the correct angle to prevent damage to the spine, reach up and grasp the ejection seat handle mounted atop the headrest and pull it down firmly over the face. It was at this stage you made doubly sure that your head didn't go forward, or else your misaligned neck could get broken as the seat fired. The handle was attached to a blind, which, by the time you had pulled it down to shoulder level, covered your head and oxygen mask. The last part of the pull-down on the blind fired the seat. Thus in real life, you would be fired out of the cockpit with the blind over your face, firmly grasping the handle, with your elbows tucked in to avoid as much bodily damage as possible from any wind blast. Obviously windblast wasn't going to be a factor when shooting ourselves up the ramp, but the mere fact that we were going to get a firm 'kick up the bum' concentrated the mind wonderfully.

I went first. The ramp was mounted in the open air in a small area surrounded by the classroom huts. It looked quite sinister. The course gathered round as I strapped into the seat. The instructor 'doctor' was on hand with advice. 'Relax, breathe normally, back straight, head back, reach up for the handle and pull it out and down.' The blind blotted out the view as the seat fired. I felt a firm jolt followed by the scream of the ratchet as the seat hurtled up the ramp. The noise of the ratchet stopped, locking as the seat came to a halt. It was suddenly very quiet. Discarding the blind, I found myself some 15 to 20 feet up in the air looking down on the upturned faces of my colleagues. The instructor winched the seat down and it was time for another guinea pig to have a go.

At the end of the short course we set off for RNAS Culdrose, located a couple of miles south-east of the town of Helston in Cornwall. The RN Jet Fighter School was based here. It consisted of 759 Squadron, equipped with the Gloster Meteor Mk 7 Trainer, and 736 Squadron equipped with the Supermarine Attacker FB 2. The three-month jet conversion course with 759 Squadron was called Operational Flying School Part 1 – OFS1 for short – and the three month – Attacker course OFS2. The squadron numbers were significant. Training, trials and non-operational squadrons in the RN were called second-line squadrons and were numbered in the 700s. All operational squadrons that formed part of a carrier's air group at sea were numbered in the 800s.

We joined 759 on 28 August, and I made my first flight in a Meteor Trainer seven days later after some ground instruction, including a swift introduction to the workings of a jet engine.

The first flight in the Meteor was quite an experience. The trainer had a tandem cockpit layout with the student sitting in the front. The cockpit canopy was a long, rigid affair, with small sections of reinforced glass set in a metal framework. With the canopy closed the cockpit felt quite claustrophobic compared to the old Harvard. With the metal framework and small areas of glass in the canopy, the view sideways seemed restricted. The Meteor had a tricycle undercarriage, so the fuselage was parallel to the ground. But, with no engine mounted at the front of the fuselage, the forward view was fantastic.

Freddie Wilcox was my instructor, and he did all the work on the first flight, although as far as I remember I had to start the engines from the front seat. We taxied out to the end of the runway. The very first impression was how everything was so relatively quiet and smooth, and the smell of a piston-engined aircraft was replaced by virtually no smell at all. This was no doubt partly due to breathing an air/oxygen mix through the oxygen mask. The second impression was of the massive acceleration as we opened up the engines to full throttle as we started the take-off. The Meteor seemed to hurl itself down the runway. Freddie lifted the nose way up into the air and we climbed steeply away from the airfield.

The next unbelievable thing was the speed. I had flown around the sky at around the 90 to 130 knot mark until now, but the take-off speed in the Meteor was 130 knots and the airspeed indicator was soon up around the 300 knot mark or more. In fact having climbed above about 2,000 feet, the only way you could tell your speed was from the airspeed indicator.

We climbed up to 20,000 feet and just flew around with me getting used to the response of the flying controls. The view was incredible. On the flight instrument panel was a new gauge that showed how fast the aircraft was going compared with the speed of sound. It was called a Machmeter. Another new feature was the airbrake control, necessary on a jet aircraft because of the lack of drag from the aircraft and the requirement to be able to slow down reasonably quickly from the high speeds achieved. In the Meteor the airbrakes consisted of a set of perforated metal slabs that extended from the top and bottom of each wing inboard of the engine nacelles. They were very effective at high speed, but less so as the speed reduced. You had to make a conscious effort to remember to retract them as you entered the landing circuit. As well as generating high drag, they also destroyed lift and, if left extended to any degree, caused high sink rates in conjunction with landing flap on final approach. In the past, extended speedbrakes had been a major cause of Meteors crashing short of the runway.

On this first flight I flew about three times as fast and three times as high as I had normally flown in the Harvard. At the same time Freddie demonstrated to me that it would become part of life to fly the aircraft at sustained high 'g' levels. Just simply turning a combat aircraft would impose much more 'g' than I had been used to in the past. The first flight ended with a session of circuits and bumps, except that now I was in the advanced world of jet flying they were called 'rollers'.

The major adjustments to flying the Meteor related to the speed at which everything happened and coping with the increased flight envelope. In particular, the final approach speed was 120 knots instead of the 70–80 knots of the Harvard, and the runway length available for landing became a significant factor. It was important to get it on the ground somewhere near the touchdown end of the runway or else you might find yourself going off the end.

Even in 1953 the Meteor was a bit 'old tech'. One weakness it had was that the tyres were of the fat low-pressure variety, and the brakes were the traditional pneumatic-powered system that existed on other old-fashioned British-built aircraft. More modern aircraft had switched to high-pressure tyres and hydraulic braking systems which could cope much better with the more demanding workload involved in stopping high-speed aircraft.

One incident occurred that highlighted these problems when taxiing out for take-off one bright and sunny day. A rather laconic call came over the radio.

'Culdrose Tower this is 411, I have brake failure.'

'Roger 411, what is your position?'

'Going through the far fence – NOW', was the reply.

It took a week and six and a half flying hours for me to go solo. In that week Freddie demonstrated all the facets of flying jet aircraft that would keep me out of trouble. They were based on the much increased flight envelope of the Meteor when compared to the Harvard. The flying at Syerston had been conducted below 10,000 feet and 150 knots. Only minor adjustments for indicated air speed (IAS) were necessary when on a navigation exercise. Otherwise the IAS had more or less been the same as the true air speed (TAS). This was not the case in the Meteor. The maximum indicated airspeed of the Meteor was around 500 knots. However, if you flew the aircraft at 500 knots at sea level, maintained 500 knots and climbed, you would eventually hit the limiting Mach number (MN). This was around 0.82 MN, or 82% of the speed of sound. At 0.82 MN the Meteor hit a 'brick wall'. In fact this phenomenon was known as the Mach stall, since it was characterised by airframe buffet and partial loss of control due to the formation of shock waves over the wing and fuselage. If you were pulling 'g' manoeuvring the aircraft the Mach stall would occur at a lower MN because the local airflow over the wing would be higher in the manoeuvre. At 35,000 feet straight and level 0.82 MN equates to an IAS of around 300 knots, so you had to learn to use a combination of the Machmeter and the airspeed indicator to be able to fly the aircraft in the useable part of the flight envelope.

Speed and height could get you lost much quicker than in the past. On the few days you could see the ground from 20–30,000 feet you knew roughly where you were by being able to see the coastline and probably the whole of Cornwall. On the days that you couldn't, you climbed up through cloud and with a combination of mental DR navigation, backed up, hopefully, with the occasional glimpse of the ground, you kept track of where you were. When it came time to return to base you relied on the CRDF from Culdrose ATC to bring you back overhead the airfield, and under their control descended through cloud to bring you out over the airfield.

This technique was known as a let down (through cloud) or a QGH in service parlance. Because of the lack of spatial reference outside the cockpit at high altitude and the necessity to spend more time climbing and descending through cloud, the ability to fly safely on instruments became paramount. Under poor weather conditions that would prevent you making a visual approach and landing, you would have to do a ground controlled approach (GCA).

Having spent the beginning of the course getting used to handling the Meteor in this new, expanded environment, I rapidly progressed to the applied flying stage. Navigation exercises were split into high and low levels. High-level navigation became more of a strategic exercise. Since you were flying at such high speed and altitudes it was sufficient to know which town or conurbation you were near as opposed to the detail of the road and railway junctions of the Harvard days. Low-level navigation was a different kettle of fish. It was a question of navigating at 300 knots at 300 feet. At this height and speed you were very conscious of the terrain, not only from the viewpoint of not hitting the ground, but that navigation relied on looking out more horizontally and landmarks didn't rely on railway, road and river junctions, but more on their vertical aspects.

The rate at which you used fuel also came into consideration. The Harvard carried enough for you not to worry about running out of fuel during your normal sortie of an hour or so, but jets use a prodigious amount of fuel, and after a sortie time of 50 minutes you were down to minimum fuel. As I remember, the Meteor carried around 200 gallons in each of two main tanks, and a 'belly' tank of around 120 gallons which was used first. On an exercise in the local area you started back to base with a minimum of '60 a side', and planned to be on the ground with more than '40 a side', so your flight instrument scan was adjusted to check the fuel gauges at regular intervals. Although we had a briefed diversion airfield, all training establishments would broadcast a general recall if the weather started to deteriorate, and I can't recall anyone being required to divert to another airfield.

Formation flying became the norm during the second part of the jet conversion. We eventually learned to do everything in formation – from formation take-offs to formation landings – and life changed from flying separately to flying with other aircraft in a tactical unit. Close formation was necessary to be able to manoeuvre a section of four aircraft precisely, but when in a hostile environment we flew in a much wider formation to attack or defend. The normal formation unit in those days was a flight of four aircraft split into two sections of two aircraft. Thus there was the Leader and Numbers '2', '3' and '4'. The leader and 2 made up one section, the

3 and 4 the other. In a hostile environment the four aircraft adopted a battle formation. This involved the two sections flying 800 to 1,000 yards apart line abreast, so that each section could see the other. The Wingmen, the 2 and 4, flew some 100 yards at about 60 degrees back from their section leaders on the outside of the formation so that they could see their own leader and look across at the other section. In this way the section leaders could concentrate on looking ahead for the enemy, whilst the wingmen could check each other's 'six o'clock' to make sure the flight wasn't being attacked from astern. Everything depended on 'eyeball' ability, since the days of airborne weapon systems were still to come and any guidance from ground or shipborne intercept radar could only put you in a ball park position to be able to attack the enemy with your guns. It was important to see them before they saw you, and under visual conditions it was also important to put yourself up sun from your opponents.

The student didn't initially take the lead positions in this battle formation, but flew in the wingman positions of 2 and 4. After some experience we had a go as the second section leader, but on the jet conversion course battle formation was only flown to get used to manoeuvring around the sky in such a widespread formation. Actually having opponents was to come on the OFS2 course.

It was important to learn how to fly the Meteor on one engine. However, the service was not interested in losing an engine in critical conditions, as would be the case in the civil aviation field. The loss of an engine related to getting the aircraft back on the ground in one piece having had it fail in a non-critical situation. For instance, the normal take-off technique in the Meteor was to get the nose-wheel off the ground and the aircraft into a 'take-off' attitude as soon as the elevator became effective enough so to do. The speed at which this occurred was well below the safe speed to be able to control the aircraft on one engine should there be an engine failure. It was assumed this condition wouldn't happen, and I can't remember being briefed on what to do if it did.

In the case of landing on one engine, the norm was to make sure the decision to land was made early and that ATC knew of the problem. Their job then was to make sure that the runway was clear so that you could land off the initial approach. If there was any doubt, you were told to go around and make another approach very early on in the situation. Your job was to get the aircraft on the ground in one piece.

As I mentioned earlier, the Meteor Mk 7 was not fitted with ejection seats. Nor was there any recommended way of baling out. The only safe procedure related to inverting the aircraft, having jettisoned the hood, undoing the seat straps and falling out under negative 'g'. In this instance the only bit of aircraft you might hit would be the tail!

Getting away from flying for the moment, life at Culdrose was quite different from that at Syerston. As students at an RAF training base we felt very much the small Naval enclave in a very permanent world. Syerston had been an established base. By that I mean that traditionally a RAF airfield has a more permanent atmosphere.

By contrast the RN put most of its finances into ships and aircraft, and although the more traditional establishments at the main Naval bases had permanent and impressive buildings, the temporary state of the airfield buildings in the RN represented minimum financial commitment. Also, it would be fair to say that the battleship mentality still pervaded the RN, and there appeared to be little enthusiasm for aviation in the main corridors of power.

Unlike RAF squadrons, which are permanently in service, an RN front line squadron's existence revolved around an aircraft carrier. When an aircraft carrier started a new commission from either a new build or a long refit, it would be with a completely new complement of officers and ratings. Squadrons would be re-commissioned with a complement of new aircraft, pilots, maintenance and administration staff who would remain together as one unit independent of the carrier. The squadron would then work up at an air station so that when it came time to embark in the aircraft carrier the pilots and maintenance crews had become used to operating the new aircraft. As a result, Naval air stations had a transient and exciting air about them, with front-line squadrons coming and going.

At the same time, we were all living in the wardroom with all the other officers of the base and squadrons, with a certain *esprit de corps* of our own. We also knew that we would only be at Culdrose until the end of October, since the RN was reorganising its airfields and it was intended to base the Fighter School at RNAS Lossiemouth (Lossie for short), on the shores of the Moray Firth in Scotland. Concurrent with our jet course was the normal piston-engined Fighter School at RNAS Yeovilton in Somerset. It was intended that their OFS2 in Sea Furies would also move to Lossie. That course would include the pilots from 31 course who were going through the normal Fighter School, which would qualify them to go to war in our carriers off the shores of Korea.

We would complete our Meteor course at Culdrose and fly the aircraft up to Lossie. There we would complete our operational training on the Attacker and be assigned to either 800 or 803 squadron, the only two operational jet squadrons in the RN, embarked in HMS *Eagle* in the Mediterranean. Although the Attacker was an operational aircraft, it appeared to be considered not operational enough to deploy to the war zone in the Far East. So the fighting would be left to our contemporaries on the Sea Fury course, who would be assigned to squadrons operating off our carriers in Korean waters. Because of this I felt that I had missed out in some way.

We also entered the world of the 'party'. The various squadrons had their own loyalties, which spilled over into the social scene, and the gatherings in the evening would start with debriefs over a pint or two in the wardroom bar. As newcomers we were also introduced to the RPC, which was short for 'Request the pleasure of your company'. The response was WMP, 'With much pleasure', or MRU, 'Much regret unable'. Soon we learnt that RPC was the generic term for a party at any venue, be it the wardroom, a private house or a pub ashore.

The move to Lossiemouth was soon upon us. Straws were drawn as to who would be able to travel straight up to Scotland by car or train and who would have to fly the aircraft up there and return for cars if necessary. I was to fly an aircraft up there and return for my car. By now I had become the proud owner of a 1929 Morris Cowley Tourer.

The date for the flight to Lossie was 30 September and the squadron stopped flying two or three days beforehand so that the engineers could ensure all the aircraft were serviceable.

On the morning of departure we had an extensive briefing for the flight. The twelve aircraft would be flown up in three flights of four. The weather was not that good. A deep depression with associated frontal systems covered the whole of the UK and we would be on top of the cloud the whole way. A letdown at Lossie would almost certainly be necessary. The total flight time was planned to be one and half hours, and to achieve this the Meteors were equipped with external wing drop tanks as well as the belly tanks. We didn't normally use the wing tanks, but as they came with the aircraft it was logical to fit them and fill them.

The take-off, form-up and climb went well. The cloud was fairly dense, but as the number 4 wingman in close formation I could see at least two of the other three aircraft in cloud. The cloud tops were very high and eventually we ended up flying at 37,000 feet, to remain in the clear. Navigation now was definitely DR. The leader of the formation called the odd naval air station en route to obtain bearings so that he had some idea where we were. We wing men just held onto our leaders since we had no idea where we were! As student pilots this was the longest flight we were making since we started to fly, and certainly the first time we had flown from one end of the UK to the other.

It wasn't until we started down that I got an idea what a very frightening trip this was going to be. The frontal system was very much concentrated in Scotland, and the cloud from 37,000 feet down to a base of about 5,000 feet over the airfield was very thick and moist. When we entered cloud I could only see the starboard wing and fuselage of my leader. The cloud also proved to be very turbulent, and I found it difficult to stay in formation. As we descended, the cockpit canopy iced up on the inside, having had a prolonged cold soak during the flight. Luckily, as a wingman flying in section, I was formating on my leader's starboard wing, so my left hand was free to flash up to the cockpit canopy to rub a small hole in the ice to enable me to see his wingtip and flash back to the throttles again to make an adjustment to the power to stay in formation. Panic surged through me when it seemed as if I was fighting a losing battle to stay with him. It seemed an age before we broke cloud over a sombre and very wet Scottish countryside. With the rise in temperature everything began to thaw out. I briefly looked down into the cockpit at one stage and to my consternation couldn't see any of the flight instruments since they were all misted up.

It was a relatively warm day for Scotland, with the surface temperature around 12°C. We had broken cloud at around 5,000 feet, could see the airfield and positioned ourselves for a visual circuit onto the westerly runway. During the short time below cloud I managed to clear most of the essential flight instruments and the bits of canopy and windscreen that would allow me to make an approach and landing.

I parked the aircraft at our new squadron dispersal. The flight had taken one hour 40 minutes, the longest flight any of us had made to date. I joined the other crews in our new crewroom. It was only then that it was realised that one of the Meteors had not arrived. With the small amount of fuel we had all had left on landing and with no news of Les Yates landing at another airfield, his aircraft was missing. Subsequently it was considered that he hadn't been able to maintain formation on the descent, had switched to flying on instruments he couldn't see because they were iced up, had lost control and crashed into the sea. As far as I remember no wreckage of his aircraft was ever found. It was a sobering fact that it could so easily have been any one of us.

We spent the rest of the day sorting out the domestic situation. If I had thought that Culdrose consisted of temporary buildings, it was nothing like Lossie. The whole of the administration and domestic area consisted of wooden huts, all painted green. The wardroom and the officers' cabins were quite snug. This time we were to live two to a room, and in the corner of each room sat the central heating system – an old-fashioned coke fire. The fire risk must have been horrendous, particularly when, having stoked it up and shut the air vent down a little to keep warm during the freezing cold night, you woke up sweating like a pig at four in the morning to see the stove glowing almost white hot. You had to shield your face to get close enough to be able to shut it right down with the poker.

Those of us who had to travel back to Cornwall for cars, etc. left the next morning by train. I thought the week allowed to drive cars up to Lossie would give time to drive over to Bognor for a couple of days before setting course for Lossie. I arrived at Culdrose after an overnight train trip, packed my worldly goods and set off next morning for Bognor. My estimate of eight hours was very optimistic. The old Morris cruised along at 40 to 45 m.p.h., but the roads were very twisty, and overtaking the lorries, which didn't do more than around 30 m.p.h., was a difficult task. The car broke down at around 9 p.m. at West End, a small village on the outskirts of Southampton.

To cut a long story short, I stayed overnight at an old people's home run by an ex-Chief Petty Officer Sickbirth Attendant (a specialist rate in the RN), who had recognised me as a naval officer from my green trilby hat and service raincoat (Burberry) at his front door and insisted on calling me 'Sir'. It was pouring with rain at the time, and he promised he would rescue the Morris from the local garage in the morning and store it in one of his unused garages at the back of the house. As it happened, when I returned to pick up the car at Christmas, it was completely useless, since the Chief had stored it under a waterproof cover that had kept the car nice and moist from its soaking, and everything had rusted up. I made a quick decision to sell it to the local scrap merchant for £15. Back to the night in question! The next day I arranged for British Rail to come and pick up my trunk and most of my baggage for onward delivery to Lossie, and left for Bognor by train with a weekend grip.

Since my parents were not on the phone, an air of concern was apparent when I arrived home a day late. I explained what had happened with the car and that I was now going on to Lossie by train.

As far as the jet conversion was concerned, there were just five flights to complete. These concentrated on obtaining an instrument rating. The final flight was to be with an Instrument Rating Examiner (IRE). His task was to ensure that you could fly the aircraft within prescribed limits and recover normal flight from unusual attitudes using the primary flight instruments (turn and slip, VSI and ASI).

On successful completion of this flight I was issued with a 'White' instrument rating, which reflected my comparative inexperience. With more experience in the future I would qualify for a 'Green' or 'Master Green' instrument rating, which enabled you to fly in worse weather conditions. Although I was now finished with the Meteor Trainer as far as the jet conversion was concerned, the instrument rating test would become an annual event when you had to demonstrate your flying ability on flight instruments to renew your instrument rating. So the Meteor would be an aircraft I would fly periodically in the future. In mid-November we all transferred to 736 Squadron for OFS2 on the Attacker.

Chapter 4

Operational Jet Training

November 1953 to March 1954

Number 736 Squadron was equipped with the Supermarine Attacker, a single-seat fighter/bomber. A brief word about this aircraft before I go any further. For a jet the Attacker looked a little odd. It had a conventional undercarriage. It was equipped with a laminar flow wing, which was exceptionally thin when compared with the Meteor. This wing would delay the onset of shock wave formation and, in theory, would give the aircraft a higher useable Mach number. The wing had actually been developed to use with the Supermarine Sprite, a piston-engined development of the Spitfire that had fallen by the wayside. Like the later versions of the Spitfire, the Attacker had been equipped with four 20 mm cannon, two mounted in each wing, and was also able to drop 250 lb and 500 lb bombs and fire 3 in. rockets. But to me it seemed to be a hybrid aircraft that hovered between the piston and jet era, and in 1953 was soon to be replaced in service by the Hawker Sea Hawk.

One significant step was to come at the very beginning of the course. The Attacker did not have a two-seat training variant, so for the first time I would be flying an aircraft by myself from the word 'go'.

Taxiing meant reverting to the techniques required to handle a directionally unstable aircraft on the ground. Once lined up on the runway, the tailwheel was locked in the fore-and-aft position to ensure stability during the take-off run. The take-off proved to be an anticlimax. One Rolls-Royce Nene engine in the Attacker produced far less thrust than the two Rolls-Royce Derwents in the Meteor. It handled quite well but the controls were heavy, particularly the elevator. You did little on the first flight to challenge yourself. It was made to familiarise you with the control and cockpit layout and to run a couple of stalls to check the slow-speed flying characteristics. Then it was back to the circuit to

Supermarine Attacker *(Crown copyright)*

practise a few rollers prior to a final landing.

The standard procedure was to complete four familiarisation flights. After these flights you had a good idea how the aircraft behaved throughout the flight envelope. It had one or two quirks that had not been apparent in the Meteor.

At high Mach number the Attacker didn't run straight into buffet. At 0.79 MN an uncontrollable nose-down change in trim occurred. No matter how hard you pulled back on the stick, the nose would go on down until you slowed the aircraft or the Mach number reduced as a result of a reduction in altitude. Although the airframe seemed very 'clean' and would reach 0.85 MN without any sign of buffet, the limiting Mach number was virtually 0.79.

Another adverse characteristic was a very strong nose-up change in trim as the flaps were lowered. Luckily the flaps were infinitely variable and could be lowered little by little to enable you to retrim the aircraft nose-down in a controllable way. However, the throttle, airbrake and flap levers were all mounted together in the cockpit. They were of different shapes, but this didn't overcome the fact that, in the heat of the moment, some pilots had extended the flap instead of the airbrake. It was said that the Attacker was the only aircraft you could loop at 30,000 feet, but it took full flap to do it!

The final quirk was one of design and not aerodynamic behaviour. The Attacker's fuel system was rather odd. Fuel was delivered to the engine from a gauged main tank with a capacity of

82 gallons. There were 290 gallons of auxiliary fuel in the fuselage and another 250 gallons of fuel in an external belly tank. The 82-gallon main tank was gauged and could be topped up from the internal or belly tank fuel. The auxiliary fuel was gauged, but the belly tank fuel was not. There was a two-position lever on the starboard console that could be set to 'AUXILIARY' or 'BELLY TANK'. Since the belly tank fuel was ungauged it was customary to use the belly tank fuel first. At around the 70-gallon mark (ten minutes flying time) on the main tank fuel gauge, a red light would come on above the gauge to indicate that the transfer of belly tank fuel was complete. At this stage you had to select the lever to 'AUXILIARY' to be able to transfer the internal fuel to the main tank. If you didn't, the main tank would run dry and the engine would stop – irrevocably. There was also nothing in the cockpit to indicate that fuel was transferring, so you spent a minute or two watching the main tank gauge to make sure it was topping up correctly. Any combat would have to be discontinued so that you could concentrate on making sure the fuel situation was OK!

Still, the human condition is one of adaptability, and it didn't take too long to get used to all these characteristics, particularly the development of a sixth sense as to when the belly tank would run dry. Pilots in general are very good at glossing over the bad points of the aircraft they fly and establishing a type loyalty. You could consider the Attacker to be the Skoda of early jet aviation in the RN.

After these familiarisation flights we got down to the real meat of the course. The main armament of the Attacker was the 20 mm cannon, and the first thing to do was to learn how to fight the aircraft using the gunsight.

The first exercise was to practise the quarter attack. We operated in section formation for these exercises, the two aircraft alternating between acting as fighter and target. The target aircraft would fly straight and level (tow) at a constant height, speed and heading, and the fighter would perch off to one side or the other, 1,000 feet above and about 1,000 yards abeam of the tow at the same speed and heading. The object was for the fighter to turn in and down in an 'S' manoeuvre, using the height advantage and engine power to get a closing speed on the target. You aimed to be about 30 degrees off the stern quarter of the tow at a maximum firing range of 600 yards, closing to a minimum of 200 yards as you dropped into line astern. A reflective gunsight was used in the Attacker, with an aiming mark and fixed ring projected onto a sloping glass screen, mounted centrally between you and the windscreen. The idea was to lay off lead ahead of the target, using the aiming mark, and to judge how much lead to apply by using the ring.

Each attack was filmed by a gunsight camera and could be assessed by our 'Range Assessor' Wrens, who were trained to analyse the films frame by frame. Results relied on your judgement of angle-off and whether the aiming mark was in line with the direction of the target. It was a similar discipline to shooting skeet with a 12 bore shotgun. Because of this we also had regular sessions of skeet shooting to get our eye in! However, there was no doubt that the best way to shoot down the enemy would be to sneak up into close line astern and open up with your cannon. Not very sporting though.

At the end of the quarter attack exercises you actually got a chance to fire the guns against a towed fabric banner. This banner consisted of an oblong sheet that was towed at some distance behind a target tug aircraft. Each individual pilot had his cannon shells colour coded with paint so that if they passed through the banner they would leave a colour trace in the hole. There were lots of safety precautions to prevent you shooting down the tug on these live firing flights, but even if you got right behind the banner and had the tug somewhere in your sights it would be out of range. More to the point, the banner would be almost invisible since you were looking at it end on.

When you fired the cannon the noise in the aircraft was horrendous and you felt a distinct retardation of the aircraft from the recoil. The one thing you wanted to avoid if possible was one of the cannon jamming. If it occurred the recoil would stop on the side of the jammed gun and throw your aim way off to one side.

Formation 'Battle Drill' took up a great deal of our flying time. The aim of the training was to get us to a proficient standard as wingmen in a combat situation. To this end we would launch two divisions of four aircraft and practise attacking each other. It was very much up to the wingmen in the defensive formation to spot the incoming enemy. We used the clock code to indicate where the threat was and called the situation over the radio. A typical call might be 'Bandits 4 o'clock high, far, closing', to which the leader would call 'Contact' or 'No contact, call the Bandits'. Bandits meant enemy aircraft, and in the latter case you would go on calling where they were. If you thought the bandits were getting into an attacking position, and neither the flight, or section leader had called for defensive action, the wingmen would call it. With bandits at 4 o'clock you would make a final call of 'Break right' if they were getting into an attacking position. The break involved going to full power, banking the aircraft steeply and pulling to the maximum usable 'g' towards the bandits. The break had to be called at the right moment: too early and the bandits could manoeuvre into another attacking position; too late and you were dead. The ideal position was with the bandits fully committed and just outside gun range. In that case you had a chance of reversing the situation and shooting them down.

The quarter attack exercises had been with the target aircraft flying straight and level. Now we were in practice combat, both the attacking and defending aircraft used their full manoeuvre margin to try and outwit each other. The manoeuvre margin related to how much 'g' you could pull, and was governed by the aircraft's buffet boundary. The stalling angle of the wing defined this boundary. The 'g' you were pulling and your altitude/IAS/Mach number determined this in turn. If you were at high altitude where the Mach number was high the boundary of your 'g' capability would be defined by the aircraft going into Mach stall (the airflow over the aircraft reaching sonic speed). At lower altitudes, where Mach number was not a factor, the wing reaching the stall angle would define the 'g' boundary. In combat manoeuvres, height, speed and MN, and therefore the available 'g' at any one moment, was constantly changing.

All very nice, but if you were pulling as much 'g' as you could and a glance behind you showed the enemy fighter still within gun range and able to pull lead, you'd better do something about it or else he'll shoot you down. The only thing left for you to do would be the unexpected which would make gunsight tracking difficult, or a manoeuvre that might persuade him to break off or might put you on his tail. Let's say that in this dog fight scenario, where all the aircraft were Attackers, the position could become very fluid.

Formation and formation form-ups were practised endlessly. If the climb-out from base was conducted in cloudy weather conditions that precluded forming the formation below cloud, we would do a snake climb. This involved the leader taking off, followed by the 2, 3 and 4 at 30-second intervals. We were all on the same radio frequency and could hear the fighter director vectoring the leader onto the incoming threat. The leader would call when he was turning onto a heading, and the remainder of the flight would turn to follow in his tracks. Thus 2 would turn thirty seconds, 3 one minute and 4 one minute thirty seconds later. When we broke out on top of the cloud we would all be just thirty seconds line astern of each other and form up visually. Sometimes it worked – at other times it was a shambles.

On one of these climb-outs I was grateful for the past anoxic climb in the Harvard. I started to feel dizzy, had difficulty seeing clearly and remembered the symptoms. I found that the oxygen check had slipped through the take-off checks and wasn't switched on!

We had an abbreviated introduction to ground attack. The only way to deliver bombs and rockets in those days was in the dive. Not that we actually dropped or fired anything air to ground. We practised dummy dive-bombing and rocketing using the fixed-ring mode on the gunsight.

The final phase of the course had been lurking in the background all the time. It wasn't much good being a naval pilot if you couldn't land on the deck of an aircraft carrier. To this end, from about half way through the course we had been practising dummy deck landings at Milltown, a satellite airfield just to the east of Lossie. The area around Milltown was dead flat, and it was ideal to pretend it was the sea and the runway the carrier deck. Unlike a normal airfield circuit based on a height of 1,000 feet, a 'batted' carrier circuit was flown at 300 feet, tapering off to around 20 feet just prior to the 'cut'. Let me explain.

In the early 1950s carrier operations were based on the straight deck, the traditional flight deck configuration since aircraft were first operated from ships. The flight deck was divided into two areas. The deck aft of the middle of the Island superstructure on the starboard side of the flight deck was used to land the aircraft. The forward end of the flight deck was used to park the aircraft that had already landed. Between these two areas was the barrier that could be lowered or raised. Aircraft would land on with the barrier raised to protect the aircraft already parked on the front end of the flight deck should the landing aircraft miss all the wires. After a successful landing the barrier would be lowered to allow the aircraft

A Supermarine Attacker takes the 'cut' *(Crown copyright)*

to taxi over it and park. The barrier would then be raised to allow the next aircraft to land on.

The landing area was equipped with a number of arrester wires rigged across the deck. These wires were held in tension hydraulically and raised inches above the deck. If you picked up a wire and stopped before the barrier, you raised the hook, cleared the wire, the barrier lowered and you would taxi over it to the deck park. If you missed the wires completely, or the lowered hook bounced over them, you would end up in the barrier, which would stop you but would also slightly disrupt the proceedings. In all probability you would do your aircraft and yourself some harm. There would also be a considerable delay in the land on whilst the flight deck was disentangled.

The responsibility for getting your aircraft onto the deck wasn't yours but the 'Batsman's'. This was the name given to the Landing Signals Officer (LSO). He stood on the port side of the stern of the flight deck facing aft so that he could see an aircraft coming into land and by visual signals guide it into a position off the end of the ship where he could give the pilot the 'cut'. At the cut an aircraft would be about 20 feet up, just coming over the back end of the flight deck. You would immediately throttle right back, ease the stick slightly forward to get a rate of descent, then ease it back to get the hook in amongst the arrester wires. Since your airspeed would be just above the stalling speed there would be no question of you 'floating', the idea being that you would arrive firmly on the deck. Whatever happened after the cut you were committed to arriving on the deck one way or the other. The batsman would have waved you off before arriving at the cut position if there was anything wrong with your approach.

Every carrier landing was filmed. This was to retain a record of what happened so that any subsequent mishap could be analysed and blame established! We watched some exciting deck landings on film as part of the training. It included spectacular prangs where pilots had bad luck or decided to overshoot instead of taking the cut. A memorable one involved an aircraft entangling just the undercarriage in the top of the barrier, resulting in a flip upside down into the deck park. The pilots did not always walk away from these crashes. All in all it had a rather salutary effect on us to the extent that we had better get it right!

The introduction to deck landings was by practising the carrier circuit and landing at an airfield. The batsman was so called because he had two large round table-tennis-type bats, one held in each hand, so that you could see him signalling to you from about half a mile on final approach. He would be an experienced carrier pilot who would have completed a course with 767 Squadron (called the 'Clockwork Mouse' squadron since it involved aircraft continuously going round and round a carrier circuit at an airfield whilst the batsman learned the ropes). He would watch each approach, and using the bats signal the pilot into an acceptable 'window' where he could give the cut. If the pilot didn't achieve the desired criteria before the window he would be waved off. The cut and wave off signals were mandatory and had to be obeyed.

The batsman's signals told you what you were doing. By judgement he could tell if you were too high or low, too fast or slow and whether you were going to be lined up with the deck at the cut. The line-up signal was the only one where he told you what you had to do. In the past this had been very necessary since single-engine piston aircraft didn't have a good view forward because of the engine cowling. Pilots would be in a banked turn, having flown a tight circuit to the cut position looking at the batsman just to the left of the engine cowling, and wouldn't be able to see if they were lined up with the deck. Although jets didn't have this visibility problem, the necessity to do a tight circuit was still required for operational reasons, which I will cover later.

On 736 Squadron, Keith Leppard was our batsman. At Milltown he would position himself at the touchdown point of the duty runway and we would fly the Assimilated Dummy Deck Landing (ADDL) circuit trying to follow his signals. Keith had a 'teller' with him whose job was to identify the pilot being batted and to make notes on Keith's comments for each ADDL approach so that the individual pilot could be debriefed afterwards.

It took a little practice to get the circuit right. We flew close into the runway on the downwind leg and commenced our turn onto the runway heading abeam the touchdown point using about 20 degrees of bank. It was a requirement that we deck land with the canopy wound open, since the circuit would be below 300 feet, and with an ejection seat envelope of a minimum of 400 feet, the only option in the event of engine failure was to crash land or ditch. For once it was a good idea to wear your goggles in the circuit to make sure that you didn't get anything in your eyes. Winter in Scotland also made the temperature in the cockpit rather bracing!

Your flying speed in the circuit was only a little above the stalling speed and so accurate speed control was required all of the time. The batsman could tell what speed you were flying at by the nose-up attitude of the aircraft, and would ensure you were flying at the correct speed once you came into visual range with him at about 45 degrees off the runway heading, but up to that point you were responsible for your own airspeed. Watching the batsman became second nature, but more importantly a sense of trust was established between pilot and batsman.

Mid-February saw the arrival in the Moray Firth of HMS *Illustrious*, a Fleet Class carrier. All our aircraft carriers were WW2 vintage and had been designed to operate piston-engine-powered aircraft of the Sea Fury and Firefly type. These aircraft were comparatively light compared to the Attacker and used approach speeds around the 80-knot mark. The planned speed at the cut for the Attacker was 110 knots, which required the arrester gear to absorb much more energy than before. The gear had been modified to do this, but all pilots were given the impression that the arrester gear was operating near its maximum energy absorption. To offset the energy requirements a little and to enable the ship to manoeuvre, a wind speed over the deck of 30 to 35 knots was common.

The morning of 12 February saw me briefing for my first deck landing. Keith had briefed us all extensively on what to expect, since actual deck operations would be a little different from ADDLs at Milltown.

I took off in section with another student pilot at 08:30 and headed to the north-east to intercept the ship. It was a grey overcast morning. I contacted the ship on its approach radio channel and got a steer towards her. I became visual at about ten miles range and was handed off to the flying control (FLYCO) frequency, which controlled the visual circuit around the ship. We lowered our hooks and joined the circuit. The ship was steaming westerly at about 15 knots against a natural wind of 15 to 20 knots. Although the wind was quite strong, the shelter of the land to the west kept the sea state low, making the conditions just about ideal. With no significant sea state it meant the ship would be fairly stable!

I flew the one minute ahead of the ship as briefed, left my wingman to fly ahead a further 30 seconds and broke downwind. I started the turn in just ahead of the ship's beam as briefed. With 90 degrees to go the position seemed impossible. If I kept the turn going at the present rate it seemed as if I would roll out on final approach ahead of the ship! And the damned thing looked so small! With 45 degrees to go I was getting to the stage of wondering what I was doing there at all when Keith's bats came into view. It seemed as if I was back at Milltown again. I followed his signals for the rest of the approach, practically ignoring the ship completely except to realise that the high relative wind over the deck was indeed sucking me into the correct position just astern of the ship. I got to the window position with Keith giving me a steady indication for the last 50 yards or so, followed by the cut. I cut the engine power and for the first time realised I was hovering off the end of this incredibly small 'runway' onto which I was about to arrive. However, since this was a session of deck landing practice (DLP), the deck ahead was clear with no aircraft parked forward and no barrier raised. I eased forward on the stick to get a rate of descent, then eased back on the stick to get the tail down. On a carrier there is no ground effect to cushion your arrival on deck, and my landing was firm. Suddenly the aircraft decelerated as the hook picked up a wire, and I was thrown forward in the cockpit. So here I was on the flight deck. It seemed so small. The wingtips looked as if they were hanging over the side of the ship and there didn't seem to be that much distance between the bow and me. I could also feel the aircraft slightly pitching. It was very obvious to me that I was sitting in an aircraft that was on a ship.

All around me was frantic activity, and my slightly wandering thoughts had to concentrate on the present. The aircraft was surrounded by flight deck crew in yellow jackets (the aircraft handlers) ready to push my aircraft back to the stern of the flight deck in preparation for my 'free take-off'. The leader of the flight deck crew was frantically signalling to me to raise the hook and release the wheel brakes. I signalled that the brakes were off and felt the aircraft rolling backwards. As I got near to the stern the leader signalled me to put the brakes back on, and I went through my pre-take-off checks before signalling I was ready to go. 'God, the deck looks so short' was my initial thought as the Flight Deck Officer (FDO), who had replaced the marshaller supervising the push-back signalled to me to run up to full power by circling a small green flag above his head. I indicated to him I was ready to go, sitting there with the engine at full power and the brakes firmly on. The FDO had a quick check with the signals from FLYCO on the Island that indicated the ship was ready as well, turned his attention back to me and dropped his flag. I released the wheel brakes and started to run down the flight deck at what seemed to be a very slow acceleration rate. It really didn't look as if I was going to get off the flight deck at all, but just as I passed the Island with at least 100 feet of deck still to go the Attacker lifted off. I climbed to 300 feet and flew for one and a half minutes ahead of the ship before turning downwind for the second landing. Meanwhile, the other student pilot was doing his first deck landing.

For the second landing and subsequent deck landings I felt far more confident. I accrued a total of 15 deck landings over the next eight days without missing a wire.

We completed operational jet training on 24 February 1954. We were now considered to be qualified naval pilots. I, along with the

De Havilland Sea Vampire F-20 *(Crown copyright)*

Giffin twins and Bob Mason, a General List Lieutenant on our flying course, were to fly to Malta, the twins and I to join 803 Squadron and Bob to join 800 Squadron, both part of the Air Group in HMS *Eagle* in the Mediterranean. However, the four of us were to hang around Lossie for a month or so awaiting a trooping flight to RAF Luqa in Malta.

Until we left Lossie I managed to talk myself into flying a Sea Vampire F-20 used in Station Flight. This was the same type of Vampire I had looked around at RNAS Ford some two years previously when Harold Bond and I had cadged our first flight as cadets, so it was quite interesting to find out what it was like. It was a charming little aircraft, relatively small compared with the Attacker and Meteor, and was fondly known as the 'Kiddie Car'. It was very light on the controls compared with either aircraft and seemed extremely manoeuvrable. You certainly got the impression it could out-turn anything.

By now I had accrued 340 flying hours since starting my flying training. My pass-out rate had been very good, obtaining a First Class assessment in most phases. This had earned me some Brownie points to accelerate my promotion to Lieutenant. We had been informed that if any of us wished to be transferred to the General

List of officers and make the RN a full career, we would be assessed for that as well. As it was, regardless of age, I was to be promoted to Acting Sub-Lieutenant straight away, as was every Midshipman on the course, since all qualified pilots on front-line squadrons had to be full-fledged officers. By early April the four of us were packed and ready to go. A night at Goodge Street Deep Shelter on the London Underground was an eye opener. This had been built during WW2 as an extensive wartime shelter complex, but was now used for accommodating military personnel in transit abroad. We had an early-morning start with a bus trip to Northolt airfield where we boarded a Vickers Viking airliner of Hunting Clan, and off we went to Malta.

Chapter 5

803 Squadron at RNAS Halfar, Malta

March to November 1954

We arrived at RAF Luqa in the afternoon and determined that we were to be accommodated in HMS *St Angelo*, the main naval base in Valetta, the capital of Malta. This was because 800 and 803 Squadrons were still embarked in HMS *Eagle*, but would be disembarking to RNAS Halfar in the next few days. Perhaps a quick resumé of what the island was like in 1954 would be a good idea.

Malta had featured as an outpost of the British Empire for some years. In 1954 it had a main airport at RAF Luqa, a fighter airfield at RAF Takali to the west of the island, and RNAS Halfar in the south-east corner. There was also a disused airfield at Qrendi in the south, which had been turned into a munitions dump. Valetta was on the north coast and surrounded the magnificent deep waters of Grand Harbour, which could accommodate a number of capital ships at anchor. Just along the coast from Grand Harbour was Sliema Creek, which usually had a flotilla of destroyers at anchor. Sliema itself was the resort end of the capital. There was also quite an Army garrison on the island, as well as the local Maltese Regiment.

After a few days we were summoned to RNAS Halfar in preparation for the disembarkation of the squadrons from HMS *Eagle*. The airfield was crowded, with some squadrons in transit to the Far East and the Korean War. We met up with some of our old course who had completed the piston-engined fighter course and were now assigned to Sea Fury squadrons. It was about this time that I learnt that Derek Evans had been killed in a Sea Fury accident off the North African coast.

The squadrons disembarked from HMS *Eagle* two days after we arrived at Halfar. It was only at this time that the twins and I learnt that our arrival made the squadron back up to twelve pilots. One had been appointed back to the UK and the other two had been killed in accidents. I had begun to accept that these things would happen, but hoped it wouldn't happen to me. The twelve aircraft and pilots were split up into three flights of four. The CO led the first flight and I was to be his wingman. The Senior Pilot (SP) was the second in command and led the second flight. The third flight was led by the most senior Lieutenant. The CO and the SP held the rank of Lieutenant-Commander and the rest of us were Lieutenants and Sub-Lieutenants.

The CO was J.S. (Boss) Bailey, a quiet man who had the reputation of being a bit of an ace, The SP was Tom Innes who had recently completed a tour as a test pilot and had been awarded the AFC. The third flight leader was Harry Bain, who had lost his hair as a result of a shock during his flying career. Harry was a great fellow, and in a squadron where most of the pilots were bachelors he and his wife Jean seemed to take us younger pilots under their social wing. There was always open house at the Bains'. They had no children and Jean had followed Harry out to Malta since it looked as if we were to be based in the Mediterranean for some time. The rest of us were a complete mixture of General List career officers and others who seemed to be on all sorts of commissions.

Becoming part of a squadron generated a different attitude in me. Until now I had been a trainee pilot with progressive loyalty to the Navy, to flying and the aircraft we flew. But none of these related to the loyalty and sense of comradeship that I felt as a member of a squadron.

Mid-April 1954 appeared to be a time of confusion and change in the Mediterranean. We new pilots had thought that we would be embarking in HMS *Eagle* with our squadrons. However, although 800 and 803 Squadrons had disembarked to Halfar on what was now a semi-permanent basis, we newcomers spent the first week flying ADDLs at Halfar in preparation for deck landing on HMS *Eagle*. On 27 April we flew out to the ship steaming off Malta. We were to make our first deck landing with the barrier raised and a deck park of aircraft on the forward end of the flight deck. If I had thought the *Illustrious* small with a clear deck in front of me, the *Eagle*'s landing area looked completely impossible as I took the cut and at the last minute realised how little distance there was between me and the barrier as I came to a stop on the deck. The barrier dropped, and I raised the hook and followed the marshaller's directions to taxi over the lowered barrier and joined the other aircraft in the forward deck park. For the first time I operated the wing-fold mechanism as I taxied forward. On the Attacker the outboard four feet or so of each wing folded into an upright position to enable it to park in a smaller space.

Taxiing an aircraft on a ship is a very precise manoeuvre and is done under the supervision of an aircraft handler, a specialised naval rating who has been trained in marshalling and parking aircraft 'on a sixpence'. To this end, a handler's repertoire of hand signals and facial expressions were so explicit that you were able to understand every slight innuendo of how much braking, turning or power application was required to park the aircraft exactly where he wanted. Although you were convinced that you were about to hit the aircraft next to you, you followed the handler's instructions exactly and once parked found you had nothing to worry about since there would be a good two to three inches to spare! As it happened, on this particular day the sea was smooth and the ship was on a steady course. The skill in taxiing and parking would be challenged in rough seas and when the ship was heeling over in a turn. By comparison today's effort would be considered an absolute doddle.

After all the aircraft on that particular land on were aboard, the deck park was rearranged for the 'launch'. This was why we new boys were operating from *Eagle* that day.

As well as the Attackers, there were 809 Squadron operating Sea Hornets, a twin-engined night-fighter, a flight of four AEW Skyraiders of 849 Squadron, and Fireflys of 824 Squadron. All these piston-engined aircraft could launch from the deck unassisted using two thirds of the length of the flight deck. The Attackers could only be realistically launched using the two bow catapults, and so would be ranged abeam the Island and launched first.

The idea was that we newcomers would be catapulted off first, hold off from the ship while the rest of the launch and land on of aircraft already airborne took place and then return to the deck for a couple of landings and catapult launches apiece.

We started up and were marshalled forward in turn to the catapults and automatically centred on a set of raised catapult chocks that ensured the aircraft was loaded symmetrically. The catapult was hydraulically operated and was just over 100 feet long. Prior to the chocks being lowered, a hold back was fitted at the rear of the aircraft and a catapult strop fitted. The strop was a long piece of steel cable with an eye on each end. The eyes would be fitted over hooks mounted on either side of the fuselage. The strop then hung down in a big loop from these hooks and was long enough to fit over the catapult shuttle. The shuttle was itself a large faired hook attached to the catapult. Once the hold-back and strop were in place, the chocks were lowered and the catapult tensioned by taking the shuttle slowly forward so that the Attacker was firmly held on the catapult with the hold-back holding the aircraft back against the tension of the strop. This hold back system was designed to take the combined force of the tensioned catapult and the thrust of the engine running at full power. When the catapult fired, the shuttle would be forced down the catapult track, taking the aircraft with it, and the hold-back would sheer away from the rear fuselage and remain on deck. The Attacker attached to the strop would be pulled down the catapult track and the strop would fall away into the sea from the aircraft as it became airborne. All this sounds very complicated, but an aircraft could be loaded and tensioned in a matter of seconds.

As far as you were concerned, you would taxi up to the catapult chocks and feel the aircraft tensioned. You would be advised by the FDO (Flight Deck Officer), who would be controlling the launch, to set full engine power. He did this by circling a little green flag over his head with his right hand. You would signal to him that you had full power set and that you were ready to be launched. He would check the visual signals from FLYCO in the Island that the ship was ready, recheck with you that you were happy and drop his flag. This was the signal to the Flight Deck Engineer Officer (FDEO) to fire the catapult. Up to five seconds later the catapult would fire and you would accelerate from 0 to 100 knots or so during the catapult run. This would take less than two seconds! That was going to be a lot of 'g'!

We had been told what to expect. The main thing was not to get disorientated by the high longitudinal 'g', to brace your body forward during the catapult run and not to hold the stick and throttle, but brace your hands behind them both. This was because if you held the stick and throttle the 'g' might well force your hands back, resulting in you taking off with the stick back and with something less than take-off power selected, setting you up for a stall off the bow. The optimum position for your right arm was with the hand cupped behind the stick at about the position the stick would need to be to fly at 110 knots and your elbow tucked into your stomach to stop your arm coming back. You were to hold the flat of your hand against the throttle and push forward on that hand as the catapult fired. As the Attacker became airborne you would feel as if you were being flung forward in the cockpit with the sudden reduction of acceleration, but the aircraft would be in trim and would fly normally until you got things under control.

So, here I was on the catapult, all tensioned up in more ways than one and ready to go. The catapult looked very short and I could feel the ship shuddering as it steamed at 25 knots. The FDO raised his little green flag over his head and circled it. I ran the engine up to full power and checked that everything was OK. I signalled the FDO that I was ready to go.

At this stage, if things had not been satisfactory I would have shaken my head to indicate that all wasn't well and the FDO would have aborted the launch. Having indicated that you weren't happy to go you had to sit there with full power on until the FDO had ensured that the catapult had been de-tensioned and that the strop had been removed. To do this he would raise a little red flag in his left hand, which would indicate to all involved that the launch was to be aborted, and would eventually lower the green flag when the strop had been removed. This lowering of the green flag was the indication to you that you could safely throttle back.

I raised my arm to show I was ready to go, the FDO checked with FLYCO that the ship was ready, checked with the FDEO on the catapult that all was well with him, rechecked that my arm was still raised, and if the answers were 'yes', dropped his arm holding the green flag. I placed my raised arm in its position ready for launch. About three seconds later the catapult fired. The bow of the ship came rocketing towards me. I thought I had tensioned my body, but it felt like a wet rag. I could feel my feet coming off the rudder pedals, but my stick and throttle hands remained in place. Suddenly the acceleration stopped and my body bounced forward

The first catapult launch

off the back of the seat. All seemed normal after a second or two, but my only thought was that the acceleration had been much fiercer than I had expected. It was nice to feel the cool air buffeting around me from the open canopy as I turned downwind to land on. It helped take the heat out of my face from the adrenaline rush. This time the deck was clear, with no barrier and no forward deck park as I landed on. 'Piece of cake', as they say.

I was ready for the next launch, and this time really braced forward to make sure my legs were going to stay on the rudder pedals. The second launch was much better, and I was more aware of what was going on during the two-second catapult ride. The third launch was even better.

I can't say that I ever got used to catapult launches during my career. Over the years I was in the Fleet Air Arm nothing very terrible happened to me on the catapult, but there were plenty of pilots who had things go wrong. They ranged from hold-backs breaking at full engine power before the catapult fired, to cold shots and engine failures. In the case of the hold-back shearing, you had to be quick to recognise that the aircraft was moving forward under its own power and stop. There were a few who didn't who ended up pitching slowly off the bow and dropping nose down the 60 or so feet into the sea, only to be hit by a carrier doing 25 knots. Many didn't survive. The cold shot related to the catapult not developing full power on the launch, which meant that you were going to be ballistic off the bow since you would be going forward quite fast but would be well below the flying speed required to stay airborne. You would possibly be in a slightly better position than trickling off the front, since it was probable that you would hit the water the right way up at about 80 knots or so some way ahead of the ship.

The only personal incident I recall related to a catapult malfunction: when the FDO dropped the flag nothing happened! The FDO raised his other hand holding the red flag. I sat there with full power on, not knowing what to expect. And with all the tension of the situation after about 20 seconds or so started to shake all over. After what seemed an eternity the aircraft was disconnected from the strop and I throttled back. They manoeuvred me back and launched me off the other catapult!

After the third deck landing we all taxied forward into the deck park, shut our engines down and had a break. We were met by a squadron pilot and taken up to the 'goofers', an area on top of the Island that was a favourite spot for off-duty personnel to watch the land on. There was a sense of excitement amongst the onlookers not unlike that which must have existed amongst the citizens at the Rome Coliseum. Carrier operations were dangerous and many

The Attacker team. *From left to right:* Muckley, Sub-Lieutenant Brian Davies and Thompson

were there not to miss the ultimate danger! The collective noun for these persons was 'goofers' and the act of watching the proceedings was known as 'goofing'. I must admit there was a certain gladiatorial aspect to flying off a carrier. It looked just as much a challenge when watching it as when doing it. After the land on, the aircraft were ranged for the next launch, which included us. We leapt back into the aircraft, did our last catapult launch and got back to Halfar in time for tea. Quite an exciting day out really. Apart from one other day when I landed on *Eagle* (and launched back to Halfar), that was the last time I would operate from her for the next fourteen years.

We, along with 800 Squadron and a flight of 849 Squadron Skyraiders, were now based at Halfar. In 803 we had a change in the hierachy. 'Boss' Bailey was appointed back to the UK, Tom Innes took over as CO and Harry Bain became the SP. The third flight was led by Maurice Tibby, an experienced pilot who had recently joined the squadron.

The flying was varied. One day we would be operating low-level interceptions under the control of the Airborne Early Warning (AEW) Skyraiders. This was an exercise to give their radar operators practice at controlling fighters to intercept very low-level targets that could not be seen by the ship's radar. The next day we would be doing the same sort of thing at high altitude under HMS *Eagle*'s control or under the control of the military land-based air defence radar in Malta. Another day we would be dropping practice bombs on the buoyed target in the sea at Delimara range just to the north of Halfar. Interspersed with these flights we would also be practising for a big flypast for Queen Elizabeth II, who would be visiting the island in early May.

All this was overshadowed by the fact that we lost four Attackers in the first six weeks of our arrival, killing three of our pilots, including Alan Giffin. Two of the accidents were probably as a result of pilot error, since the exercise being conducted was formation aerobatics on a hazy day over the sea. No one was absolutely sure this was the case, since no trace of the aircraft or pilots was ever found. Tom Innes had an engine failure at altitude and managed to force land the aircraft at Qrendi. Rather than being given a pat on the back, I think he was castigated for arriving in amongst the crates of ammunition instead of ejecting. The aircraft was a write-off. Finally, Alan Giffin was killed on take-off at Halfar. The engine failed just as his wheels left the runway and the aircraft crashed into the stone walls surrounding the fields at the end of the runway. Because of the two engine failures so close together, the Attackers were grounded until the cause of the failures could be determined.

Since we now didn't have anything to fly, I nipped along to see Alan Fife, a QFI/IRE who ran the 'Instrument Flight' at Halfar. He had training aircraft available to allow any pilot to take an

Fairey Firefly trainer *(Crown copyright)*

instrument rating. The aircraft included a Meteor 7, a Sea Fury T 20 trainer, and a Firefly trainer. I persuaded him that I should check out in the Sea Fury and the Firefly, as well as flying the Meteor.

Tom Innes gave me a quick dual check in the Sea Fury. It was quite a handful. It had a long main undercarriage and a relatively short fuselage. So with the tail-wheel on the ground the aircraft sat with a very nose-up attitude. With the Centaurus engine mounted in front of you the view over the nose was non-existent. On take-off you looked out of each side of the cockpit ahead of the aircraft until you had enough speed to get the tail-wheel off the ground and were able to see over the nose. Once airborne the Sea Fury was a joy to fly, very manoeuvrable when compared to many of the jets, but of course not so fast. The real challenge was to get it back on the ground again! The Sea Fury would just about be in the stalled attitude to achieve a three-point landing, and it was recommended I 'wheel it on' to begin with. Even then it was a bit of a handful after landing because of its directional instability.

As well as flying the Meteor, I checked out in the Firefly trainer with Colin Casperd. He was one of the more experienced pilots in 803 and had flown the Firefly before. The Firefly trainer had two pilots' cockpits, one in the normal position and another mounted in place of the observer's cockpit. Colin flew in the rear cockpit and I checked out in the front.

My third flight in the Sea Fury was to prove eventful. I rejoined the circuit at the end of the flight to do some more circuits and bumps. The Centaurus was such a powerful engine that there was no need to retract the flap to take off again on the roll.

One of the golden rules after landing is to clear the runway before starting the after-landing checks. However, that particular day I felt in a really slick mood since the circuits and bumps had gone very well. While still moving on the runway I decided to 'clean up' the aircraft. I reached out to the flap and undercarriage quadrant (they were mounted adjacent to each other) and put the flap control into the 'up' position. Suddenly the aircraft seemed to hit a hole in the runway as the starboard wing dipped down. I realised it was a huge hole as the starboard wing hit the runway. Then the port wing started to drop and I realised there was something seriously wrong. The Sea Fury dragged along the runway making a horrible grinding noise, and the engine ground to a shuddering halt as the outboard ends of the propeller contacted the runway surface and bent.

'By God,' I thought, 'the bloody undercarriage has collapsed.'

I looked vacantly around the cockpit in a certain amount of shock and then noticed that the undercarriage lever was firmly in the 'UP'

'Doing a Dilbert.' The Hawker Sea Fury T 20 *(Crown copyright)*

position. I had done a Dilbert and retracted the undercarriage instead of the flaps! 'What a stupid idiot' (or words to that effect) was my immediate reaction. Perhaps I could force the undercarriage lever down and say there must have been some sort of failure. But honesty reared its head and I decided to stick with the truth.

I heard the sirens of the crash wagon arriving, and suddenly the station Doc was on the wing alongside the cockpit.

'What's wrong?' he asked.

'I pulled the undercarriage up', I said, still sitting there in disbelief.

'Well, I think you'd better get out before this thing catches fire', was his suggestion.

'Too true', I thought, switching off the magneto switches and the fuel. I hopped out feeling an absolute prat.

No one said anything at the time, but shortly afterwards I was paraded in front of the Commanding Officer of Halfar, who was himself a pilot and held the official title of 'Captain Air Mediterranean'. Richard Smeeton was his name, not that we were on first name terms, you understand. Captain Smeeton could look very fierce indeed, mainly by raising one eyebrow and fixing you with a stare. He told me what he thought about me severely damaging the Sea Fury – none of it complimentary – and then informed me I would get a station logging. I was somewhat relieved by this since it meant that I was on probation with him, but nothing would be noted officially on my records.

The next day the Attacker was back in the air. I don't know what had happened in the case of the CO's engine failure, but Alan's had been caused by fuel starvation. There was a switch in the cockpit that isolated the barometric pressure control (BPC) for take-off. If the switch was 'ON', the BPC was integrated with the system, but could be the cause of an engine flameout due to air getting into the fuel system. If the switch was 'OFF' the BPC was isolated, but could be the cause of a flameout due to over-fuelling if the throttle was 'hammed' too much on a formation take off. In the past, flameouts had occurred due to the over-fuelling problem caused by pilots forgetting to put the isolation switch 'ON' after take-off and subsequently changing power quickly. Presumably Alan had the switch selected to 'ON' for take-off.

It became a bit of a Catch 22 situation. A design fault where the buck had been passed to the pilot. I think the recommendation was that we took off with the switch 'OFF', but most of us mentally tossed a coin at the take-off point and selected the switch where we thought it ought to be. Tuesdays and Fridays it was 'ON'. And why not?

Some of our interception exercises were conducted using the Malta Air Defence Radar, when a flight of Attackers would be matched against a flight of Vampires from an Australian squadron based at RAF Takali. Honour was at stake. Because they were the official defenders of Malta, our Attackers were nearly always the enemy. But we could cheat, since we were all listening out on the same radio frequency. The final 'Tally Ho' from the Vampires would generate a heightened awareness in us all and an improved lookout from the wingmen. However, we also knew from which direction they were coming. The Vampire usually had the measure of us since it could out-turn the Attacker. On our side we seemed to be able to out accelerate them, particularly in a dive, probably because the Attacker weighed more than the Vampire! Nevertheless, the small dog fight at the end of the intercept was regarded with eager anticipation. There was always tremendous confusion on the radio at this stage, since both fighters and targets were calling instructions and warnings to each other on the same frequency. You also had to keep your wits about you, since with eight aircraft in the same piece of sky there was also the possibility of a mid-air collision.

When operating with the AEW Skyraiders at low altitudes, we, as fighters, would often be pitted against the Westland Wyverns of 813 Squadron. The Wyvern was originally designed as a torpedo bomber, but in 1954 I can't recall a requirement for a torpedo bomber to attack ships. So the Wyvern had become a ground attack aircraft. By Naval standards it was quite large and was powered by a single turbo-prop contra-rotating propellered engine. The fuselage was designed to give the pilot a good view forward. It had a long nose that sloped down from a high cockpit. It had a conventional undercarriage layout with long mainwheel oleos, which provided plenty of room underneath the aircraft to load bombs and rockets.

It had a high wing loading and didn't manoeuvre well. Mike Teague, one of the members of my pilots' course, had recently been killed in one, how I'm not sure. Whenever we jumped the Wyverns on these intercepts, they would all go into line astern and start to go round in a circle. This was a defensive manoeuvre developed by Mike Crosley, the CO of 813, and was called the daisy chain. At least it meant that if you ended up on the tail of a Wyvern, there would be another Wyvern sitting on your tail ready to shoot you down.

The Wyvern had a poor reputation, and I was lucky enough never to fly one. It was alleged that the first naval test pilot to fly it was not impressed. He summarised what he thought in the long climb you had to make to reach the cockpit. He had apparently written, 'Access to the cockpit is difficult. It should be made impossible.'

Malta with its small fields surrounded by stone walls was nothing like the green fields of England. Any sort of forced landing was out of the question. However, if the engine stopped and you were out of reach of the sea or below 400 feet, you would have to take your chances with the stone walls. The media are very fond of headlines that show the pilot of a crashing aircraft heroically avoiding built-up areas. I can assure you it is very much a case of self-preservation. I would rather try and land in an open space than run headlong into a stone wall.

The social life tended to match the professional one. Malta was geared to the requirements of the British Services, and there were plenty of bars around. Alcohol had a calming affect on the adrenaline-filled days. Near Halfar was the small fishing village of Birsebuga. The favourite bar for the aircrew was, as I recall, Jimmy Dowdall's. It had a nice view over Marsaxlokk Bay, and we would all congregate there in the evening and sink a few beers. The overall impression of Malta was summed up by the expression 'Yells, Bells and Smells'. The Maltese were very vocal, the bells of the various Catholic Churches were always ringing and the drains left something to be desired. Their main occupations appeared to be working for the British, the Catholic Church, farming, and shop- and bar-keeping. They probably had the highest number of priests and nuns per square yard outside of the Vatican.

Now, where was I? The Attacker was back in the air and we spent a week attacking Sicily. The island provided a good variety of terrain and targets. Various bridges, viaducts and prominent buildings in some of the central and coastal towns of Caltanissetta, Agrigento, Licata and Gela had been well documented by aerial photography. Sicily itself had been designated a low-flying exercise area with virtually no restrictions on how low you were allowed to go, so we were looking forward to it!

Having completed our week of dummy attacks, the squadron flew to Castel Benito, an airfield about 40 miles south of Tripoli in Libya, for a ten-day detachment to exercise with the 14th/20th Hussars, a tank regiment based at Zuara on the Libyan coast. In those days we were obviously still friendly with the Libyans!

The 14th/20th would deploy their tanks in the desert. Our objective was to find and attack them. We were going to pretend to use 20 mm semi-armour-piercing shells from our guns. When you think about it, a tank is a very small object when seen from the air, and can only be destroyed or disabled by a direct hit. To get the accuracy required the 20 mm SAP shells were considered to be the only weapon available to us.

Before exercising with the tanks, we had a quick couple of days' strafing practice at Tarhuna range nearby. As far as I remember, the dive angle was around ten degrees and each burst was commenced around a height of 1,200 feet, which equated to the maximum effective range. You continued down to a height of around 500 feet. Unlike bombing and rocketing, you fired your guns over a number of seconds and you needed to adjust the aiming point during the dive. The shells fired at 1,200 feet had further to go than those fired at 500 feet, so needed more elevation to hit the target. To compensate for this effect the gunsight alignment was depressed. This had the effect of increasing the dive angle towards the end of the strafing run. Thus the shells would be concentrated on the target and not sprayed around as in the movies!

Strafing was fun. You could see where the first shells were hitting during the last part of the dive, and there was a tremendous tendency to remain in the dive to ensure that you scored as much as possible. We had been warned about this target fixation effect. Ignoring it could mean eventually piling you and the aircraft into the target as well!

The result of this strafing was quite impressive in that we all managed to get a high percentage of shells on the target, and towards the end of the practice some managed to rip the target apart completely. So when the day of the first exercise against the tanks arrived, we were all confident our gunsight cameras would show 100 per cent success.

The tanks operated out in the desert. To make our task as difficult as possible they would be stopped and camouflaged. To begin with it was difficult to isolate the tanks from the surrounding scrub and rocks, but after a couple of sorties we could pick them out quite easily. It was the first time most of us had operated against live targets. There were Pongos actually watching what you were doing and by Jove you were going to show them a thing or two! To make sure the camera was going to record a kill, you stayed locked on the target until you could see the whites of their eyes. Target fixation reared its ugly head. The first and only time it happened to me scared me witless. I suddenly realised I had gone way below the minimum height for the attack and instantly heaved back on the stick. In the high temperatures over the desert the aircraft tended to 'mush' on the pullout, and I was convinced I was going to hit the rising ground behind the tank.

It was arranged that during the five days of the exercise two pilots would spend each twenty-four hours looking at it from the Pongos' point of view. Late every afternoon, an army Land Rover would arrive at the officers' mess to drop off two of us and pick up the next two to be whisked off to the desert. Brian Giffin and I went off for our stint. The trip took about an hour and a half, most of it off road before arriving at the 14th/20th encampment. We went straight to the officers' marquee. It was laid out for dinner in a most formal way. We were introduced to the detachment commander – a five-foot four-inch Major with a black patch over one eye. His first words of greeting included an offer of a pint of gin and tonic!

The next morning started just before sunrise. After breakfast, Brian and I were allocated to individual Centurion tanks. The commander of my tank was a young subaltern. I sat with him in the opening at the top of the turret and was not really aware of what the rest of the tank crew were doing in the bowels. But there was no doubt that a tank in the Sahara desert in June was not the most comfortable place to be. Sitting on top of it was probably less uncomfortable than sitting inside it. We started up and lurched off over the terrain with the subaltern talking into a two-way radio using a hand microphone and earphones. Continual reference was made to a map on his clipboard, and we were obviously heading for some sort of map reference point. We came to a halt in a flurry of sand and camouflaged the tank. The subaltern said he had been very impressed by our low flying. In fact one of our aircraft had come so low it had hit the top of his 15-foot whip aerial. I wondered whether it had been me or someone else with a touch of the target fixations!

Some 803 Squadron aircraft appeared and we came under

dummy attack. I must admit it was most impressive from the ground, but since it was now around Day Three there were no last minute pullouts or whipping of aerials. However, you definitely got the impression of being identified and could tell which aircraft was attacking you. The exercise finished with a party at the Pongos' officers' mess in Zuara. The next day we all flew back to Malta

In August the next big change was to come. The Attacker was to be replaced by the Hawker Sea Hawk Mk 3. The Sea Hawk was a very pretty aircraft for a fighter and it flew much better than the Attacker. Its main armament was 4 x 20 mm cannon mounted in the nose of the aircraft. It could also carry a similar ground attack load to the Attacker. It was equipped with a tricycle undercarriage and powered ailerons, which made it more responsive and more controllable at high MN. Although equipped with a Rolls-Royce Nene engine, it had a better performance than the Attacker. It could reach around 0.85 MN in mach stall buffet and could still manoeuvre. The Attacker had never been able to turn very well at high altitude.

When you first saw a Sea Hawk you could be forgiven for thinking it had two engines. There was an air intake at the wing root leading edge of each wing and a jet pipe protruding from the trailing edge wing root of each wing. However, the intakes fed into a common single engine intake and the exhaust expelled into a bifurcated jet pipe taking the hot gases through individual exhaust outlets. This was so that the aircraft could use a short jet pipe, giving space to install a rear fuselage fuel tank. Although suitably protected against hot gas leaks, there was a Tank Fire Warning light located on the right side of the pilot's instrument panel in the cockpit. The pilot's action if the light came on was to eject before the aircraft blew up! The light was located almost out of view under the cockpit combing so that the sun didn't shine on it and cause an inadvertent ejection! While I'm on the subject, the ejection seat envelope had been improved with the introduction of the Sea Hawk. As I recall we could now expect to get away with it above 200 feet.

Associated with the installation of this new ejection seat the Sea Hawk, unlike the Attacker, was fitted with a clear cockpit canopy. This innovation also required us to use the new flying helmet, known instantly as the 'bone dome', to replace our much loved leather flying helmets and goggles. The bone dome consisted of an inner cloth flying helmet incorporating the microphone, earphones and oxygen mask attachments. Over this fitted the hard hat to protect the head in a crash or when ejecting through the canopy. There was a certain amount of resistance to this new helmet since it weighed more and restricted the ability to look back over

No. 803 Squadron, Autumn 1954.
Back row from left to right: Brian Griffin, Maurice Tibby, Brian Davies, Dicky Jenkins, Ken Kemp, John Ellis, Nobby Hall, Brian Young, Sam Janes, Colin Casperd and Tim Savage. *Front row from left to right:* Eddie Ward, Harry Bain, Tom Innes, Dicky Carne and the AEO *(Crown copyright)*

your shoulder. On the other hand the clear canopy provided a better view. The other change was that we would now land on airfield or carrier with the canopy closed, since ejecting and the use of goggles with an open canopy was now not compatible with the new helmet.

The Attackers were being flown back to the UK and the Sea Hawks flown out to Malta by our own pilots. We were replacing the aircraft in flights of four, and I was now number 4 in the SP's flight. Harry Bain, Nobby Hall, Ken Kemp and I flew our aircraft back in separate sections. It reflected something of the limited range capability of the Attacker when we had to ferry them back via Rome, Orange, a French Airforce base with a RAF detachment at it, Dijon, Lee-on-Solent and then up to RNAS Abbotsinch (the present-day Glasgow airport), which was then a main RN Aircraft Repair Yard. We then travelled down to RNAS Stretton, near Warrington, where we spent ten days or so checking out in the Vampire T 22, the new training aircraft to replace the Meteor 7s, and flying acceptance flights on the new Sea Hawks. Most of us didn't think much of the T 22. It was a dual side-by-side seat trainer based on the single-seat version and powered by the de Havilland Ghost 3 engine. It didn't have the performance of the 'Kiddy Car' and wasn't so pleasant to handle. The cockpit was a bit cramped; if there were two of you in the cockpit things got very cosy.

On completion of the re-equipment we were now sitting at Halfar awaiting the arrival of HMS *Albion*, a light fleet carrier, which along with HMS *Centaur*, also operating in the Mediterranean, had been modified with an angled deck and mirror landing sight (MLS). The introduction of the MLS meant that pilots would make their own approaches to the deck and would be responsible for their speed and line-up. The batsman was now redundant and became the LSO, monitoring the MLS and each individual approach. He could activate the go-around red lights on the MLS to indicate that he wasn't happy with your approach or there was something wrong with the MLS. A similar mandatory wave-off could be given by FLYCO by firing a red flare if the ship or deck wasn't ready to receive you. The angled deck meant that the landing area of the flight deck had been angled off to port. If you missed the arrester wires you could open up to full power, roll along the deck and get airborne to have another go without hitting any of the aircraft in the forward deck park. If you did a practice landing without lowering the hook and ran along the deck to take off again, it was known as a 'touch and go'. If you landed on with the hook lowered and didn't catch a wire it would be known as a 'bolter'.

Anyway, an MLS had been installed on the main runway at Halfar, and the squadron went through a programme of mirror dummy deck landings (MADDLs) to learn the procedure. The circuit was flown at 500 feet, reducing to 300 feet on the final turn and with a little more straight away, since the MLS couldn't be used until you were nearly lined up with the runway. The MLS was located on the left side of the runway at the

No. 803 Squadron's 1954 Christmas card. Brian Davies is flying aircraft 143 *(Crown copyright)*

touchdown point. The mirror itself was square and slightly concave so that it reflected a ball of light from a battery of spot lights mounted in front of it. The mirror could be adjusted to shine a beam of light at a suitable angle to provide a visual glide slope to the pilot on approach. On either side of the mirror was a horizontal bar of green lights mounted at its mid-point. The total presentation given to the pilot was a square mirror with a bright ball of light shining in it, which he attempted to keep lined up with the green bars. If he went low on the glide slope, the 'meat ball', as it became known, would drop below the green bars; if he went high the Meat Ball went above the green bars. Keeping the meat ball in the middle and lined up with the green bars meant that the pilot was on the ideal glide slope to make a safe arrested landing.

At the end of October HMS *Albion* arrived in the area and we prepared to embark. We did one or two sessions of touch and goes without the hook lowered, and then on 15 November embarked aboard *Albion* to complete her complement of squadrons.

Chapter 6

803 Squadron, Carrier Operations

November 1954 to November 1955

Embarking a squadron in a carrier was quite a logistical task. Flying the aircraft on board was no real problem. Getting all the manpower, stores and equipment on board at more or less the same time, and sorting out the domestic situation, required most thought. Having no helicopter support to speak of in those days meant that there couldn't be any last minute airlift of men or material. All the aircraft had to be flyable on the day, so the engineers had their work cut out to repair the hangar queens (the aircraft that had been robbed of spare parts to keep the others flying).

We flew out to *Albion* in three flights of four aircraft, forming into sections line astern to join the carrier circuit. My deck landings to date had been very much for my own benefit. However, we were now landing on for the carrier's benefit, which meant that the ship wanted to spend the minimum amount of time steaming into wind.

In a war situation, an aircraft carrier steaming on a steady course at a fixed speed would give an enemy submarine advanced information and a steady target at which to launch a torpedo attack.

The object was to land on the aircraft at intervals of between 20 and 30 seconds, and it was up to you to position yourself in the circuit to achieve this. The initial problem was to convince yourself that you weren't too close behind the aircraft ahead before you yourself landed. It often looked completely impossible for him to land on, roll back to clear the arrester wire and then apply power quickly enough to clear the landing area. If it looked as if he would be able to clear the deck in time, you were probably too far behind him and would get a bollocking for not being close enough. If you were too close and had to be waved off you'd get a bollocking as well. If the LSO waved you off because you weren't flying the approach correctly, you'd get a bollocking. If the ship waved you off someone else would get a bollocking. To enable everyone to judge their position it was most important that you did a tight circuit onto a short final approach.

The MLS proved very easy to fly in the calm weather conditions prevailing on the day. The glide slope angle had been set to four degrees, one degree steeper than the airfield setting. This was for two reasons. Firstly, the high wind speed over the deck had the effect of decreasing the glide slope angle, making it equivalent to three degrees in more normal wind conditions. Secondly, the steeper glide slope was also necessary to ensure adequate clearance of the round down at the stern of the flight deck under rough sea conditions when the stern of the carrier would be pitching up and down. It seemed a little strange not to be watching a batsman so that now you were responsible for your own speed. The line-up on the angled deck didn't present a problem either. The circuit was flown to slightly overshoot the ship's wake and end up on a short final approach, rolling the wings level at around 200 feet, which put you 'on the meat ball' about 400 yards astern of the ship.

The angled deck on *Albion* was more of a cosmetic feature than the angle we are used to seeing on current American aircraft carriers. The port side of the flight deck had been built out a little abeam the island, and the designated landing area had been painted on from the starboard aft part of the flight deck at an angle of about five degrees to the ship's centre line. It finished on the port edge of the flight deck just ahead of the island.

As you came over the round down you concentrated on keeping that meat ball lined up with the green bars, your speed at 110 knots and ensuring you were on the angled deck centre line. There was no question of you flaring the aircraft to 'grease it on'; you just flew it into the deck. Any easing back on the stick would almost certainly mean you missing all the wires and doing a bolter, particularly since there were only six arrester wires instead of the multitude on *Eagle*. Even if you flew a perfect approach and landing, there was still a chance that you might 'bolt' anyway.

The MLS had been set up so that under ideal conditions your hook would engage number 3 wire. Although the hook was damped, it was still possible for it to bounce over 4, 5, and 6 wires. In this case the port side of the carrier would rapidly disappear under the aircraft and you would find yourself airborne again. To allow for this occurrence you didn't cut the engine power just prior to touchdown as with a batsman. Approach power was maintained until you felt the deceleration from the arrester wire. If you missed all the wires you pushed the throttle fully open and by the time the wheels were rolling off the deck edge you had enough power to climb away normally.

As soon as you felt the wire arrest the aircraft you closed the throttle. At the end of the wire runout, you allowed the aircraft to roll back in the high wind until the handler controlling the deck operation indicated you were clear of the wire and signalled you to raise the hook and apply the brakes. The handler controlling the land-on would hand you off to the handler controlling the forward deck park, who would be indicating to you to fold your wings. At this stage the main object was to get your aircraft clear of the landing area ASAP. To get the aircraft going you would slam the throttle wide open until you achieved the power you wanted and then throttle back.

We old hands hadn't found much difficulty with the new system. However, it was seven months since I had joined the squadron, and we had had a few new arrivals since then. Back home these pilots had trained on the Vampire T 22 and Sea Hawk, but had not had any deck landing training at all! Talk about the deep end. Unlike the security of the batsman on my initial deck landings, they were confronted by the do-it-yourself technique of the angled deck and MLS. The crowds on the goofers were something to behold when the new pilots were scheduled for their first catapult launches and deck landing practice.

As I mentioned, *Albion* was a light fleet carrier considerably smaller than *Eagle*, with only one hangar instead of two. We were embarked with 898 Sea Hawk Squadron and a flight of 849 Skyraider AEW aircraft. Both 898 and the 849 Flight were embarked before the ship arrived in the Mediterranean.

The role and the armament capability of the Sea Hawk were the same as the Attacker. We exercised under the control of the ship's radar for high and medium level intercepts and with the AEW Skyraiders for low-level intercepts. Normally our opponents were 898, in either the defensive or offensive roles.

We were now part of the ship's complement, and yet operated separately. We had become part of the 'Air Department', headed by 'Commander Air', or 'Wings' for short. He was responsible for all aspects of the operation of aircraft from the ship. The air department of a carrier included ship's officers who were qualified pilots. Overseeing the whole of the launch and land-on operation was 'Lieutenant-Commander (Flying)', 'Little F' for short. His domain was FLYCO, a glazed structure sticking out from the port side of the island. From there he could survey the whole of the flight deck. He was responsible for executing the flying programme and ensuring safe deck operations, including adequate wind speed over the deck to launch and land aircraft, wave-offs and launch and land-on sequencing amongst other things. Flyco was also the control tower of the ship, and all radio communication with aircraft airborne in the circuit or manned on the flight deck was from there.

The FDO was in charge of the flight deck, and under him were other junior FDOs. The job of the FDOs was to run the flight deck. This included the manoeuvring of aircraft around the deck, moving aircraft between flight deck and hangar via the lifts and sequencing aircraft for launch and land-on. He had teams of aircraft handlers and tractors to assist in these matters. Even though we now had the angled deck we still retained the ability to rig a barrier amidships in case an aircraft that couldn't use the normal arrester gear landed on. Associated with this we had 'Jumbo', an enormous mobile crane parked alongside the island that could lift any one of the aircraft on board and move it.

Some of the FDOs were qualified LSOs who looked after the operation of the MLS and batted on the Skyraiders, which, because of their restricted view, still used a batsman.

The Aircraft Control Room Officer (ACRO) operated from the ACR located at flight deck level at the aft end of the island. The ACR was equipped with scale models of the flight deck and hangar on which were scale models of the aircraft on board. Aircraft side numbers were used to identify individual aircraft. The ACRO overlooked the organisation of aircraft on the ship and liaised with the individual squadron duty officers as to their requirements with respect to which aircraft were to be used for each launch. With the restricted space on board, this could become a bit of a nightmare. Unserviceable (U/S) aircraft that had landed might need to be 'struck down' to the hangar to be worked on and replaced by aircraft in the hangar that had become serviceable. The ship normally worked on a 45-minute launch cycle. Having launched and landed on into wind, the carrier would then steam in the direction that fleet operations required until launching and recovering aircraft into wind 45 minutes later. There was nothing magical about the 45 minutes. In the case of the *Albion* in 1954, it was based on the fact that the Sea Hawk in particular couldn't stay airborne for longer than 45 minutes without running out of fuel. Having completed the land-on, there were about 35 minutes available to rearrange the flight deck, refuel and service the aircraft, before the next launch. It was the job of the ACRO to organise it and the job of the FDO to execute it.

Finally, we had the ship's flight, which, consisted of a ship's flight aircraft that would be flown by a ship's flight pilot. New to the game in *Albion* were the ship's flight helicopters, two Sikorsky S 51

'Dragonfly' to be used for SAR and 'plane guard' duties. Until quite recently the rescuing of aircrew who ended up in the sea had been the job of the plane guard frigate or destroyer which steamed astern and to one side of the carrier during the launch and land-on sequence. The helicopter was now replacing this role.

On the engineering side, the squadron maintenance task was overlooked and supported by the ship's air engineering department, although the squadron Air Engineer Officer (AEO) was in charge of the maintenance and was responsible to the squadron CO. There were few ship's aircraft maintenance men, and squadron maintenance personnel were seconded to the various specialist workshops on board. The ship's supply department provided spare parts. Thus the overall task of the ship was to provide the wherewithal to operate and maintain the aircraft.

A typical daily training programme started at a gentlemanly hour. First launch was around 08.30 and continued throughout the day, normally consisting of six deck cycles.

Number 803 Squadron was embarked in *Albion* from November '54 to March '55, with the occasional return to Malta, where we would disembark a few aircraft to Halfar so that we could keep our hands in whilst the ship was in harbour. At sea the ship's programme varied. We would operate under the control of the ship's air defence system most of the time. Occasionally we would have ground attack exercises involving rocketing, bombing and strafing using a 'splash target' towed behind the ship, with the fall of shot measured from ships' observations. On these occasions the goofers would be full, since reputations could be gained or lost depending on your ability.

We would often be involved in exercises made up of two opposing forces. The American Sixth Fleet was based in the Mediterranean and would provide opposition to *Albion* and HMS *Centaur*, another light fleet carrier with a similar air group to us. During these clashes we would often spend a lot of time at 'Condition One' readiness on the flight deck. This meant sitting in our aircraft, fully ready to be launched instantly to intercept an incoming raid. There would be up to eight aircraft at Condition One, and we could expect to be launched in pairs. In the 1950s the slang word for an aircraft in the RAF was a 'Kite'. In the Navy it was a 'Cab' and I had never known why. However, the NATO term for a number of aircraft waiting at Condition One on the flight deck was 'Cab Rank' – thus 'Cab'.

We were often matched against the Grumman Cougar, the United States Navy's latest swept-wing aircraft. It was interesting to see that although they could outpace us with their ability to fly at a higher Mach number, the Sea Hawk could outmanoeuvre them if it came to a dog fight and they tried to stay with us.

We also gained experience of carrier operations using the MLS under less than ideal conditions. The Mediterranean in winter can be a very hostile place. Turning into wind meant turning into sea as well, and we became used to operating off a pitching deck. A ship the size of *Albion* doesn't go up and down in the sea. In fact a large ship steaming into a high sea will only pitch a maximum of about three degrees. However, if you're on a large ship pitching three degrees it can be very sick making. If you fly an aircraft down a four degrees glide slope, onto a deck pitching three degrees it can be very unnerving. One minute the deck angle is showing you a one-degree glide slope the next a seven-degree glide slope. Those who fly will know what an extreme this is. You couldn't land on if the deck was pitching much outside two degrees. However, the MLS was gyro stabilised, and because it was amidships maintained a constant height above the sea. It was therefore projecting a constant beam of light up the glide slope. The LSO monitored the MLS continually under these conditions and if necessary could hold the MLS steady by manually tracking the horizon. High winds also meant slower ship's speed, since more than 35 knots of wind over the deck introduced problems in just standing up on the flight deck and keeping moveable things lashed down.

If you came over the round-down while the ship was pitching nose down, the relative glide angle would be around two degrees and you would taxi smoothly into number one wire. If the ship was pitching nose up, your relative glide slope would be around six degrees and you would be lucky to catch number 6 wire and keep your undercarriage intact from the high impact with the deck.

The ship would synchronise itself with the waves and achieve large pitch angles. But every so often it would get out of synchronisation and stop pitching. The trick was to catch the ship in the steadier periods when the deck pitch was within limits to land. This wasn't a decision you made. This was Little F's problem, and if it was decided that the deck would be outside pitch limits at touchdown the red wave-off lights would be illuminated on the MLS and a red flare would be fired from the forward end of the flight deck. However, we learnt that the more impossible the situation looked with 20 seconds to go the more likely we were to land on.

The last thing you tried to do was to 'eyeball' the deck. It was important to follow the glide slope and ignore the gyrations of the ship. There was a tremendous tendency to try and get yourself synchronised at the last minute. If you approached the round-down with the stern dropping away from you, it was important that you resisted poling forward to chase the deck. By the time you got over the end of the ship the stern would be coming up!

The final problem was the ship's heading. During 'Flying Stations' you had one of the most experienced helmsmen on the wheel. But under conditions of high wind and heavy seas, where the ship was probably only making about ten knots, it was impossible to hold the ship steady within one or two degrees. So you were always having to make slight adjustments to your heading to stay lined up at the last minute.

The other aspect to the pitching problem was of course the catapult launch. Here it was very much up to the FDO to time the launch to coincide with the bow of the ship pitching up. However, the delay between his dropping the flag and the catapult firing was variable, and it was inevitable that the occasional launch was made with the bow pitched down. This resulted in you launching through heavy spray or skimming the waves. One of the pilots who was prone to seasickness really didn't mind when he was launched providing he got off the deck before he threw up.

It was decided that the MLS could become disabled and that we should practise mirrorless deck landings. A calm day was picked for this exercise to ensure maximum ship stability. The approaches were monitored by the LSO through the MLS with the Meat Ball lights switched off, and surprisingly no one had much of a problem making a safe approach and landing. We had obviously become used to judging the aspect of the ship to be able to establish the correct glide angle!

Number 803 Squadron was to spend two more months embarked in *Albion* before the ship returned to UK. Then we were to embark in *Centaur*. Our brother Sea Hawk squadron in *Centaur* would be 806, famous at the time as the 'Ace of Diamonds' squadron that had unofficially taken the mantle of the Fleet Air Arm's formation aerobatic aces as well. Unofficial because the days of public relations were yet to come, and formation aerobatics were considered to be more of a morale booster than anything else. The CO of 806 was John Kelly, who did an individual aerobatics routine in synchronisation with a 'box four' formation. He had gained a certain notoriety as a dare devil pilot.

It was at this stage that I thought our mirrorless deck landings on *Albion* had an ulterior motive. *Centaur* was configured exactly the same as *Albion*, except that it didn't have a workable MLS system. It had only recently been installed and for the first few days of our embarkation would be inoperative. 806 used the angled deck but still with an old-fashioned batsman. By now half the pilots in 803 had never seen a batsman, and there was no time to give them any instruction. So it was decided to embark using the mirrorless deck landing technique until the MLS became operational. One of the LSOs from *Albion* had also transferred to *Centaur* and would be instrumental in getting *Centaur*'s equipment, LSOs and 806 up to speed on the new system within a couple of days!

We in 803 were very much the newcomers onboard *Centaur*, and lacked the glamour of 806. That is until the first land on. Using the mirrorless technique we established a new land on record for the ship, with an average of 18 seconds between landings for twelve aircraft. *Centaur* remained in the Mediterranean for three months or so before returning to UK.

After the ship's final ritual stop at Gibraltar, *Centaur* set sail for the UK. In early June, 803 and 806 Squadrons, aircraft disembarked to RNAS Ford and the Skyraiders disembarked to their home base at RNAS Culdrose.

For the first ten days or so we operated periodically from *Centaur* on a 'shop window' exercise. This was one of the early efforts at Public Relations, and concentrated on showing the capabilities of an aircraft carrier to the influential but uninitiated. The audience included senior Army and RAF officers and influential MPs. The routine consisted of *Centaur* putting to sea from Portsmouth without the inconvenience of having aircraft aboard, and the ship's officers briefing the visitors on the day's action. Then they were shepherded up to the goofers just in time to see the Sea Hawks arrive overhead to provide a quick firepower demonstration against a splash target towed astern. This was followed by a land on, re-arm and refuel, and a launch. More firepower demonstrations after the launch were followed by a general 'beat up' of the ship, and we all got back to Ford for tea.

You could say that the 'shop window' began the start of the silly season. This period was a feature between June and the end of August in the UK in the 50s. It meant that a lot of our time was spent rehearsing for and flying in the various air days and open days at Naval Air Stations and Dockyards throughout the South of England.

One of the first occasions was the Ford Air Day. Both 803 and 806 Squadrons were to take part. But 806 took the lion's share of the aerobatic content. They were to fly their normal precise 'box four' formation aerobatics interspersed with John Kelly's solo aerobatics. As well as his general routine he was famous for his slow loop, a manoeuvre which involved a great deal of risk as well as flying skill. Under normal conditions you would start a loop in the Sea Hawk at around the 300-knot mark, and expect to cover a vertical height of 3,000 feet or so. John Kelly started his loop at around 200 feet and 200 knots and didn't get much above 1,500 feet at the top. The power to weight ratio of the Sea Hawk was nothing like the modern-day fighter, and although he applied full power at the beginning of the loop, the aircraft was well below stalling speed at the top and on the initial pullout. It was necessary for him to lower take-off flap going over the top to give extra lift.

In the past I, as well as many other naval pilots, had watched this manoeuvre with heart in mouth as John had pulled out at 100 to 200 feet above the ground, obviously pulling to the stall. If you got it wrong you were dead. On one of the practice days the flaps didn't extend at the top of the loop and John's Sea Hawk just simply didn't pull out. It crashed short of the runway off the airfield. He was killed instantly.

He was undoubtedly a very skilful pilot and everyone admired his guts, but his demise had certainly taught me a lesson. The only people who had realised that his slow loop had been a manoeuvre requiring skill and courage were other pilots. It was lost on the general public, who would probably have been more impressed by lots of speed and noise. At the same time, it was probably not a good idea to commit yourself to a manoeuvre that required a change of configuration half way through to ensure its safe execution.

The squadrons re-embarked in *Centaur* on 31 August, and the ship set sail for Northern Norway and the autumn exercises. Whilst operating in the Moray Firth on the way north, a flight deck accident occurred which wrote off three of the squadron's aircraft. I was up in the goofers watching a land-on of two flights of 803 aircraft. The first flight landed on and was marshalled into the starboard forward part of the flight deck. Maurice Tibby, the leader of the second flight, landed on and cleared the landing area normally by opening up to full throttle to get the aircraft going. However, when he throttled back, the engine kept on winding up to full power. With tyres smoking from the application of full brake Maurice's aircraft ploughed into the forward deck park, catching Nobby Hall's half-folded port wing with his half folded starboard wing. This slewed Maurice's aircraft to the right, and he disappeared over the side of the ship, crashing into the sea with the aircraft inverted. The Sea Hawk drifted down the starboard side of the carrier. The rescue helicopter peeled off and was hovering over the aircraft as it cleared the stern. Maurice popped up out of the water alongside his aircraft.

As well as hitting Nobby's aircraft, Maurice's aircraft had hit another Sea Hawk and knocked over a number of maintenance and flight deck personnel. Sam Janes, the squadron electrical officer, had been hit by Maurice's aircraft and carried over the side on the nose-wheel door. Luckily, the helicopter had spotted him floating

Maurice Tibby's flight deck accident.
Sam Janes can be seen hanging from the nose of an aircraft in the third photo
(Crown copyright)

WM978
WM931
148
WM987
145
100

face down in the sea and had hauled him out. It was a bit touch and go whether Sam would live. However, he did recover, but required considerable convalescence afterwards. Remarkably, no one else was hurt. However, with Maurice's aircraft in the sea and two others badly damaged, the squadron was down to nine aircraft.

From the middle of September to the middle of October our operations ranged from Kristiansand in the south to Bodö in the north and the Lofoten Islands inside the Arctic Circle. We picked up the odd Russian 'Elint' (Electronic Intelligence) spy ship. We did a lot of pretend ground attack on targets in Norway. Often we found the targets required a specific attack direction to avoid hitting high ground in the area. Most of our aerial opposition came from the Norwegian Air Force flying F-84 Thunderjets, but we didn't see a great deal of them.

At the end of the exercise, *Centaur* made her way back to UK waters still battling away against 'enemy forces' from RN and RAF bases in Scotland. She was planned to pay off (decommission) at the end of October, and our last flights were to be made to RNAS Lee-on-Solent and the RN Aircraft Repair Yard at Belfast Lock (now the Belfast City airport).

All the squadron pilots had been informed of their new appointments. Mine was to join 751, a second-line squadron based at RAF Watton in Norfolk. I had been told that I had been selected to fly a newly equipped de Havilland Sea Venom Mk 21, which was planned to be the first RN jet aircraft fitted with electronic countermeasures (ECM) equipment. The reason the squadron was based at RAF Watton was because ECM operations were top secret and the RAF had a number of squadrons dedicated to the role. Number 751 Squadron was the naval element. I can't say that I was looking forward to my new job. I knew absolutely nothing about ECM. The Sea Venom was a one-off aircraft which wouldn't have a fighter role. It would act as a 'fast vehicle' full of electronics for an observer to operate.

Chapter 7

751 Squadron

November 1955 to August 1957

I spent a short leave with my parents at Bognor. My main purpose was to buy a car, since in rural Norfolk life would be just about impossible without private transport. I ended up with a 1937 Riley Adelphi sports saloon with a pre-selector gearbox, which set me back £175.

I arrived at RAF Watton in the first week of November. I checked into the officers' mess. I was back in the permanency of the RAF. That evening I met a few of my new squadron colleagues in the bar and began to find out about the job.

The next day it was good to get back to the temporary feeling of the RN! Number 751 Squadron offices and hangar were located on the far side of the airfield, known as the Griston Site (Griston being a small hamlet just outside the back gate of the airfield). It had all the temporary buildings. The squadron offices were wooden huts akin to those at Lossie, suitably heated with the standard coke fire.

The morning was spent meeting all the other squadron aircrew. The squadron CO, Bill Cooper, was an observer. In those days it was unusual to have an observer as a CO, but this reflected the specialised nature of the squadron's task. Electronic countermeasures (ECM) required brains and not brawn. He explained that although I had been sent to the squadron as the 'jet jockey' for the new Sea Venom, the aircraft was somewhat delayed and in the meantime I would have to fit in with the normal squadron operations. Bill Sabey, the SP, would sort out my conversion to the main squadron type, the Grumman Avenger Mk 6.

The Avenger was a USN WW2 torpedo bomber. It was the largest single-engined aircraft built during the war and had been used extensively in the Pacific against the Japanese. It was powered by a Wright Cyclone 2600R double-banked radial engine and had the

The 'Ruptured Duck' – Grumman Avenger Mk 6 *(Crown copyright)*

reputation of being a very rugged machine. The six squadron aircraft were the last remnants of the RN machines, and had been converted to the Mk 6 configuration, where the rear gun turret had been faired in to provide a large rear cockpit for the observer. The belly gun position had been converted to provide a cockpit for a telegraphist. The large bomb bay provided more than enough room for the ECM equipment, and a small radome was fitted underneath the fuselage associated with this equipment.

During my four familiarisation flights I flew the Avenger solo. It was very much a do-it-yourself conversion. I must admit it did seem a huge aircraft compared with the Sea Hawk. The cockpit was quite the largest I had seen. It looked as if it had been built for someone the size of John Wayne. It wasn't until I lifted off on my first flight that I realised I would have to be as strong as John Wayne to fly the damned thing. Compared with the Sea Hawk, the control forces were so high that my initial reaction was that someone must have left the control locks engaged. After the familiarisation flights I was called into the CO's office. I was told to pack my bags and travel down to RAF Benson on the Thames to help the RNVR squadron there convert from Sea Furies to Attackers! It was only for a week, but proved very interesting. The RNVRs had a Vampire T 22 at Benson where they were progressively converting to jets with the help of a couple of RN QFIs. My jet instrument rating was also up for renewal, which I suspect was the real reason I had been seconded to Benson. There were no RN IREs at Watton. I needed to take my instrument rating on a jet since in those days it was considered that if you passed a jet instrument rating test you would be able to fly a piston-engined aircraft on instruments but not vice versa.

The week at Benson also showed me that the reputation of the Attacker as one of the more dangerous aircraft to fly had got around. Most of my time was spent closeted in the RNVR squadron CO's office helping him make a case to show that the RNVR shouldn't be equipped with Attackers. My little sojourn in the jet world came to an end and I found myself back at Watton adjusting to the slower pace of life.

The Avenger wasn't the only aircraft on the squadron. We also had a Firefly Mk 6 and an Avro Anson, but were about to get rid of both of them. I managed to cadge three flights in the Firefly before it left, but wasn't allowed to fly the Anson since I wasn't a qualified twin-piston pilot.

To begin with, the job was a bit of a novelty. Being able to chat to other people who weren't sitting in the same cockpit was a bit different. It was also unusual to have someone else doing the navigating and being told where to go. However, when the observer was fully occupied with the ECM gear, it was very much up to the pilot to do the navigating, so brawn was mixed with a little brain.

Compared with current ECM equipment, our 1950s gear was very basic. A wide range of radio and radar frequencies could be monitored, and if necessary individual frequencies or frequency bands could be jammed. The pilots had nothing to do with this process, but we could listen in on the passive side. We all developed a 'musical ear' by listening to the different radar frequencies and working out what sort of radar was 'illuminating' us at the time. Low-frequency radars were used for long-range target detection. These low frequencies gave a low pulse repetition frequency (PRF) which sounded like a 'raspberry'. You could only hear these sounds at comparatively large time intervals, since the rate of rotation of a long-range radar aerial was very slow. As the useable range of radar reduces, the PRF increases and the aerial rotation rate increases. These higher frequency radars gave a more accurate picture than the long-range radars and were used as intercept radars. The days of SAM and long-range airborne missile systems were still well into the future and didn't come into our sphere of operation. The flying proved a little boring since all we seemed to do was wander around East Anglia in particular and the UK in general just listening to radar transmission to give the observers practice in listening to various radar signatures.

However, things started to get a little exciting in January 1956. The six Avengers were to be flown to Malta to operate in the ECM role during the winter exercises in the Mediterranean. We set off from UK on 31 January, the day the bad weather hit Europe.

We didn't make our first destination of Istres, a French military base near Marseilles, but diverted early to Chateauroux. We all ended up on the GCA at this American Air Force base in France in extremely bad weather conditions. It was the first time I had been controlled by an American voice, and I found it a little difficult to understand. It was obvious that many of the instructions being given were of a standard nature required by their system, but as I was directed around the pattern onto final approach, the American voice came up with 'Approaching final glide slope, stand by to descend. The United States Government takes no responsibility for any damage done to your aircraft off this approach.' I began to wonder what was wrong. I didn't know whether this statement related to some degradation of the GCA equipment, or that language and terminology might induce a mistake, or whether they thought we were lousy pilots. We all landed OK in probably the worst weather conditions I had yet encountered.

We stayed the night since weather conditions were 'out' at Istres. That evening, in the American officers' club, we met up with our GCA controller. I enquired about the warning given on the GCA that afternoon. He explained that the statement was now a requirement when controlling other than US military aircraft. It would appear that some few weeks previously a formation of G91 Italian jet fighters had diverted into Chateauroux and had all crashed short of the runway as a result of running out of fuel. One of the reasons given for the incident was the protracted nature of the procedures when compared to those of the Italian Air Force. The Italian government was in the process of trying to lay the blame on the Americans and demanding financial compensation!

The next day we flew on to Istres and again landed in very adverse weather conditions, with the *Mistral* gusting up to 50 knots. Istres decided to shut after we had landed and didn't open again for another five days. There was a transit mess at Istres which was well known for its appalling conditions, but luckily it was chock-a-block with other transit crews. We had to be accommodated in the local village at the Hotel de Poste.

Five days later saw us airborne again on the non-stop flight to Halfar. We arrived very late for the exercise and were only involved for about a week before commencing the return journey. This time it was planned to stop at Cagliari in Sardinia on the way to Istres because of very strong head winds. We landed at Cagliari in torrential rain some two hours later. We were beginning to smell. The days of drip dry were still to come. Most of our shirts and collars required laundering, and we hadn't stayed anywhere long enough to have them laundered.

Having spent so much time not at a British base, which would have allowed us access to banking facilities (no credit cards in those days), we were also running short of money. At Cagliari we found that Istres was shut again because of the bad weather. The CO decided to contact the local British Consul to obtain funds, but found he had died recently and had yet to be replaced! So we stayed the night as the guests of the Italian Air Force. We were determined to leave the next day, but half way to Istres found there were no airfields open and turned back to Cagliari. We spent another miserable night in the damp of Sardinia.

We departed for Istres the next day, even though we knew the place was shut! The idea was that the telegraphists would communicate with all and sundry *en route* to find somewhere for us to land. It was eventually determined that Perpignan, a small French civilian airfield on the Mediterranean coast just to the north of the French/Spanish border, was open, and we set course for there. We were cleared to land to the north-west on a very short asphalt runway with a slight tailwind. It wasn't until we were rolling out on the runway after touchdown that we realised just how short it was. The only way to avoid running off the end was to take a smart right turn onto the dispersal just before the end of the runway. The next day a picture of the line of Avengers appeared in the local paper with the headlines that 'Six British Naval Fighters' had landed at the small civil airfield as a last resort because of the appalling weather elsewhere.

We explained our financial difficulties to the airfield authorities when the problem of landing fees was raised, and within minutes the CO was in contact with the local British authority. He established funds and accommodation for the night. Two days after our arrival we departed for the UK.

The detachment to Malta had enabled me to get to know the other squadron members well. My service life to date had revolved around the squadron as a 'team' at sea doing an operational job. I was beginning to look at 751 Squadron more as a family existence instead of just belonging to a team. I was, at the age of 23, the youngest member of the squadron. The oldest squadron members seemed Methuselah-like to me, although they were around 45 years old. Some of the older observers had been Telegraphist/Air Gunners (TAGs), and one in particular went back to the Fairey IIIF days between the wars.

Life in 751 Squadron was proving much less boring than I expected. March saw us practising ADDLs on the airfield at Watton with our own batsman, Ted Scoley, before embarking in HMS *Bulwark* for yet another exercise. We embarked somewhere in the North Sea. The next day the pilots had a quick session of DLPs before commencing four days operating in our ECM role. I found deck landing a piston-engined aircraft a pleasure. *Bulwark* had an angled deck and MLS like *Albion* and *Centaur*, and like the Skyraider AEW aircraft in the past, we were required to use a batsman because of the restricted view from the Avenger. We launched one or two aircraft at a time for the exercise requirements, but this didn't involve catapult launches.

The flying was a bit boring. Flying an aircraft at low level over the sea for up to four hours at a time wasn't very exciting. It did become a little exciting on one of my sorties. After about thirty minutes transiting out to our jamming station, the telegraphist came on the intercom. to inform me that his cockpit window was covered in engine oil. I decided to return to the ship, having informed it of my problem. On joining the circuit, FLYCO informed me that I was trailing black smoke. The deck had been cleared and I landed on. An inspection of the aircraft showed it was lucky that I decided to return to the ship when I did. The oil return pipe to the sump had a partial leak and I had only about ten per cent of my oil capacity left on arrival!

At Watton the summer drifted by. I had been promoted to Lieutenant in the spring of '56, and was summoned to the Admiralty for an interview. I had let it be known that I was interested in a full naval career and was now eligible for consideration. At the same time the RN was rationalising all the various commissions on which officers were serving, and had decided to establish the Supplementary List in addition to the General List. The Supplementary List would contain all the officers on other short-service commissions and offer a limited aircrew specialist career to a pensionable age. As a result of this revision, one of our 'old and bold' Senior Commissioned Observers, Jackie Lambert, became a Lieutenant-Commander overnight. Along with the restructuring of the career options came the deletion of the specialist colours between the rings of rank on an officer's sleeve. Whereas in the past engineer specialist officers had been identified by dark red, electrical by green, supply by white and medical by crimson, all, except the medical branch which retained the crimson colour, became unidentifiable from the executive officer, who didn't wear any colour. Aviators were in general selected from the Executive Branch, although there were many engineer pilots and at the time at least one from the Supply Branch. Most of us thought it wasn't a good idea to get rid of the colours since it was convenient for most personnel to know which specialisation an officer was.

My day of the interview arrived and I set off for the Admiralty in my best lounge suit. Awaiting my turn I felt a little uneasy surrounded by other interviewees in dark suits with rolled umbrellas and attendant bowler hat of the London 'mufti' brigade. I relaxed a little when my turn came, since Derek Empson, the Commander (Air) at Halfar when I was there in 803, was chairing the committee, so at least there was someone on the board who knew me personally. I learnt within the week that I was now a General List career officer. Nevertheless, from the Navy's viewpoint I wasn't a fully qualified naval officer. I would have to go to sea as a seaman officer to gain the experience of 'fish-heading' that I hadn't obtained during the courses I would have done as a Sub-Lieutenant had I been a Dartmouth Entry officer cadet at the beginning of my career. In particular I would have to obtain a Bridge Watch Keeping Certificate and an Ocean Navigation Certificate, which meant I could navigate out of sight of land using astral observations of the sun and stars. Incidentally, 'fish-head' was the term used by naval aviators to refer to Executive Branch officers who didn't fly. They used to call us 'flyboys' in derogatory response, but you could get much more venom into 'fish'ead' than 'flyboy'.

October 1956 came around and it was autumn exercise time again. It was planned for us to fly to Holland and operate with the Dutch Navy from their Naval Air Station at Valkenburg near the coast just to the north of The Hague. The two-week detachment proved to be very social without a great deal of flying. My main recollection of this period was the fact that every Dutch officer and rating spoke very good English and that the Dutch draft beer was excellent!

I have deliberately kept personal history to a minimum until now, but the 1956 Christmas Ball at the RAF Watton officers' mess was a bit of a milestone in my life. I spied a gorgeous girl across a crowded room and fell in love. I'm not sure that Anne felt the same way about me at the time since in a true naval aviating tradition, I was slightly inebriated when we met. However, I engineered another meeting after the ball, and we started going out together.

January 1957 saw the Sea Venom Mk 21 I had joined the squadron to fly getting close to arriving! I was sent to 764 Squadron at RNAS Ford to do a jet refresher course and renew my instrument rating. I then went to 766 Squadron at RAF Merryfield in Somerset to do a Sea Venom conversion course. Normally 766 would have been based at RNAS Yeovilton, but the main runway was being

Sea Venom Mk 21 *(Crown copyright)*

extended ready for a new generation of aircraft, and RAF Merryfield, a little-used air station nearby, had been utilised as its temporary home.

The conversion was semi-formal. Although larger than the Vampire T 22, the Sea Venom was a two-seat night-fighter from the same stable, and apart from the fact that the Sea Venom had hydraulically powered ailerons, the aircraft was very similar. I was given the pilot's notes to read, accumulated six hours and was then considered suitably experienced to fly the Sea Venom. Since I was not to become a night-fighter pilot, I wasn't offered the full course, and apart from one flight with an observer, flew the aircraft solo. The ECM version of the Sea Venom I had joined 751 to fly arrived in June 1957. I managed to fly it five times before leaving the squadron in August 1957.

By the time it arrived I had already received an appointment to a new job. Much to my surprise I had been selected as one of the nine pilots to join 700X Flight. This flight was to be formed six months before the introduction into front-line service of the Vickers Supermarine Scimitar, a swept-wing, single-seat, two-engined fighter/bomber that could go supersonic in a shallow dive. The object of 700X Flight was to evaluate the aircraft operationally and to iron out any design or engineering faults prior to the aircraft entering squadron service. The flight was to be based at RNAS Ford. I wondered why on earth I had been selected for the job, until I found out that 700X Flight CO was to be Tom Innes, my old boss of 803. He had been promoted to the rank of Commander, and I could only think that he had asked for me by name. I was quite flattered.

Before joining 700X Flight I went back to 764 Squadron in July to do an Instrument Rating Examiner (IRE) course on the Vampire T 22 to become the examiner for the flight. This involved a number of flights 'under the hood' to demonstrate my instrument flying ability, followed by a final flying test and ground examination to establish my credentials as an examiner with the specialists at RNAS Yeovilton.

Although I was very pleased to be involved in the forefront of naval aviation, I didn't want to leave Anne and all my friends at Watton. I told Anne I would be up to see her as often as possible in the 'Ice Cream Van'. During my two years at Watton I had decided to join the ranks of new car owners and had bought a cream-coloured Austin A35 van. This was the cheapest way of getting into the new car market, since vans didn't attract purchase tax (old VAT). At the same time vans were restricted to a maximum speed of 30 mph, but I didn't take much notice of that. The main thing was that it provided the reliability of a new car! I packed my belongings in the van and left Watton for the last time at the end of July 1957. I attended a week's course at the Rolls-Royce Engine School in Derby learning about the Avon jet engine installed in the Scimitar, and then motored to Ford.

Chapter 8

700X Flight, the Scimitar Intensive Flying Trials Unit (IFTU) – RNAS Ford

August 1957 to January 1958

The Supermarine Scimitar was the first-swept wing aircraft to enter service with the Fleet Air Arm and the last of the old-fashioned day-fighter/bombers. It came from the same stable as the Attacker and the Swift. However, compared with the Swift the Scimitar was considerably larger, and being equipped with two Rolls-Royce Avon axial-flow jet engines had considerably more power and two-engine reliability. Until the introduction of the Scimitar, RN aircraft had in general been powered by one engine. Although few had been lost as a result of an engine failure, it was considered a good idea to have aircraft with more than one engine in future.

The Scimitar was also the strongest aircraft I was to fly. It was built like the proverbial brick chicken house. Although it had a 'Coke Bottle' fuselage, a design concept at the time that went some way towards reducing Mach drag, the aircraft was equipped with a thick wing. It accelerated extremely well in level flight until it reached significant shock wave drag at around 0.95 MN, and then behaved as if it had hit a brick wall.

Number 700X Flight formed in mid August with one Vampire T 22. It appeared that the Scimitar deliveries would be slightly delayed, and the Vampire was allocated to provide us with flying practice. A couple of the flight's pilots had served on exchange postings with RAF Hunter squadrons and had experience of flying swept-wing aircraft. Tom Innes and Jock Tofts, the SP, also had swept-wing experience, but the rest of us hadn't. So Tom Innes had arranged for those of us who hadn't flown swept-wing aircraft to fly Hunters with 'A' Squadron at the Aeroplane and Armament

Experimental Establishment (A&AEE) Boscombe Down in Wiltshire. 'A' Squadron tested RAF fighter aircraft. We all travelled over to Boscombe Down, expecting to stay a few days whilst accumulating experience with the Hunter. Day One started with a brief on the Hunter. A two-seat training version of the Hunter was yet to come, so our first flights would be solo. For myself the briefing was followed by a flight in a Rolls-Royce-Avon-powered Mk 4, followed by a flight in an Armstrong-Siddeley-Sapphire powered Mk 5. This second flight frightened the life out of me, since one of the Sapphire's characteristics was to make all sorts of rumbling and wailing noises during normal operations. The next day I flew the Hunter Mk 5 one more time. That was to be my lot. 'A' Squadron couldn't afford to give us any more flying.

This brief experience of flying swept-wing aircraft showed up different flying characteristics in various areas. Swept wings were used to delay the onset of shock waves and the associated increased drag as the aircraft operated in the transonic area. In those days wing structures couldn't be made thin and strong at the same time. Thickness to chord ratios of ten to twelve per cent was the norm. By that I mean that the depth of the wing couldn't be made thinner than ten to twelve per cent of the distance between the leading and trailing edge of the wing, partly because the wing structure included the fuel tanks. But imagine a twelve per cent straight wing that is swept back. In the direction that the air is flowing, the distance between the leading and trailing edge increases, thus making the wing 'thinner'.

At the same time the overall proportions of swept-wing aircraft had changed. They were designed to go as fast as possible. As a result the ratio of wing span to fuselage length had reduced. In all piston-powered aircraft the wing span was greater than the fuselage

Vickers Supermarine Scimitar *(Crown copyright)*

length. In the Attacker and Sea Hawk the wing span and fuselage length had been about the same. In swept-wing fighter aircraft the fuselage was longer than the wing span.

This change in shape and proportion changed the way the aircraft flew. With reduced wing areas and higher weights, the landing speeds had increased. Most swept-wing fighters now had an approach speed of 120 to 130 knots instead of the 110 knots of the Attacker and Sea Hawk. Also, because the aerodynamic characteristics of the swept wing, the angle of attack of the wing at these speeds was much greater, resulting in an increased nose-up attitude at touchdown.

The reduction of wing span relative to fuselage length made the aircraft more manoeuvrable in the rolling plane. Combined with very effective powered flying control systems, the rate of roll of the Hunter compared with the Sea Hawk was very much increased.

Another major change related to flying a swept-wing aircraft near to the stalling angle at slow and high speeds. With a straight-wing aircraft the stall occurs over the whole wing at the same time. With a swept-wing aircraft the air tends to flow from the wing root to the wing tip, as well as straight back over the wing. As the angle of attack increases at high speeds in a manoeuvre, or as the aircraft slows towards the stalling speed in level flight, it becomes more marked and results in the outer part of the wing stalling before the inner part. This results in the total reduction of lift, and it would be desirable for the nose to pitch down to recover the situation. However, exactly the opposite occurs, since what lift is left acts on the forward, inner part of the wing and pitches the nose up, forcing the aircraft into an even worse stalled attitude. This is an unstable situation and relies on the pilot pushing the stick forward to stop the nose going up. At high speeds when pulling 'g' to the stall buffet, this characteristic would produce a sudden pitch-up which could be recovered quite quickly by easing off the 'g', but at slow speeds recovery had to be much more positive. As a result slow-speed flying in a swept-wing aircraft was done with caution, and the speed was never reduced below the onset of pitch-up. Full-blown stall practice was banned, and spinning was out of the question. Any slow flying practice near the stalling speed had to be conducted at a considerable altitude, since stall recovery could use up 10,000 feet if you got it right and considerably more if you got it wrong. Still, regardless of any legislation on the banning of stalls and spins, there had been the odd occasion when pilots had inadvertently spun the Hunter, and a few had managed to recover safely. Others had had to resort to the ejection seat when spin recovery didn't occur. At one stage it was thought that a Hunter would come out of a spin if the pilot's canopy was jettisoned. However, canopy jettison could be the preamble to ejecting, and it was likely that the recovery was as a result of the pilot letting go of the flying controls!

Along with the aerodynamic changes there were changes in engine design. The engines in the early post-war jet aircraft had used a centrifugal compressor. The characteristic of this compressor was akin to a vacuum cleaner. The air was sucked into the 'eye' of the rotating compressor and thrown outwards into a surrounding gallery to compress it before delivery to the burner section of the engine. The main problem with the use of this type of compressor in aircraft was that any increase in compression ratios could only be achieved by increasing the diameter of the compressor to an unacceptable size for aircraft use. Over the years the axial compressor had been developed for use in aircraft. It had originally been considered impractical since turbine blades in jet aero engines couldn't be made strong enough to cope with foreign bodies entering the engine intake. The axial compressor worked on the turbine principle. This meant that the frontal area of an engine could be kept relatively small, whilst the compression ratio could be increased by adding more stages to the turbine.

The three 40-minute flights in the Hunter had only been enough to wet my whistle as far as these aspects of flying went. Nevertheless, the one thing the Hunter did that no other aircraft I had flown to date could do was go supersonic. Regardless of anything else, I had to do that. Mind you, it didn't leave much time to do anything else since to go supersonic required a climb to 35,000 feet followed by a full power dive.

It was a bit of a non-event. It was just like a Mach run in a Meteor, except that instead of reading 0.85 MN the Machmeter in the Hunter read 1.02 MN. You didn't experience any noise from the sonic bang in the cockpit, and the aircraft, pointing down in a 20-degree dive, couldn't manoeuvre to any great extent. The only difference was that the aerodynamic buffet levels were a little lower in the Hunter.

The areas you could explore quite safely in the Hunter were numerous, since it didn't handle in any extreme way. The stalled wing pitch-up was recognisable but quite controllable. Its powered flying controls were very responsive and well balanced, making it an excellent aircraft in which to fly aerobatics and formation. It had a fantastic rate of roll compared with any aircraft I had flown to date. All in all it was a pilot's aircraft.

We returned to Ford at the end of August and had to wait until the middle of October before the first of the Scimitars turned up.

The Scimitar seemed enormous compared with the other jet

fighters I had flown. With two Rolls-Royce Avon engines it also produced a hell of a lot more thrust. The first impression on take-off was of the incredible acceleration. The second impression was of the high nose-up attitude to maintain the climb speed of 400 knots. The briefing for the first flight didn't include a supersonic run. The idea was to get used to the increased performance of the aircraft and to get the feel of the controls. Most of this was done at around 20,000 feet.

The Scimitar was equipped with fully hydraulic-powered flying controls that included an all-flying tail (stabilator). The advantage of having the all-flying tailplane was that shockwave interference was very much reduced, making pitch control very much easier in the transonic range of 0.80 to 1.20 MN. Unlike other aircraft, the flying control system didn't have a manual reversion enabling the aircraft to be flown with the hydraulic power disconnected. Each engine powered a separate flying control system, so it was possible to fly the aircraft with one engine shut down. If both engines stopped, the flying controls froze and you ejected. Made life simple anyway!

The Scimitar was also the first RN aircraft to be equipped with a navigation facility. The Service had adopted the tactical air navigation beacon (TACAN). RN airfields and aircraft carriers would be equipped with this navigation system. It operated on a VHF frequency and provided the ability to home onto the ship or air station. The TACAN system became universal in the UK and the USA.

On my first flight I thought the Scimitar handled very well. The flying controls were well balanced and the overall impression was of a stable, yet manoeuvrable, aircraft. Flying at landing speeds showed that the high nose-up attitude was something I'd have to get used to. A new feature was the blown flap in the landing configuration. To reduce the landing speed, high-pressure air was bled from the engine compressors and ejected over the leading edge of the flaps. This had the effect of increasing the available lift and enabled the aircraft to fly slower at a given angle of attack.

Ford only had a 6,000-foot concrete runway, and the introduction of the Scimitar coincided with the introduction of the first airfield arrester gear. Apart from the wheel brakes, the Scimitar had no other form of retardation. Since the aircraft had been designed to operate from a carrier, there had been no thought of installing a drag chute to be deployed after landing to aid in the retardation. On landing off an approach speed of 125/130 knots, 6,000 feet of runway could prove to be insufficient when relying on wheel brakes alone, particularly if there was no headwind or the concrete runway was wet and wheel adhesion poor.

The airfield arrester gear consisted of a carrier arrester wire rigged at the upwind end of the runway. The idea was that if you thought you were going to run off the end of the runway, you could lower the arrester hook and pick up the wire. Each end of the arrester wire was attached to yards of anchor chain flaked out (a naval expression) on either side of the runway edge. On engaging the wire, the anchor chain would be pulled out behind the aircraft, rather like the chains restraining a ship being launched, and stop you before the end of the runway. Mind you, there was only a fixed amount of energy in the chain, so it rather depended on how fast you picked up the wire as to how much further you would travel before stopping.

The runway arrester gear had its limitations. It was a question of first come first served. If a Scimitar used the arrester gear on landing, it meant the runway would be unusable until the aircraft was disentangled from the arrester gear. Unfortunately it then took ages before the arrester gear could be reset. It would have been unwise for other Scimitars still airborne to land without the arrester gear rigged if the reason for its original use was because of a runway limitation. Tangmere, an RAF station just down the road, was operating Hunters at the time. Tangmere's main runway was of asphalt, had good braking qualities and was slightly longer than Ford's. It was just as well that Tangmere was so close, since the Avon engine in the Scimitar didn't have the same sort of starter as the Avon in the Hunter. The Scimitar required its own special air starting system. Each time we landed away from base, a starter and engineering personnel had to be sent over by road.

The progressive flying of the Scimitar highlighted its strengths and weaknesses. It didn't manoeuvre well at high altitude. It had the power to climb quickly, could reach 0.99 MN in level flight and 1.1. MN in a shallow dive, but couldn't turn to save its life. The thick wing associated with a high wing loading meant that as soon as you tried to turn, the aircraft would go into Mach stall buffet. With its main armament of four 30 mm cannon it required the ability to track a target. Pulling any sort of 'g' at high altitude would make this task nigh impossible. However, at low levels where high indicated airspeeds were not associated with very high Mach numbers, the Scimitar performed extremely well. With an indicated airspeed limit of around 630 knots and the engine power to maintain that speed in level flight, there were few aircraft in the world to match it at the time. It was obvious that it would make a successful low-level attack aircraft and a relatively unsuccessful high-altitude fighter.

The task of 700X Flight was to fly the aircraft as much as possible and to establish performance data and basic operational procedures. To this end most of our work consisted of fuel consumption runs at various altitudes, climb performance at various weights, manoeuvre capabilities, descent procedures and formation tactics. These we achieved with limited success. The other task, which governed the overall programme, was to determine the aircraft's reliability. Unfortunately this proved the limiting factor, since a number of maintenance and serviceability problems arose which meant that the Scimitar spent more time in the hangar than it did airborne. In the five months of 700X's existence I managed to amass a total of 58 flying hours, nearly half of which were in the Vampire T 22 doing instrument flying training. At around twelve hours per month that hardly kept me in flying practice.

On the personal side I spent Christmas with Anne and her parents at RAF Watton so that we could celebrate our engagement. She had said 'yes' when I proposed marriage, but we both realised that the exigencies of the Service meant that a firm date couldn't be set, since I didn't know what I would be doing in the near future.

The final memory of 700X Flight was tragic. Driving north one weekend Tom Innes ran off the road in his car on the A29 at Bury hill and was killed. No one else was involved and it remained a mystery as to what exactly had happened.

Number 700X Flight disbanded in January 1958, and all the other pilots were appointed to the new 803 Squadron, which was to be formed at Lossiemouth to eventually embark in HMS *Victorious*, a light fleet carrier that was slightly bigger than *Centaur* and *Albion*. She was being modified to incorporate a full angled deck and the new steam catapults, which had been developed to replace the hydraulic catapults used to date. On the air defence side, she had been equipped with a new radar system called 3D radar. This system was a big improvement on previous shipborne radar installations in that it incorporated an electronic management system that could give instant height readout on radar returns. Previous systems had only been able to give range and azimuth information and had relied on a separate height-finding radar to measure target height.

I was to join 700 Trials Squadron at Ford as the specialist Scimitar pilot for any further trials that might come up, and then subsequently to join 807 Squadron, the next Scimitar squadron to be formed. Some of the trials would involve deck-landing the Scimitar on *Victorious* when she carried out her sea trials later in the year.

Chapter 9

700 Trials Squadron

January to September 1958

Number 700 Squadron was the RN squadron that looked after trials relating to aircraft and equipment that had already been accepted into service. We also flew as a Fleet Requirements Unit providing aircraft to ships that needed an aircraft target with which to practise intercepts or gunnery. We had a selection of aircraft representing most of those in service at the time. They were the Vampire T 22, the Sea Venom Mk 20 and 21, the Sea Hawk, the Scimitar and the Fairey Gannet, which had replaced the Firefly as the anti-submarine aircraft of the fleet.

The only aircraft I hadn't flown before was the Gannet. It was a turbo-prop aircraft equipped with an Armstrong Siddeley (known in the trade as 'Um-Tum-Tiddly') Double Mamba. It had two engines driving separate propellers on concentric shafts. The propellers were contra-rotating, but the overall visual impression was that they were driven by one engine. The propellers were mounted one behind the other within the same propeller boss. The idea was that fuel economy could be achieved on patrol by shutting down one engine and running on the other. In this configuration of one engine stopped and its propeller fully feathered, the casual observer would have the immediate impression that the aircraft's one and only engine was stopped!

The Gannet had three separate cockpits. The pilot's cockpit, equipped with a bubble canopy, had a fantastic view forward and to either side. Immediately behind the pilot's cockpit was that of the observer, and towards the rear of the upper fuselage the telegraphist's cockpit. The underneath of the fuselage was taken up by a weapons bay with opening doors that carried the anti-submarine sono-buoys and ordnance.

I did the standard four familiarisation flights in the Gannet. It was stable, had a super view, and was comfortable and quiet. The engines gave very good power response. From the initial airfield landings it was very apparent that it would be an excellent deck landing aircraft. I nicknamed it Queen of the Skies. Aircraft do not have genders, but for a military aircraft it was very feminine.

Number 700 Squadron didn't use the Gannet in its operational role. The aircraft was a test vehicle for various bits of radio equipment, and was also fitted with photographic survey cameras.

The spring of 1958 drifted by with a series of small trials on different aircraft and operating fleet requirement flights in the English Channel. As the only permanent IRE at Ford, I also found myself in demand to renew pilots' instrument ratings.

June proved to be a busy month involving a scenic tour of Scotland in a Gannet, combining a voice single-sideband HF trial with survey photography of Stornoway and Lossiemouth airfields. The voice HF was something new. At the time voice communications were only available on the VHF band and were limited in range to line of sight. Long-range communication over thousands of miles was achieved by using HF radio and telegraphy (Morse code). But recent experiments had developed voice communication using the single-sideband, HF-enabling long-range voice communications, and the Gannet had been equipped for this trial. So the Scottish trip included regular conversations with Cove Radio, an experimental section located at the village of Cove near RAE Farnborough in Hampshire.

On my return to Ford I found myself practising MADDLs in preparation for the deck trial of HMS *Victorious*. She would put to sea at the end of July, having completed her refit. It was normal for 700 Squadron aircraft to be employed 'pulling the wires' and

The Fairey Gannet AS 4 *(Crown copyright)*

checking out the catapults before the ship was considered operational and able to embark her squadrons. As experienced pilots flying the Sea Venom, Sea Hawk, Gannet and in my case the Scimitar, we would check the ability of the flight deck equipment and ship's personnel to operate aircraft. In my case, the CO, 'Sheepy' Lamb, had decided that I would fly the Sea Hawk, Sea Venom and Scimitar, so my MADDL sessions were flown on these aircraft.

Came the day, the first aircraft I deck-landed on *Victorious* was the Gannet! It was planned that I would be the last pilot to get airborne from Ford with the Scimitar after the lighter jets had done the initial wire pulling. However, a last-minute requirement had arisen to fly four Chief Petty Officer Technicians on board who were vital to the deck trial, and I was the only pilot available. The only aircraft that had spare seats to fly these chaps on board was the Gannet. Although I hadn't flown an intensive session of MADDLs in the Gannet, I had a very good idea of the way it would handle on a carrier approach, and I was quite happy to take these CPOs on board two at a time in the spare cockpits.

None of the four had flown before and there was a certain amount of trepidation in their faces. I set off with the first two for *Victorious*, which was only some twenty minutes' flying time away from Ford. There was little time for conversation on the way, but the inevitable questions were raised on the intercom. of how dangerous it was, and how many times I had deck-landed the Gannet. Well, I didn't like to tell them the truth, so I fudged around it by saying that I hadn't deck-landed a Gannet on *Victorious* before, but all aircraft carriers were the same. The Gannet handled impeccably in the carrier circuit and the land-on was a piece of cake. As we taxied forward out of the wires I congratulated the Chiefs on their first deck landing with a pilot who had not previously deck-landed a Gannet. They jumped out, and the flight deck crew pushed me back to the stern for a free take-off. I returned to Ford for the other two Chiefs. The same questions arose on the flight to *Victorious*, but this time I could be a little more honest. I told them I had deck-landed the Gannet before and that I was the only pilot to have deck-landed a Gannet on HMS *Victorious*!

The next day I took the Scimitar on board. Being a much larger aircraft than I had previously deck-landed, there were one or two differences between it and the Sea Hawk. The first was the increased approach speed, some 15 knots higher than previous jets, which meant that things happened a little faster. Combined with the increased inertia of the aircraft, this meant that the margins for error were reduced. The swept-wing configuration of the Scimitar resulted in a much steeper nose-up attitude on final approach, and the view out of the front windscreen wasn't as good as that of the Sea Hawk. With this high nose-up attitude the engine thrust line would be much more instrumental in maintaining the glide slope angle. It would be very much more a case of controlling rate of descent with power and the airspeed with elevator, compared with the Sea Hawk.

Finally, because of this high nose-up attitude associated with a long arrester hook hanging down from the rear fuselage, the vertical distance between the pilot's eye and the hook was very much increased. This resulted in the necessity for the cockpit to be well above the deck to ensure the hook arrived in the middle of the arrester wires. The impression from the cockpit of the Scimitar was that you were going to be far too high to even land on the deck. *Victorious*' angled deck wasn't that long, and a projection of the glide slope through the cockpit gave the impression that you would just about spear into the sea off the end of it! In fact *Victorious*'s MLS was the first to have a large vertical range of adjustment to compensate for a range of hook/eye distances depending on the aircraft. It was set somewhere near the top for the Scimitar.

The one last problem that could arise was the nose wheel 'falling through' quickly on touchdown and compressing the nose oleo sufficiently for the hook to miss all the wires should the hook touch down short of number 1 wire. This problem was slightly overcome by easing the stick back as the main wheels hit the deck to stop the nose falling through. It was also a reminder not to land short!

The bolter needed a different technique as well. If you missed all the wires, or were just doing a touch and go, it was necessary to rotate the aircraft very quickly to its normal flying attitude to prevent a sink off the end of the deck. However, the rotation had to be precise as well as quick, since over-rotation could induce pre-stall pitch-up at these low speeds.

All these things were revealed to me on the first two or three touch and goes before lowering the hook for the final landing. There didn't seem much deck ahead of me after the arrested landing. Once on the deck there seemed even less room than in the Sea Hawk since the Scimitar was so relatively large. However, time was precious, and it was a matter of being taxied forward straight onto the catapult for my first Scimitar launch.

Unlike previous catapult launches in the Sea Hawk, which were made with main and nose wheels on the deck, the Scimitar's nose rose slowly into the air as the catapult was tensioned against the hold back. The geometry of the aircraft was such that the tail was pulled down until the aircraft was in a large nose-up attitude sitting

A Scimitar is launched off the bow catapult *(Crown copyright)*

on the main wheels and the tailskid, which lowered with the undercarriage. This was necessary to ensure the Scimitar was in the correct flying attitude as it left the catapult. Having the cockpit hoisted so high above the deck had an unnerving effect on me. The increased cockpit height above the deck had the effect of foreshortening the distance between me and the bow, thus giving the impression that there was a completely inadequate catapult run to achieve any sort of safe flying speed. My only thought was that, since this was a trial, the ship would ensure that I had more than enough catapult end speed to ensure I would be well and truly airborne. Catapult end speed relates to the speed an aircraft achieves off the end of the catapult. The energy produced by the catapult has to increase as the weight of the aircraft, and therefore the minimum flying speed, increases. Minimum flying speed could only be obtained by the aircraft carrier steaming into wind and generating a wind over the deck. However, the crunch point was approached when the aircraft's launch weight was at a maximum and the natural wind at zero. In this case the carrier had to steam at maximum speed, the catapult had to produce its maximum amount of energy, and the pilot had to accept being launched at minimum airspeed. I went through the pre-take-off checks, wound the engines up to full power, signalled the FDO that I was ready to go and braced myself for the launch. The catapult fired. The ride was remarkably smooth on this new steam catapult and the Scimitar flew off with no problems. I did two sessions of three launches and arrested landings in the Scimitar that day, followed by a session in the Sea Venom the following day, and that was it as far as *Victorious* was concerned. HMS *Bulwark* was around in the Channel at the same time, since my log book records my flying there the next day in a Gannet for a short session of seven deck landings to check out their wires.

A week after the deck-landing trial I set off in a Gannet with two observers, Malcolm Carver and Hugh Damerell, for a two-week trek down to the Mediterranean on an extended trial of the HF voice equipment. Cove Radio wanted to check out the frequency ranges to use, based on the time of day or night and the distance over which we were to transmit and receive, and to see if there was any difference if we were airborne or on the ground.

The first sector was from Ford to Orange, a French Air Force base in Southern France that had an RAF detachment used for servicing Transport Command aircraft *en route* to the Middle and Far East. The remnants of Empire were still around in the late 50s! From Orange we set off for Pratica di Mare, an Italian Air Force base south of Rome, as our second refuelling stop.

We arrived at Halfar in the evening of the day of our departure from the UK. The Gannet was scheduled to go in for a 'Maincheck 4', which meant it would be out of commission for a few days. Unlike modern maintenance schedules which can be completed on a flexible basis, the old Fleet Air Arm servicing schedules were based on taking the aircraft out of service for maintenance on a calendar basis, stripping it down, doing the check and putting it back together again. This often meant the aircraft didn't work properly for some days afterwards. We had four days off while the station engineers did the maintenance check.

The following morning I was sitting in the wardroom after breakfast, reading the Malta Times newspaper, when I was approached by a bespectacled gentleman in civilian clothes.

'Lieutenant Davies?' he enquired. I said I was he.

'I understand you're a Gannet pilot.' I said I was.

'I was wondering whether you'd like to drop a torpedo from a Gannet for us?' I said that I'd love to drop a torpedo for them. It turned out that he was a boffin in charge of an acoustic torpedo trial. He had his team, a torpedo and a Gannet, but no pilot. I didn't enquire how he and his aircraft had arrived in Halfar, or where his pilot was, in case I lost the chance of dropping a torpedo.

We set up the drop for the next morning. Malcolm Carver would act as the test observer. The current airborne anti-submarine equipment in use in the RN consisted of sono-buoys that were dropped in the sea to listen for and locate enemy submarines and airborne depth charges, which would then be dropped on suspected contacts. The idea was that the acoustic torpedo would be dropped instead of the depth charges, circle in the water and home onto submarine 'noise', exploding on contact.

For the purposes of the trial an acoustic source had been set up underwater near the small rocky island of Filfla, just off the coast near Halfar. I was to get airborne in the Gannet, run in at low level towards Filfla and drop the torpedo about 400 yards short of the target. The torpedo would then circle, home onto the target and explode on contact at the base of the rock.

The next morning Malcolm and I made our way over to the far side of the airfield where the trials Gannet was parked. A team of technical ratings led by a CPO and supervised by two boffins was preparing to load the torpedo into the weapons bay of the Gannet. One or two other civilians were around who I assumed were company reps associated with the torpedo. There was probably the odd Russian spy as well! With the torpedo under the aircraft all ready to load, the boffins and the civilians all disappeared. They made their way down to Kalafrana Bay, where a flat-topped aircraft lighter was waiting to take them out to view the drop.

The team of ratings spent the next hour or so loading the torpedo into the weapons bay and checking the various circuits. Malcolm and I had received our brief on the switchery in the cockpits and the dropping technique required by the boffins. We got airborne and I established two-way radio contact with the lighter.

We ran in on the dropping line, having prepared all the switches and opened the weapons bay door. I released the torpedo at the planned speed and height and it entered the water at the planned range from the target. I pulled up and circled the island at about 500 feet. The sea was calm and crystal clear and we could make out the torpedo circling in the water. It did this until the battery ran out, and made no attempt to home onto the acoustic source. The drop was a failure.

The radio communications from the lighter were very unprofessional. The subjects the boffins were talking about were meant to be top secret. I thought that if there were any Russian Elint spy ships listening in, they must think we were stupid.

The torpedo eventually did nothing and I landed back at Halfar. Malcolm and I talked with the trial team afterwards, but it became apparent that they didn't have a clue as to why the torpedo hadn't worked. I'm not even sure there had been any check on the serviceability of the acoustic target. I suggested that next time it might be a good idea if they remained behind to ensure the correct loading of the torpedo before rushing off to see the successful result of their efforts. I have related this incident at length to indicate the cavalier 'string and sealing wax' way in which many trials were conducted in that era. An academic as opposed to a practical approach seemed to be the order of the day.

Over the next two weeks we flew our own Gannet on the HF trial. I took pictures with my own camera of Mount Etna in Sicily and the islands of Lampedusa and Pantelleria. We also flew over Libya and Tunisia. There seemed to be no restrictions as to where you could fly in those days. We also flew at night in the vicinity of Malta to check on the frequency shift between day and night transmissions. We completed the trial on 31 July and flew back to Ford.

August and September saw me flying the Sea Venom and Scimitar off *Victorious* again, mainly on maximum-weight catapult launches in both aircraft. The initial deck trial had gone well and they were now in the process of ensuring that they could launch both of these aircraft under maximum-weight conditions. This was a slightly different matter from the original launches that had been made at low weights and high catapult end speeds just to prove the catapults.

The minimum-airspeed launch at maximum weight was a challenge for the pilot. If you thought you were too near the stall and eased off the angle of attack you could end up hitting the sea. If you thought you were sinking excessively and eased the stick back too much, you could pitch up and – you've guessed it – end up hitting the sea! The launches I did in the Scimitar on this occasion were at maximum weight and for the benefit of the catapult trial. There was enough natural wind blowing to ensure that I wasn't launched at the minimum flying speed. However, the launch speeds weren't that much more than minimum. Handling a heavy Scimitar off the end of a catapult launch at a large angle of attack at slow speed required a certain delicacy.

The last job before leaving 700 Squadron was another deck trial in mid-September. The Dutch Navy had asked us to do the deck trial on their new carrier, the *Karel Doorman*, which had just finished a refit. The *Karel Doorman* was a light fleet carrier of the Bulwark class that had been purchased from the Royal Navy. I suspect the British government, as a 'guarantee', instigated the deck trial. I think the Dutch were also buying some Sea Hawks from us to operate from her deck.

I was leaving 700 Squadron to join 807, the second Scimitar squadron commissioning at Lossiemouth, as an experienced Scimitar pilot and the squadron IRE. Keith Leppard, the batsman who had trained my flying course in deck landing, was to be the CO.

Looking back on it, my time in 700 Squadron proved to be one of the happiest and most varied nine months of my naval flying career. Along with the varied flying I had seen a lot of Anne. Her father had retired from the RAF and had joined the Civil Service as a technical officer (he was a radar and electronic specialist). He had accepted a position at RAF Medenham, a part of 90 Group, Signals Command, based at an old priory of that name located on the Thames between Marlow and Henley. The family had moved to Marlow in the summer of 1957. We had definitely decided to marry, but 'when' was going to be the problem.

Another tragedy happened as I was changing squadrons. Having completed the deck trial, *Victorious* embarked her squadrons. The BBC was invited to cover the occasion and to film the arrival of our new swept-wing aircraft into service. Des Russell, 803 Squadron's CO, was the first to land on the deck. He made a perfect landing, picked up a wire that didn't retard the aircraft properly and broke at the end of the runout. Des's Scimitar, with not enough flying speed, went off the end of the angled deck into the sea. The Scimitar floated for a while with Des in the cockpit apparently unable to release the canopy, and the Scimitar sank with him still in it. The whole incident had been filmed by the BBC and was broadcast on TV news that evening. The Fleet Air Arm community was outraged that such a thing had been allowed to happen and that the BBC could be so sensationalist to show someone dying on TV. A bit different nowadays I suppose. No doubt those pilots who had watched the incident, as I had, all thought 'there but for the grace of God . . .'

Chapter 10

807 & 803 Squadrons

October 1958 to December 1959

I loaded up the Austin A35 van with my worldly goods and set off to Lossie to join 807. I would miss Anne very much. It looked as if it would be back to writing letters, with the odd visit on long weekends.

Lossie was its same old temporary self. By the time I arrived, 807 was in possession of most of its Scimitars. My first task was to check out in the Hunter T 8, introduced into service to replace the Vampire T 22. As the squadron IRE I would be required to perform instrument rating renewals in this aircraft.

Number 807 Squadron's Scimitars had been modified to deliver a tactical nuclear bomb using the Low Altitude Bombing System (LABS for short). LABS bombing would put as much distance as possible between the bombing aircraft and the nuclear explosion, with the aircraft flying away from the explosion. You would only have to deal with the flash of the bomb going off. The idea was that you approached the target 'on the deck' at very high speed. You flew over an easily identifiable landmark called an 'Initial Point' (IP) that was on your attack heading at a known distance from the target. As you passed over the IP you started your stopwatch and pressed the 'pickle button' which armed the LABS equipment. You then flew for a pre-calculated number of seconds to the 'Pull Up Point' (PUP). The timing used was based on the distance of the IP from the target, the speed you were doing, the forward throw of the bomb and the wind effect you had calculated would affect you and the bomb. You pulled up into a loop at the PUP, using a fixed amount of 'g' (around 4 g if my memory serves me well) and, having pressed the pickle button, the bomb release circuit was completed on the gyro stabilised LABS equipment at around 45 degrees of aircraft elevation to the horizon. The bomb came off the aircraft and was thrown forward towards the target, while the aircraft completed half a 'Cuban 8' manoeuvre, a loop with a roll-off on the way down, and headed away from the target as fast and as low as possible. The distance from bomb release to the target was three to four miles and didn't require you to even see the target. This technique was known as the 'Long Toss', and to this end you had to make sure that the delivery switch in the cockpit was set to 'Long Toss'.

The other position of this switch was 'Over The Shoulder', or OTS. This technique was used if you missed the IP or you were attacking a ship where there would be no IP. In this case you used the target as the PUP. Let me explain. With the cockpit switch set at OTS, the bomb would be released slightly beyond the vertical so that it was thrown well up in the air and would more or less drop vertically onto the target. You then completed the Cuban 8 manoeuvre. There were two problems using this technique. Firstly, if the target was well defended you were going to get shot at. Secondly, you would be four miles closer to the atomic bomb when it went off.

There were many problems associated with LABS bombing, the major one being how accurately we would be able to deliver a bomb. I had just started running this trial when I got a 'pier head jump' to 803 Squadron. Des Russell being killed meant they were one pilot short. I sold the van, packed my bags and headed south to Portsmouth.

I joined 803 in mid-February 1959. By the end of March we were disembarked back to Lossie. The six weeks in between, we had operated in the Atlantic out of range of diversion airfields. We used

Hawker Hunter T8 *(Crown copyright)*

the spare deck principle. *Victorious* operated in company with HMS *Centaur*, so that if one carrier had a problem landing-on aircraft they could divert to the other, negating the requirement for diversion airfields.

The fighter tactics had changed and we didn't have the mass launches of the Sea Hawk era. Instead of a flight of four aircraft being the tactical unit, the Scimitar operated in sections of two aircraft. The change had come about as a result of the increased capability of the 3D radar to detect aircraft, and the new electronics had aided the fighter direction staff to put you in the right place at the right time at the right altitude. Our Sea Hawk days had reflected WW2 tactics, which envisaged the threat would come from mass attacks of fighter/bomber type aircraft. The theory now was that the main threat would come from large land-based aircraft of the Soviet Navy, and that the Scimitar would be used as an interceptor and not have the dog fight role imposed on it. On the last day of the exercise using the spare deck operation, I found myself orbiting *Victorious*, waiting for them to fix a problem on the deck that was preventing us from landing on. John Beyfus and I were the only two left airborne at the time. After some considerable delay with no indication that things were going to be fixed, we persuaded FLYCO to divert us to *Centaur*, some thirty miles away. The weather wasn't very good, with low cloud and rain. We eventually found *Centaur* steaming into wind on a long swell with the deck pitching quite badly.

With both aircraft on low fuel states we had to make an approach straight away and ensure we picked up a wire off the first landing attempt. *Centaur* in the days of the Sea Hawk looked quite big, but today she looked extremely small on final approach. Rain wasn't the ideal weather in which to land, since it stuck to the windscreen and cut down the visibility (no windscreen wipers on fighter aircraft). The deck was moving quite a lot as I came over the stern of the ship, but no flares or red lights on the MLS showed the ship was happy with the situation. I flew the Scimitar slightly low on the meat ball to ensure my picking up a wire. My hook was on the deck well before number 1 wire, and I breathed a sigh of relief as I felt it retard the aircraft. I taxied forward to park alongside John in the deck park. As we got out of the aircraft we suddenly realised the goofers was full of spectators. No one had seen a Scimitar before, but the fact that we were both on low fuel states, associated with our unfamiliarity with the *Centaur* deck and the poor weather conditions, indicated that there might be something exciting to see!

The next day we flew off *Centaur*, bound for Lossie. During our time disembarked at Lossie, 803 Squadron aircraft were modified for LABS bombing. This involved removing one of the nose-mounted 30 mm Aden gun packs to take the LABS equipment, leaving us with the other pack of two Aden guns as our air-to-air armament. Since I was the only pilot to have operated the system before, the CO, Jeff Higgs, decided to make me the squadron LABS bombing expert, and assigned three other pilots to the role. We spent the rest of our disembarkation tossing practice bombs at West Freugh range in Luce Bay on the Mull of Galloway. The range was run under the auspices of the Royal Aircraft Establishment (RAE) and was equipped with kine-theodolite cameras. These could track and film anything on the range, be it aircraft or missile, and then produce a three-dimensional plot of their position at any one time. The limiting factor was visibility and cloud base, since they obviously had to see what they were filming.

The one advantage of this range was that it had a floating ship target at the northern end of the bay and a large rock at the southern entrance to the bay towards the Isle of Man. The rock would make a good IP with the attack heading towards the ship target. Poor visibility proved to be one of the problems for the exercise. Trying to line up to fly over a rock on the attack heading at around 600 knots flying over water wasn't easy. The odd jink was often necessary at the last minute. With the requirement to leave the rock on an exact heading, this didn't do much for compass stability!

The initial bombing results were disappointing. The average fall of shot was well outside the accuracy we expected and there weren't enough results to determine a trend. The bombs fell at random around the target. If you were on the receiving end of a tactical nuclear bomb, the fact that it exploded 300 yards away as opposed to on top of you sounded pretty bad news anyway. Nevertheless, when you looked at the variables involved it was no surprise that the errors were large. Assuming a still air condition, with no wind at all at any level, the accuracy of the compass would be critical. An error of just one degree on heading meant a 50-yard fall of shot error. Apart from anything else it was difficult to steer within one degree on the type of compass we used. For the other attack parameters, half a second out on the timing meant a 200-yard error, a slack pull up to four 'g' and inaccurate 'g', I don't know what. If you included adjustments for wind on heading and timing and during the flight of the bomb, it was something like contemplating how much to lay off for wind on a four-mile 8 iron shot to the green!

Outside flying I had managed to get the odd long weekend down south to see Anne. On one of these visits we managed to settle on a

The Residents

▲ All tensioned-up *(Crown copyright)*

▼ Ready to go *(Crown copyright)*

▲ Over the 'Round-down' *(Crown copyright)*

▼ No. 1 wire? *(Crown copyright)*

The Visitors

▲ F-8 Crusader *(Crown copyright)*

▼ A-4 Skyhawk *(Crown copyright)*

F-4D Skyray *(Crown copyright)*

wedding date of 15 August. Although the ship would still be operational, it was planned that she would be in dock in mid-August and that we would all get two weeks' summer leave. The wedding was to be at All Saints, a beautiful church right on the river Thames by Marlow bridge.

May saw the squadron back on board *Victorious* operating in the Channel. It was the beginning of the year's silly season, and our part in it was to run another 'shop window' to show off the ship and its capabilities. I didn't do any flying but looked after various VIPs on our days out at sea. Before the ship left port to start the day's operations, a tour of the flight deck and hangar was arranged for the visitors to show them the various aspects of flying from a carrier.

When a carrier was entering or leaving harbour and on other occasions when flying operations weren't being conducted, we normally had flagpoles rigged on the bow and stern of the flight deck to carry the Union Jack and the White Ensign. Both of these flagpoles could be taken down quite easily. However, one MP asked, 'How do you avoid the flagpole when you land?' A comment came from a General whilst inspecting the pitot heads, tubes which looked like .22 rifles which were mounted on the leading edge of each wing of a Scimitar. He said, 'I would have expected your guns to be of a larger calibre than this.' These comments were obviously made from ignorance, which, hopefully, a day at sea would overcome.

July of 1959 saw us set sail for the USA. We were to be the first British aircraft carrier to visit the country since WW2. In between flying periods we were to visit Norfolk, Virginia, the main US naval base on the East Coast, Boston and New York. For this visit we had Rear Admiral Charles 'Crash' Evans, Flag Officer Aircraft Carriers (FOAC) and his staff on board. I think 'Crash' must have been some shortened form of Charles, since he wasn't famous for crashing aircraft. But he was famous for being the first British pilot to shoot down a German aircraft at the beginning of WW2.

Our visit to Boston was brief. It was customary for the ship to hold a cocktail party on the evening of the arrival in a foreign port. It was hosted by the ship and squadron officers. The party was normally held in the aft part of the hangar. It would be decorated with flowers and bunting (signal flags) for the occasion. Towards the end of the party the guests and hosts would be taken up to the flight deck, using the hangar lift, to witness the Royal Marine guard and band perform the 'Beat the Retreat' at sunset.

However, the object of the more mercenary officers at the cocktail party was the 'Baron Strangle'. The idea was to try and pick the richest and most amenable group of guests to come aboard, introduce yourself and look after them in the hope that you might be invited back to their place – which with any luck might be the local castle. It also helped if the Baron had a young and attractive daughter in tow. All too often the Baron appeared as a frog, only changing into a Baron at midnight. By accident, that evening I ended up with the frog, and was invited out for the evening and the next day to the New England mansion along the coast. My first taste of the USA was impressive.

The ship set sail for an area off the Virginia coast where we conducted two or three days of exercises before putting into our next port of call, at Norfolk, Virginia. This visit was to be a little more serious, since the local media would be more interested in the carrier and its aircraft. Norfolk was very much a US Navy town, and was the headquarters of East Coast Naval Aviation. It was a deep-water port, and *Victorious* was able to berth alongside one of the quays in the harbour. Our entrance into Norfolk harbour was made with the ship 'dressed', that is to say with all flags flying and the flight deck manned all the way around the edge with ship and squadron personnel. Most of 803 Squadron officers manned the forward end of the flight deck, and so I had a good view of our arrival. And that view was impressive. There appeared to be more USN ships in Norfolk harbour than in the whole of the RN. We eventually ended up in our berth at what could only be called Carrier Row. There must have been three or four carriers alongside, and we were parked opposite one of the latest. The USS *Saratoga* seemed twice as long and twice as high as the *Victorious*. The scale of things was quite beyond my belief.

As the PR man for 803 I was seconded onto the ship's team of officers who were to meet the Press. There was no question of any sort of media event, as we know it today. Television was comparatively new, even in the USA, but no TV cameras were around. This was strictly specialist journalism. I had been briefed by the Admiral's staff not to divulge any performance figures for the Scimitar. All that sort of stuff was secret.

I got a bit of a grilling. My rather coy attempts at not divulging aircraft statistics, and in particular the implication that the Scimitar had a superior performance, were taken apart by these very professional journalists. One of them told me exactly what the Scimitar's performance was. Not because he had read it anywhere, but by just looking at the aircraft, gauging its intake and exhaust areas and the fact that the engines weren't equipped with reheat. Also, he noted, it had a thick wing, and it was obvious to him that the aircraft couldn't go supersonic in level flight, could it? I found the whole exercise fascinating and somewhat embarrassing.

At the official cocktail party that evening I met up with Bill Conklin and his wife 'Buzzie'. Bill had been an exchange pilot from the USN on 700 Squadron at Ford. They invited me to stay the weekend at their house in Virginia Beach, a resort area on the Atlantic coast close to Norfolk. At the end of the party I rushed off to grab some clothes for the two days away, but remained in my formal white uniform whilst travelling to their home.

The food at the cocktail party had only consisted of snacks, and so we stopped at a drive-in hamburger stall on the way. It was a very warm night and the high collar of my dress uniform was proving uncomfortable. I decided to take the top off, and sat in the car bare chested. Within a few minutes a cop strolled over and informed me that there had been a complaint from a lady in the area about my lack of clothing, and did I realise that I was violating a Virginia State Law. I was indecently exposed. Having been raised on the apparent informality of American films, I was surprised by the non-conformist Christian ethic in the country. Many of the laws relating to public behaviour were restrictive by British standards. In fact, my first and only pair of Bermuda shorts were bought the next morning. Another bylaw of Virginia Beach was that you could be in bathing attire on the boardwalk (promenade) side of the beachfront, but if you crossed the road to the shops then a shirt and suitable shorts had to be worn. English shorts weren't suitable. Anything much above the male knee was considered indecent exposure.

The weekend was great: lots of beer and barbecues and my first introduction to water-skiing. The Saturday night party included other members of Bill's squadron, and the talk was about aircraft. They were currently flying one of the new USN fighters, the 'Skyray' by name, the F-4D by designation. The name described it best, since it looked like a ray fish. The pilots called it the 'Ford', after its designation. No performance was discussed and we didn't come across them in the subsequent exercise, so I have no idea how good they were compared to the Scimitar.

On Monday morning we put to sea for the main exercise. Our initial part in it was to use the Scimitar in the tactical nuclear bombing role against targets in North Carolina. These had been selected well away from areas of main population in order not to alarm the local residents. I would imagine that any US citizen who had knowledge of aircraft recognition and managed to identify a Scimitar at 600 knots and 200 feet as a foreign aircraft might initiate a certain amount of panic. The American public were very much in a 'the Russians are coming!' state of mind in those days, and the USA wasn't used to being 'attacked' by other than their own military aircraft.

The main target for our pretend nuclear bomb was the resort of White Lake Beach on the shores of a lake inland from the Carolina coast. We selected our approach heading and IP. I flew three attacks in one day. I missed the IP on the first run, remembered to switch the mode to OTS and continued the run in to the target. The IP had been selected because it was on one side of the lake with the target on the other, which it was thought would prove less disruptive for the holiday makers using the lake's facilities. However, having missed the IP, continuing on the attack heading took me slap-bang over the middle of the lake. The resort was deafened by a Scimitar at 600 knots on the deck scattering sailboats and water skiers as it approached over the lake. The second attack went as planned.

The third attack was made in the late afternoon on that hot and humid day. I had to fly through a line of thunderstorms on the way in, and was able to avoid them visually. However, on the way back the thunderstorms had amalgamated into one long, unbroken barrier between the ship and me. It is the American boast that things in the USA are much bigger than anywhere else, and when it comes to thunderstorms that is very probably true. In this instance I was limited in the fuel available to be able to get back to the ship, and there was no question but that I would have to fly through them. Shades of Dilbert. Flying into thunderstorms is not recommended. Turbulence and icing could be extreme. However, the Scimitar was a very strong aircraft and I reckoned that I wouldn't be in the storms for long. I entered the storm at around 20,000 feet. All hell let loose. The aircraft was thrown around, and just trying to fly straight and level involved coping with a lot of positive and negative 'g'. The noise of the precipitation hitting the aircraft was deafening, and the aircraft started to ice up. Military fighter aircraft were not equipped to cope with airframe icing. The only ice protection systems related to heating the pitot heads and the air entering the engine intakes. I had these on so all should be well! However, it became apparent that the static vents had probably iced up since my height was rock steady at 22,000 feet on the altimeter, but the aircraft was going up and down like a Yo-Yo in the turbulence. I flew the aircraft on attitude alone and became not a little alarmed. I suddenly burst out of the cloud into clear air the other side of the line of storms. I didn't know what height I was at and the airspeed looked a little unreal for the amount of engine power set, so I just flew the aircraft on attitude at a cruise power that seemed reasonable and set off back to the ship.

I eventually picked up the ship's TACAN beacon and homed in on it. I called the ship on the radio and explained the situation. They vectored another Scimitar on to me and we flew in formation back to the ship. We compared airspeed and altimeter readings and it was obvious that my static vents were still blocked. I explained that I would be short of fuel on arrival, and the ship was heading into wind ready to receive me as it hove into sight. I stayed in formation with the other Scimitar as we flew an approach to the deck. With 100 yards to go he pulled away and I landed on without airspeed reference. I was very glad to be down and not a little chastened by the whole experience.

The exercise finished a couple of days later and we set sail for New York. The Manhattan skyline looked interesting as we entered harbour and tied up alongside at Pier 92, the Cunard pier, which was vacant for a day or two. My initial run ashore took in the normal sights of the city and involved me in another brush with the law. 'Jay'-walking' was trying to cross the road at other than the designated pedestrian crossing points. The New York cop isn't like your English Bobby. There was no question of a polite approach. It wasn't 'Excuse me, sir, I wonder if I could have a word', but rather 'Hey, Bub, com'ere. What the hell do you think you're playing at?' I explained in my best British accent that I was unaware of the rules on crossing the road.

'You an American?' he asked. Assured that our visit had been well publicised and that every New Yorker was well aware of the arrival of the British aircraft carrier, I said, 'I come from *Victorious*.'

The cop looked dumbfounded. I think he must have thought that *Victorious* was some sort of principality in central Europe.

'You sure speak good English for a foreigner,' he said, 'but you're in America now, so just watch the jay-walking. Beat it!'

We set sail for England at the end of July and disembarked to Lossiemouth for summer leave before the ship went into dock at Portsmouth for an extended maintenance period. We wouldn't re-embark until mid-September.

I set off for Marlow and my marriage to Anne. All the arrangements had been made by my future father-in-law and we had a lovely day. After just a weeks' honeymoon, Anne and I separated again, she to go back and live with her parents and I to return to Lossiemouth and the squadron. We had married in the summer because the squadron was due to disband at the end of the year. I would probably be appointed to a shore flying duty for the next two years, which would mean that we would be able to set up home in four months' time wherever the Navy sent me.

Jeff Higgs had asked my preference for a new job. I had asked him to recommend me for the Experimental Test Pilots' course at the Empire Test Pilots' School, then based at RAE Farnborough. He had duly done so and I was called for interview. This lasted two days.

The first day required you to take a maths test in the morning, involving questions in algebra and calculus. In the afternoon we were all interviewed by the School's tutors. The maths paper was a bit of a challenge and I answered as much as I could. The professional interview didn't seem to go quite as well.

'Tutor' was the term given to those pilots who would be teaching us how to test fly. There were four of them on the board in addition to the Chief Test Flying Instructor. The CTFI was a Wing Commander, and the tutors were three Squadron Leaders from the RAF and a Lieutenant-Commander from the RN. They were all qualified and experienced test pilots. I had filled in a questionnaire before being interviewed. It included a list of the aircraft types I had flown to date, eighteen in all. Some I had flown only once. For twenty minutes or so they fired questions at me. If my answer was 'I don't know', there would often be a long silence accompanied by serious looks from all the board which were meant to encourage me to attempt an answer (I presumed). Since technical details are specific and not a matter of opinion, it was difficult to speculate. At the end of the interview there was no indication from the board as to how well I might have done.

The 'political' interview with the Commandant of ETPS, Captain Ken Hickson AFC RN, and two senior boffins from the RAE came the next day. In this interview they covered your career based on the sort of flying you had done. It eventually got around to my current involvement in LABS bombing. What did I think of it? Not a lot was the basic theme of my reply. I explained the difficulty of maintaining an accurate attack heading and the large errors that small variations in flying technique and wind calculations introduced into the ability to deliver the bomb accurately to a target. They seemed interested, but again I didn't get any impression on how well I might have done.

I returned to the squadron at Lossiemouth. The LABS bombing at West Freugh continued, but this time based at RNAS Abbotsinch (today's Glasgow Airport), which put us nearer to the bombing range. It was about this time that I was told that I had been accepted for test pilot training. I was surprised, but subsequently learnt that ETPS was not only interested in your mathematical and technical prowess. Flying ability and honesty came into it as well. What they didn't want were pilots who would 'bullshit' when put under a bit of pressure.

Number 803 Squadron disbanded in December, and Anne and I started to look for accommodation in the Farnborough area where we would live for the next year.

Chapter 11

No. 19 Course, Empire Test Pilots' School

RAE Farnborough 1960

The first priority on returning from sea was transport. We bought a 1952 Morris Oxford. Anne and I set off to look for accommodation in the Farnborough area. We eventually settled on a small, rather tatty bungalow by a railway embankment in Aldershot. We called the place Railway Cuttings after Tony Hancock's pad in East Cheam on the 'Hancock's Half Hour' TV programme.

There were a total of twenty-four pilots in No 19 course, split up into four syndicates, giving each tutor six pilots to look after. As well as pilots from the RAF and RN, we had an Australian, two USN pilots, one of whom had a degree in nuclear physics, a USAF Captain and two Indian Air Force pilots. The rest were British. On the first day the first words from our ground instructor were 'Gentlemen, if it's all right with you we'll start at the Binomial Theorem.' The maths got deeper and deeper into theoretical aerodynamics. I amazed myself by being able to keep up, more because of an interest in flying than for any innate mathematical bent.

Around the middle of February we started flying, and from then on would operate a similar routine to that on my initial flying course – half a day of flying and half a day of ground school each day. For our conversion onto the fleet of aircraft we were to use on the course we would be given three sets of pilots' notes a week to swot up before actually flying those aircraft. There were fourteen different aircraft types on the fleet and we checked out in all of them. Some I had flown before, others fitted into a category similar to these. Larger aircraft, like the Handley Page Hastings and Avro Shackleton, were a new experience, but after the first couple of flights we adjusted to their size. The exception was the English Electric Canberra B 2. It

Empire Test Pilots' School, No. 19 Course *(Crown copyright)*

had only one pilot's seat and one set of flying controls. It could be a bit of a tricky aircraft in some areas of the flight envelope, so another course member who had flown it previously would come with you on the rumble seat. This was a pull-out strap alongside the pilot's position. He would be there during your first flight to advise you if any problems arose. The trouble was that, having done your one flight, you then became qualified on type and found yourself on the rumble seat checking out some other pilot the next day! You became used to switching from one aircraft to another, somehow remembering the different features and technical facets of each one. We were also required to fly a helicopter, but only under strict dual control as an introduction to flying these aircraft.

Many of the aircraft had particular instrumentation installed to conduct certain tests, the very first of these being the calibration of an air thermometer. This was installed in the Vampire T 11 and was our first introduction to test flying. Test flying didn't mean adrenaline-pumping action. In fact rarely at all. If adrenaline came into it something had gone wrong.

Anyway the air thermometer calibration proved very unexciting, as did the fuel consumption in the Vickers Varsity. It became apparent at an early stage that we weren't going to get much flying, since every flight seemed to generate about four days of paperwork and calculations. But it was most important not to miss anything since we couldn't continually nip off for another flight to measure something we'd forgotten.

Performance reduction seemed to take an endless amount of time to produce the tabulated results required by the test flights. All our sums were calculated using a slide rule, which gave an accurate enough result, but many of the performance figures involved massively large or small numbers, and it was necessary to count exactly where the decimal point should go. This sort of test flying was called quantitative. Qualitative was more fun.

By qualitative I mean writing about how an aircraft behaved in certain areas of the flight envelope. This was done using a formalised vocabulary. For instance, you couldn't say that a flying control was not very effective. A flying control was either effective or not. Effectiveness, if you will, was called response, so a control could be effective but its response poor.

Before undertaking a particular test programme, the tutor lectured his syndicate on the procedures to be followed and what specific flying characteristics we were looking for. From then on, if we had any problems, the tutor would give us advice. My first qualitative test was to evaluate the Hunter at high Mach number. Now I had flown a Hunter at high MN before, but describing what happened and evaluating the flying control effectiveness and response was something else.

Spinning tests for me were allocated on the piston Provost. I had not spun an aircraft for years. I would have to go back to the Sea Hawk as the last aircraft I had spun, and even then not that often. It may seem a little silly for a trainee test pilot to be nervous about spinning a basic training aircraft like the Provost. Part of this nervousness was because the spin testing followed the requirement of all these qualitative tests. It wasn't sufficient just to get the aircraft in and out of a spin; you had to record the effect and response of control deflections in the stabilised spin. At the same time there were quantitative parameters to measure: how many turns of the incipient spin, rate of rotation, height lost per turn, angle of tilt of the wing, angle of dip of the nose, number of turns and height lost during recovery action, total height lost in the spin, etc., etc.

The very first spin was enlightening. Although a voice wire recorder would be the main way of recording data, you were still expected to back this up with kneepad notes in the spin! I climbed up to a safe height and put the Provost into the first spin. On the playback my voice came over with all the things I was planning to measure on this first spin, followed by 'Full pro-spin controls NOW...(a lot of deep breathing)... recovering NOW'. My kneepad was also blank. It was a lesson that I wasn't producing the goods.

After two one hour flights I was producing the goods. Although a spin is a fairly violent manoeuvre, I found myself able to write notes, time turns, check control effectiveness and response, estimate angles and, luckily, read an altimeter. This last ability became very necessary. Having overcome spin nerves, I was happily sitting there measuring things in a detached way. This remote attitude had to be checked. It had been a cause of accidents in the past and you could suffer a severe case of deceleration sickness (kill yourself, in layman's terms). Many had in the past. Just spinning into the ground wasn't an uncommon way of being dropped from the course.

Report writing became the dread. Was the layout correct? Was the terminology correct? Was it logical? Was the data right? And finally – was it time for it to be submitted? There was always a deadline for reports to be handed in, and hand-written reports were not acceptable. If you used the typing pool the draft report had to be in five days before you required the final report. Luckily Anne was a qualified secretary. Reports seemed to dominate life. Me writing them and Anne typing them. Some of the technical terms threw Anne, and over the months I started touch typing myself to keep up with the flood.

The tests progressed. Longitudinal stability in the Vickers Varsity nearly came to a sticky end at the very beginning. Although it was a two-pilot aircraft, you flew the Varsity by yourself with a staff engineer in the right-hand seat. There were two or three flight engineers on the staff of ETPS who would fly with you on tests like this, where they were the experienced crew as far as the technical aspects of the aircraft were concerned. Their favourite aircraft was the Hastings since you couldn't fly it without two pilots and an engineer. The Varsity flights weren't too popular since they knew that most pilots didn't have much experience on the aircraft, and they probably thought they were taking their lives in their hands just coming with us.

On this particular flight we took off on the easterly runway. I opened up to full power, rolled down the runway and rotated to get airborne. Right at that moment, Bill the engineer said, 'You've lost oil pressure on the starboard engine'. I looked down at the gauge, which was firmly reading zero, called for him to raise the undercarriage and feather the starboard engine. Apart from shutting down the bad engine, making sure you had full power on the good engine, the undercarriage up and sufficient airspeed, there was nothing else to do. In those days you just coped. The one thing the aircraft wasn't doing was climbing. Bill had been very swift to shut down the engine, which had left us at about 20 feet on one engine heading for the Black Sheds (large hangars at the eastern end of Farnborough airfield). I glanced around the cockpit and saw three green lights still glowing on the instrument panel. 'Get the effing gear up Bill, or we're going to hit the sheds.' Bill had the gear up before I finished talking. I dragged the Varsity into a low left-hand circuit and landed straight away. It was eventually found that the oil pressure limiter on the 'failed' engine, which normally kept the oil pressure at a fixed maximum below the oil pump's capacity, had failed. As a result, with the engine running at maximum r.p.m. for take-off, the oil pressure was very high and the needle on the pressure gauge had gone all the way round to zero again. We hadn't lost oil pressure – we had too much! The rest of the longitudinal stability tests weren't quite so exciting, thank goodness.

By the time the summer leave break came we had completed all the individual test programmes required by the course. Some tests wouldn't be conducted on some aircraft. For instance, both 'Stability and Control' and 'Stick Force per 'g'' tests would be flown on fighter aircraft, but Stick Force per 'g' wouldn't be necessary on transport aircraft. It was a good idea that transport aircraft had very stable characteristics that would not require a lot of attention from the pilot under straight and level conditions. On the other hand a fighter would require less stable characteristics to enable it to manoeuvre well, with reasonable control forces so to do. 'Stick Force per 'g'' tests would determine this latter characteristic as a number; 3 to 5 lb/g would be a good fighter design number. So to pull 5 'g' would take 15 to 25 lb pull on the elevator. On something like the Hastings you'd be lucky to get 1 'g' for a 25 lb pull!

It was around this time that I flew the Supermarine Swift Mk 5, the only one in the ETPS fleet. It had spent all of its time U/S in the hangar, since spare parts were hard to come by. As it happened, only three or four of us flew it, since something went wrong with it shortly after its exposure to sunlight and it spent the rest of the year in the hangar. The Swift Mk 5 had a reheated Avon engine and had only been used in small numbers in the RAF as a fighter/reconnaissance aircraft. The one flight I did in it reminded me of the Attacker for size and the Scimitar for performance. It gave the impression of being fairly useless at altitude.

Anne and I hired a boat on the Thames as our summer break, and enjoyed the peace of the river before getting back to the academics.

On our return the Commandant called all the students together. He explained that our final term at the school was aimed at producing two reports, the 'Pilot's Assessment', a brief assessment of an aircraft for its role, and the 'Preview', which did the same sort of thing but in more depth. This last term was apparently not to be so demanding, since we intended to visit various aircraft manufacturers in the UK to learn about their newest projects. The other subject the Commandant covered was jobs at the end of the course. Apparently ours had been the first course to have reached the final term without some sort of loss. No one had failed and no one had been killed. The course complement had been established assuming this would happen, and unless someone killed himself before the end of the course, two of the pilots would not have jobs to go to.

For this final term, test flying was interspersed with the visits. Most consisted of a classroom presentation of the company's latest project, followed by questions and a tour of the production line of what they were currently building. If we were lucky it also included a pub-crawl in the evening funded by the company. Undoubtedly the star of the visits was the one to Fairey Aviation at White Waltham near Maidenhead.

Fairey was an old-established firm of aircraft manufacturers. It had been purveyors of aircraft to the Services since the year dot. It had supplied some of the first aircraft to enter service with the RAF. Most of the aircraft that had operated from carriers between the wars were of Fairey origin, and on the takeover of the FAA by the RN, Fairey had supplied sea-going aircraft for the Navy. The Fairey Swordfish was probably the most famous. The last line of naval aircraft was the Gannet AEW Mk 3. There was no other aircraft in prospect for Fairey Aviation. They hadn't produced commercial aircraft and had no experience of modern jet aviation outside the Fairey Delta 2, a current research aircraft in 1960. They were the object of the first takeover in the British aircraft industry. They were about to merge with Westland Helicopters.

Morale at Fairey's was not good. However, the visit was being funded by Westland and was something of a Fairey swan song so they were going to town. White Waltham was the home of the West London Aero Club. Our first pleasant surprise was to be taken out to the airfield just after morning coffee and shown a dozen or so light aircraft. By each aircraft was a pilot 'qualified on type'. The idea was that we would select aircraft in turn, get a quick cockpit brief from the pilot, nip off for a couple of circuits and come back and try another one. With 24 pilots there was no chance we would fly them all, but I managed a couple of circuits in the Tipsy B, the Tipsy Nipper, and the Tiger Moth, none of which I had flown before. Lunch was a prolonged affair at the Aero Club, followed by a coach trip down to Kew Bridge, where we picked up a steamer loaded with booze and food for a trip down to Tower Bridge and back.

There were Westland people on board the steamer to help entertain us, and we stopped off at the Embankment to pick up a few naval officers who had been invited from the MoD and Min. Tech. The SBAC Farnborough airshow had been held just before this visit, and Westland had demonstrated the Rotodyne. This was a large hybrid helicopter/autogyro. The fuselage was quite long and shaped like a small airliner. Two stub wings were mounted on the fuselage, which housed conventional turbo prop engines. The idea was that the rotor power would get you off the ground pretty quickly, and as the aircraft gained forward speed using the turbo props the lift would be supplied by the stub wings and the rotor, now acting as an autogyro. It was quite an innovative design, but in practical commercial use the tip jets produced such a screaming noise that your ears hurt and no one could hear or speak while the Rotodyne lifted off. As the beer flowed on the steamer I was talking to a man from Westland, giving him the benefit of my opinion of the Rotodyne, most of which wasn't very flattering. At the end of my side of the discussion I asked him what he did. 'I designed the Rotodyne', was the reply. I apologised for my appraisal of his work. If he was offended, he didn't show it, but it was my first lesson in the politics of aircraft production. Don't express an opinion without facts.

Final examinations and reports completed, the course ended in December 1960. I had enjoyed the flying but the academics had been quite a battle for me. I ended up in the bottom half of the list of merit. However, as it was pointed out by the Commandant in his final address, the ETPS had been established to train pilots in the field of observation, and to communicate those observations to the technical specialists who knew about these things. So regardless of how well we had done on the course, our success in the testing establishments would be based on how well we did in the field.

The majority of the graduates would go on to serve at A&AEE Boscombe Down. Nick Bennett, John Carrodus and I were to join 'C' (Naval Test) Squadron. Pete Lovick, another naval officer on the course, volunteered to convert to helicopters. He would join 'D' Squadron. Most of our RAF colleagues joined either 'A' (Fighter) or 'B' (Bomber) Squadron to test those aircraft types. One or two pilots joined the Aerodynamic Flight at RAE Bedford, which dealt with advanced projects. They were working on the Handley Page 177, a 'one-off' designed to explore low-speed aerodynamics of a delta wing and the Fairey Delta 2, another 'one-off' looking at high-speed and supersonic characteristics of delta wings.

You could say that ETPS had been based on getting as much data from each flight as possible: thousands of words as opposed to thousands of flying hours. For the year I had amassed 86 flying hours on 15 different aircraft types (excluding the White Waltham flights).

Anne and I had to move house. We settled on renting a two-up-two-down cottage in the village of Abbotts Ann, just outside

Andover. It had the novelty of central heating. The single coal fire was in the middle of the house!

I persuaded myself to buy one of these new 'Minis'. Living fifteen miles from the base required new car reliability and economy. By January we were ensconced in our thatched cottage ready for the three years test flying at Boscombe Down.

The certificate proving qualification to test fly landplanes

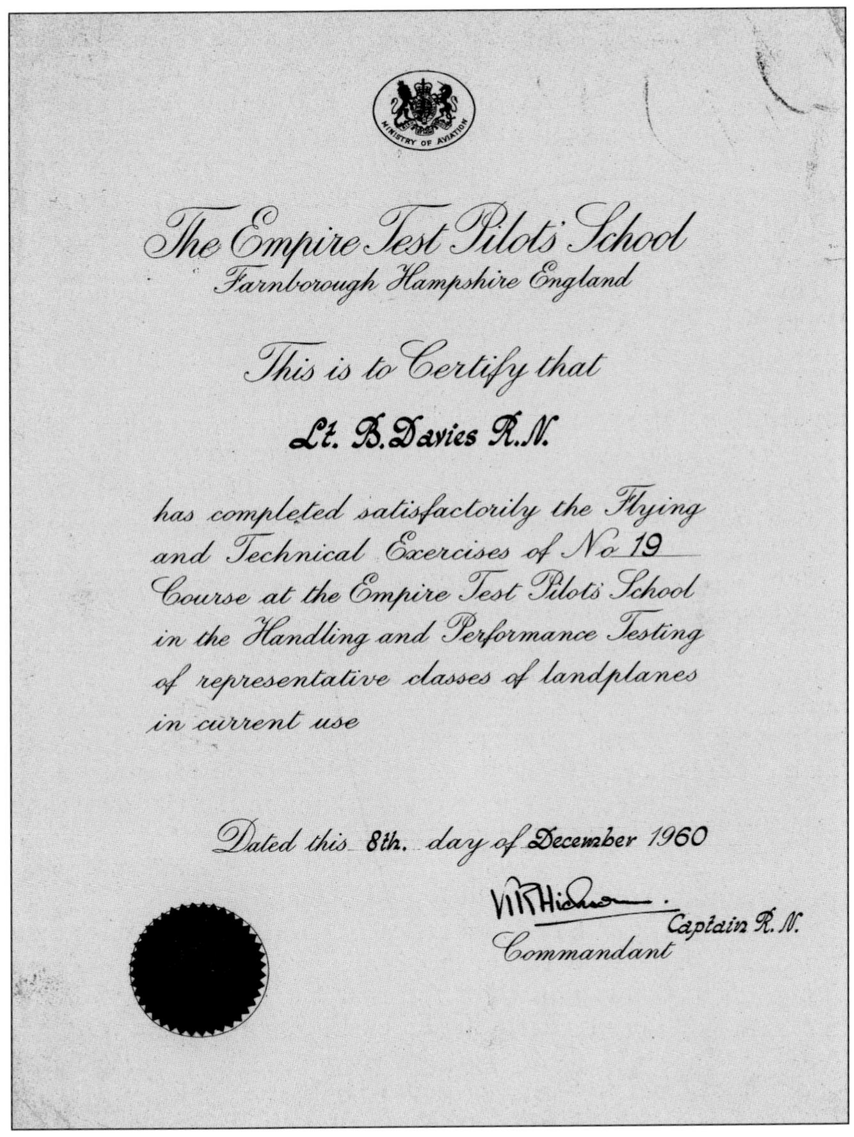

MINISTRY OF AVIATION

The Empire Test Pilots' School
Farnborough Hampshire England

This is to Certify that

Lt. B. Davies R.N.

has completed satisfactorily the Flying and Technical Exercises of No 19 Course at the Empire Test Pilots' School in the Handling and Performance Testing of representative classes of landplanes in current use

Dated this 8th. day of December 1960

Captain R.N.
Commandant

Chapter 12

A&AEE Boscombe Down

1961

In 1961 A&AEE was the agency used to test military aircraft and ordnance for its suitability for service use. Three Divisions looked after the major aspects of evaluations. 'Performance' looked after all the flying aspects, and 'Engineering' and 'Armament' are both self explanatory, but 'Armament' had a subdivision called 'Weapon Systems', since ordnance delivery was beginning to rely on aircraft radar and electronics as opposed to the Mark 1 eyeball of the pilot. Any project arriving would be administered by one of them.

The Division concerned would allocate a project officer who would work with the test aircrew allocated by the Squadron CO. I said 'test crew' because, in the case of the RN, a policy decision had been made to adopt two-engine, two-seat aircraft for the future. A number of RN observers were now on the staff of C Squadron to provide the expertise to evaluate the weapon systems installed in these aircraft. A test programme would be agreed with the divisional project officer and a report written by the aircrew on the flight tests carried out. This report would be strictly internal. The final report to Min. Tech. would be written by the Division and would take into consideration all aspects of the project.

The first job for us new boys was to visit the Blackburn Aircraft Company to complete a technical course on the Buccaneer S Mk 1. The Buccaneer would shortly enter naval service, but still had a long way to go to be cleared for operational use.

The only permanent aircraft we had in C squadron was a Boulton Paul Sea Balliol. It was a two-seat trainer equipped with a Rolls-Royce Merlin engine and had quite a 'hot' performance. It had not featured much in the RN, and the Sea Balliol name meant it was equipped with an arrester hook for deck landing. We used it as a communications aircraft. However, it came into its own on deck trials. If there was a person or spare part that needed to be delivered on board, the Sea Balliol could fly them there.

We used other station flight pooled aircraft to do the ordinary communications work as well. The Meteor 7 was used for destinations further afield, and if there were three crew involved we used a Canberra. If there were more than a total of three people to fly around we used the Avro Anson C 19. It was quite a thing for me to check out in an Anson. Not that it was difficult to fly, but a lot of stories I had read as a boy during the war involved the Anson, and I never dreamed I would fly one. However, at a cruise speed of 110 knots it wasn't the most popular of aircraft to take any distance.

I gradually eased in to helping out with the projects already running. Not having done any inflight refuelling before, I was sent off to Flight Refuelling Ltd, at their airfield of Tarrent Rushden near Bournemouth, to familiarise myself with the technique. I flew

The Buccaneer Course certificate

Blackburn Buccaneer Mk 1 XK523, No. 5 DB aircraft *(Crown copyright)*

with a Mr Hornidge in a Canberra equipped with a flight-refuelling probe mounted on the nose of the aircraft. It was a Canberra B 2 with one set of flying controls. Pat Hornidge demonstrated how to do it using a drogue towed from another Canberra, with me looking out of the front from the rumble seat. Then we changed seats for me to have a go. After three or four good contacts I was considered qualified.

To get used to flying the Buccaneer, I flew HF trials similar to those in the Gannet in 1957, only this time we were flying around the south of England talking to someone in Malta!

A word about the Buccaneer might be appropriate at this time. It had been designed to the OR NA/39, which required the FAA to have its first specifically designed strike aircraft. Its primary role in this era of East/West confrontation was to deliver a tactical nuclear bomb against a ship, using the LABS technique. Its secondary role was to deliver conventional weapons using LABS, 'Dive Toss' or normal dive-bombing techniques.

The Buccaneer proved to be very stable and yet manoeuvrable, capable of high indicated airspeeds at low level. To reduce the deck landing speed the trailing edge of the wing had been designed to allow the ailerons to droop as well as the flap extending, thus changing the whole of the trailing edge of the wing into a flap. This provided extra wing camber and therefore extra lift.

There was one slight snag to this design. At the large wing camber obtained with full flap and droop in the landing configuration, the wing would stall early. To delay the stall, narrow ducts had been installed on the leading edge of the ailerons and flap, which allowed high-speed air bled from the engine compressors to be blown over the whole of the drooped aileron and flap. This 'boundary layer control' (blc) retained the streamline airflow over the wing down to the approach speed. This design worked well enough, but meant the aircraft was completely dependent on the blc at maximum droop and flap deflection. If the blc failed or an engine failed or lost power in this configuration, the aircraft would drop out of the sky.

The only engine available at the inception of the design was the de Havilland Gyron Junior, which developed about 7,500 lb of static thrust at full power without compressor bleeds for the blc. With two of these engines producing a maximum of 15,000 lb of thrust, the Buccaneer was somewhat under-powered. The Gyron Junior was equipped with a set of inlet guide vanes (igv's) which controlled the engine intake airflow. They weren't very reliable and would occasionally fail to the full closed position, cutting down the mass airflow through the engine and therefore the thrust and blc if selected. This characteristic would be the cause of a number of crashes in the blown landing configuration in the next few years.

In April I had my own little trial to do. The Scimitar was to be equipped with the Sidewinder air-to-air infra-red missile system. It had been realised that 30 mm cannon were not the best weapons for interceptor work in this aircraft. The Scimitar installation simply required the missiles to be hung on the wing pylons, an acquisition audio system to be installed, and 'Bob's your uncle'. The fact that the missile could 'see' the target was communicated to you by a growl in the headphones. This wasn't a tactical trial, but rather to ensure the missile acquisition head worked out to maximum range from the target and that the engines weren't adversely affected by the firing of the rocket motor.

In May it was decided to conduct inverted spinning trials on the SeaVixen, and I had been selected to do them! I was the ideal pilot to do this trial since I hadn't spun a swept-wing aircraft and I hadn't yet flown the Sea Vixen! Why they wanted to spin the Vixen inverted, God only knew. It was arranged that I do some inverted spin training with Hawker at their Dunsfold airfield near Gatwick airport in their Hunter 66, a civil version of the Hunter T 7.

I flew over one day in the Sea Balliol and spoke with Hugh Mereweather, a Hawker test pilot who would demonstrate spinning to me. He gave me a lecture on spinning, followed by a briefing for our first flight. It would appear that the spin recovery action used in the Hunter was different from the conventional recovery action in a straight-wing aircraft. The rudder wasn't very effective – sorry, was effective but the response poor. The only effective control to stop the spin rotation in a swept-wing aircraft were the ailerons. Deflection was applied to increase the drag on the outboard wing and reduce it on the inboard wing whilst in the spin. To do this, the outboard aileron had to go down and the inboard aileron up. This meant applying 'INSPIN' aileron, that is aileron applied towards the direction of the spin, a completely unnatural control input, since under normal unstalled flight conditions this control input would have had the opposite effect. But spinning the aircraft inverted required an opposite control input. The outboard aileron had to go up and the inboard aileron down. To achieve this, 'OUTSPIN' aileron had to be applied. Swept-wing spinning aircraft fell like a stone. Spins were commenced above 30,000 feet, with spin rotation stopped by 15,000 feet. Full recovery had to be completed by 10,000 feet.

Hugh briefed for the flight. Since I hadn't spun the Hunter before, he suggested we do three upright spins before going inverted. We got airborne and climbed to 35,000 feet. On the first spin Hugh demonstrated what happened if you applied rudder against the spin rotation – nothing. 'INSPIN' aileron was the only control deflection that had any effect. We recovered. We climbed back up to 35,000 feet and I had a go at the upright spin. Hugh suggested we make the next one inverted – and that I fly it, but he would monitor my actions all the time.

Now, to get a Hunter into an inverted spin requires extreme mishandling. Speed back to 180 knots at 35,000 feet and apply full aileron to get the aircraft rolling. Then gradually feed in full opposite rudder. The aircraft departed from controlled flight. You suddenly found yourself hanging in the seat straps to the tune of minus 3 'g'. After a couple of turns it settled into an inverted spin at a steady 1 'g' negative. Hugh was definitely in charge of the spin. He talked me through it and we recovered. I noticed that although there was some negative 'g' on the aircraft, the visual cues were very similar to the upright spin. You had to look out to the side of the aircraft to check where the horizon was to determine whether you were upright or inverted. It also took some few turns for the Hunter to stop spinning, and on each turn of the spin there was a necessity to continually check you had the correct control inputs applied. After another couple of spins I was reasonably happy. We landed, debriefed and I mounted the Sea Balliol for the flight back to Boscombe Down. After the spinning Hunter, the Balliol was welcomely sedate!

The good news was that after about three weeks it was decided not to carry out the inverted spin trial in the Sea Vixen.

Towards the end of May, John Carrodus and I were called into the CO, Mike Crosley's, office and informed that we would be off to the USA in a few days to evaluate a radio-controlled, rocket-boosted bomb called the Bullpup. Jacksonville in Florida was the home of a large US Naval Air Station of the same name. John and I were heading for VA 66, an A-4 Skyhawk squadron. Perhaps a brief word about USN squadron, aircraft and ship designations is appropriate at this stage. The USN gave their aircraft names, but always used the aircraft designations. To start from the beginning – C stood for Carrier, A for Attack, F for Fighter, P for Patrol or Anti-Submarine, V for HeaVier than air, L for Lighter than air, H for helicopter, N for Nuclear, etc., etc. So a CVN was a carrier that operated heavier-than-air aircraft and was nuclear powered, VF a heavier-than-air fighter squadron, LP a lighter-than-air (airship) patrol squadron, VA 66 a heavier-than-air attack squadron. If anyone ever developed a fighter airship, the USN could designate a squadron of them!

VA 66 was a large training squadron equipped with the latest A-4s, the D-2 and the D-2N. They were very welcoming and we were looked after by Dan Mealey, one of the Lieutenant-Commanders on the squadron. The A-4 was made by the Douglas Aircraft Corp.

A-4 Skyhawk *(USN)*

It was a small but very versatile aircraft. It could carry a vast range of ordnance or fuel tanks on five external underwing pylons. It had been designed for simplicity. On start-up everything came on line as the generator cut in, and you were ready to go. If the generator failed in the air you could extend a small turbine into the airflow which would provide sufficient electrics to get you home.

Simple it might have been, but they gave us three days of intensive ground school instruction before letting us loose on the aircraft. We did three familiarisation flights before getting down to the Bullpup evaluation. These flights were very necessary. Apart from getting used to the A-4 there was the small matter of getting used to flying from a USN airfield, in a USN environment using USN terminology. A slow-talking Southerner in air traffic control was not the easiest person to understand, and I'm sure he had difficulty with my British accent. You had to keep a nimble ear on what was being said. It was also important to get to know the local area.

At the same time as the familiarisation flights, we were being briefed on the workings of the Bullpup. It had been designed and built by the Martin (Marietta) Aircraft Corporation. The concept of the Bullpup had been based on a requirement that had arisen from the Korean War. The Korean terrain had been mountainous, and conventional dive-bombing had proved comparatively inaccurate because of the high altitude of bomb release required to ensure subsequent terrain clearance on the pull-out. It was thought that a great improvement in accuracy could be achieved if bombs could be radio controlled, rocket boosted and guided onto the target. With these attributes it could also be launched at a higher altitude above the ground, with the advantage of keeping the aircraft further away from defending ordnance.

So, the Bullpup was a radio-controlled, air-to-ground missile, carrying a 250 lb warhead that could be guided visually by the pilot. The attack profile envisaged an entry height of 5 to 6,000 feet above the terrain into a 30 degree-ish dive. The Bullpup would then be launched using a three-second booster rocket and would glide on down towards the target. At the end of the booster phase the radio control would be activated and the pilot would guide the Bullpup onto the target, using a flare on the back of the missile ignited during the booster phase.

The guidance system was simple. It consisted of a four-way switch on top of the stick which was spring loaded to the central (neutral) position but could be deflected to make the missile go up, down, left and right. This was called a 'Bang bang' control system. Selecting a channel on this switch would signal the missile to put full deflection on the control vanes. If you wanted to maintain the missile on the sight line to the target you would have to blip the up-channel more or less continuously to overcome the effects of gravity, occasionally blipping it left, right and down as required to maintain the line of sight.

To familiarise us with the control technique, Martin had devised a monochrome video game/simulator dedicated entirely to the Bullpup. This was before the advent of video recorders and colour video and monitors. Various dive angles and target ranges could be selected to vary the parameters to get used to the missile's handling characteristics. This reinforced the fact that this was a 'stand off' missile, since shallow dives combined with short flight times meant that you couldn't get the Bullpup stabilised before target impact. Shallow dives with long flight times meant that you'd run out of 'up' command capability because the progressive deceleration of the missile meant that it would drop off the target line due to gravity, even with full 'up' command continuously selected.

The only live firing range available at the time was some way up the coast near to Cherry Point, a large Marine Corps air base. The plan was that we'd fly to BT-9, the live firing range, fire the two Bullpups and land at Cherry Point to refuel before returning to Jacksonville. We had an excellent target to use at BT-9 – a beached freighter. It was about 300 feet long and painted dayglo orange. But it wasn't that easy to see on a hazy summer afternoon rolling into the dive at 6,000 feet. I stabilised the dive and fired the left Bullpup. It left the aircraft in a flurry of flame and smoke. I thumbed in full UP command on the 'bang bang' switch. The A-4 started to pull out of the dive. I looked down at the control and found I had operated the wrong switch. I was selecting full nose-up trim on the electric trimmer. I quickly retrimmed the aircraft back into the dive, relocated the flare on the back of the Bullpup, which by now was well below the line of sight to the target, and thumbed in full UP command. The Bullpup reacted slowly at first, but then started to close the sight line rapidly. I found myself over-controlling the thing for the last few seconds. Luckily for the statistics, it hit the target as it flew through the sight line. The second firing was more successful and I managed to fly the Bullpup onto the target in the published manner.

Three days after the first firing we completed the assessment, packed our bags and bade a fond farewell to the USN and the USA. On our arrival at Boscombe Down, John and I wrote our report. It recommended we didn't buy the Bullpup for the RN. The main reasons we had against it were that with a maximum warhead of

250 lb. the missile would only have a limited effect, that it would be difficult for the pilot to see a target in poor visibility and that the weather and cloud base would have to be pretty good in the target area for the Bullpup to be used. In addition to these basic objections, we considered that the Bullpup couldn't be used against small targets like tanks. The flare on the missile was so relatively bright that it obscured small targets when on the line of sight. It was at this stage that we found out that ours had not been an evaluation visit to VA 66, but a visit to familiarise ourselves with the Bullpup, which had already been ordered.

The last three months of the year involved me in two projects requiring my first real contact with the manufacturers and the Min. Tech. They required me to attend meetings at South Marston, the Supermarine works just outside Swindon, de Havillands at Hatfield, Aberporth, administering the range in Cardigan Bay, and RAE Bedford, where the Bullpup installation would be tested on catapult launches and arrested landings. Since it also involved two or three others attending the meetings, and all the destinations were reasonably close to Boscombe, we commuted in the Anson.

These meetings were an eye opener. The manufacturer's representatives presented the good aspects of their equipment, leaving us to find out about the less satisfactory aspects during the tests. The various other agencies had their own axes to grind, and unless run by an iron-handed chairman these meetings could get into protracted discussions on minutiae. They also gave me my first impression of the characters who attended these meetings. On all occasions you had the 'next meeting' and the 'hat' people. Next meeting people would always overcome a problem by deferring it to the next meeting; mainly it seemed to ensure there would indeed be a next meeting. Their lives seemed to revolve around meetings. Then there were the hat people who represented more than one agency. If you got two or more overt hat people together, the rest of us could leave the meeting and let them get on with it. They would eventually establish their own importance, but achieve very little.

It was around this time that we thought it would be a good idea to write away to the heraldic person to establish a squadron coat of arms. We eventually ended up with a crossed quill and sword superimposed on a pair of angel's wings. The Latin motto was *Ex Caligne Veritas*, which freely translated means 'Truth from Obscurity'.

A Scimitar had been modified to conduct the Bullpup trial. It had been fitted with the radio control system, and I was to run it through its service acceptance trial. This involved a number of flights establishing the polar diagram, or transmitting pattern, of the controlling radio, to determine that the signal strength ahead of the aircraft was sufficient to be able to control the missile out to its maximum range.

The live firings were made at Aberporth range during December, an excellent month in which to show up the tactical restrictions imposed by other than excellent weather; three of the flights were abandoned because of poor visibility and low cloud base. The other three were successful and two Bullpups were fired on each occasion. The target used at Aberporth had been agreed after long discussions at various meetings. The missiles had to be fired into the sea, and since Aberporth was mainly used for surface-to-air and air-to-air missile trials, they didn't have a regular surface target to use. In the end it had been decided to fire the Bullpups against a standard-pattern buoyed target enhanced by dayglo meteorology balloons. It was not intended that the trial was in any way an operational evaluation, and there was no requirement to hit the target. The aim of the trial was to determine that the radio power was sufficient to control the Bullpup out to maximum range, and the target was necessary to evaluate the response of the missile at these extreme ranges. The Pullpup worked well enough, but firing against a small target like a met balloon proved the point that small targets would be a problem. If you got the missile flare superimposed on the target, you couldn't see the target.

Compared to the test pilots' course, 1961 proved quite an active year, and I managed to accrue 152 flying hours, about half the hours I would have achieved on a squadron, but the variety and interest made up for this.

Chapter 13

A&AEE Boscombe Down

1962

1962 started off with a bang. I commuted to RAE Bedford in the Scimitar to be launched off their catapult and arrested by their deck arrest gear. Part of the programme was to try to determine what had happened to a Scimitar that had pitched up off the carrier's catapult and crashed, and partly to clear the Bullpup for catapulting and arresting.

The boffin in charge of the pitch-up trial briefed me on how he thought it should go. I didn't agree with him on the technique he proposed because I didn't want to end up in a heap of wreckage off the end of the catapult. After a couple of days and some six launches it was agreed that nothing probably would happen. Unlike a carrier's flight deck that is some 60 feet above the sea, the Bedford catapult was about five feet off the ground, and the Scimitar was in ground effect after the launch. Ground effect modifies the airflow over an aircraft, and in the case of the Scimitar very much reduced the nose-up pitch. In the end the incident was put down to mishandling by the pilot. The Bullpup launches and arrested landings went well.

Our beautiful daughter Lynne arrived in Andover hospital on 18 February. I was given a couple of days off for the event, but wasn't welcomed in the delivery room. Fathers didn't help in those days.

The Bullpup installation in the Sea Vixen was different from that in the Scimitar. Instead of the 'bang bang' switch on the control column, the Sea Vixen had been equipped with a proportional control system. However, the missile control was mounted away from the control column and you had to get used to flying the aircraft with the right hand and the missile with a small joystick mounted on the left-hand console. This left the throttles looking after themselves!

March was a little slack because the Hunter GA 11, a project

Hawker Hunter GA 11 *(Crown copyright)*

allocated to me, was a little late in arriving. The GA 11 had been procured for the FAA to be used for the operational conversion of new pilots, and was a very slightly modified Hunter Mk 4. But it would appear that it was considered sufficiently different to require a full test programme. After five or six flights I duly cleared it for service use.

In early summer a Gannet AEW 3 arrived for a handling assessment with external stores. Nick Bennett, who had flown many hours in the Gannet, had the project. At the end of the trial I persuaded him to let me have a quick flight since it was a model of the Gannet I hadn't previously flown. On this one flight, two of the squadron observers, both ex-AEW men, were coming with me in the back to keep their hands in operating the radar.

One of the poor features of the Gannet was that it had no nose-wheel steering facility. It was an old-fashioned design and relied on differential braking to steer the aircraft. It also had a complicated wheel-brake system. The brakes were hydraulically operated but electrically controlled. A foot-operated electrical actuator was positioned at the top of each rudder pedal. Foot pressure on these actuators transmitted the pilot's braking demands to the hydraulic system. There was also a manual parking brake located to the left and behind the pilot's seat, which applied both brakes mechanically. The twin nose wheel was a little uncontrollable. It was difficult to castor out of the fore-and-aft position, and was directionally unstable when castored. Manoeuvring the aircraft accurately on a flight deck was difficult, and in the past the Service had requested it be modified with a suitable nose-wheel steering system. This would have cost some £1 million to modify all the Gannets in service, an unacceptable sum of money in those days.

I required to make a sharp turn to get out of the dispersal area. I operated the left brake two or three times to get the nose-wheel to castor. To get to the holding point of the westerly runway I had to taxi past the V bomber dispersal, but my route required me to point at them before turning left again on the taxiway. As I approached the centre line of the taxiway I started to apply the left brake again, but nothing happened! I was now heading straight towards the line of V bombers, but too close to them to attempt a right turn. I decided instantly that the left brake electrical actuator must have failed, since the brake had worked only seconds before. I reached behind the left side of the seat and applied the parking brake. The right brake locked up, but the left didn't and I slewed sideways. I thought I was going to get squashed under the nose of a Vulcan that was ahead and to the right of me. I shut the engines down as the starboard brake locked up, and the propellers hacked into the Vulcan's fuselage

The taxiing accident, outside view. Brian Davies is partly obscured by the propeller whereas Nick Bennett can be seen in the cockpit with the Supt. of flying *(Crown copyright)*

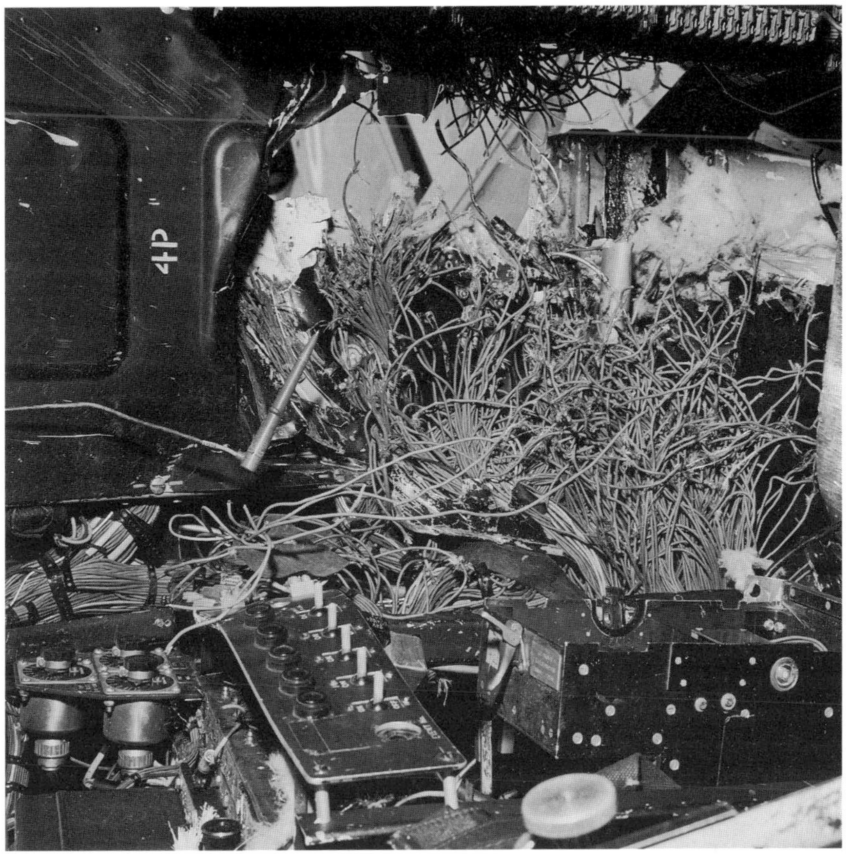

The flying accident, interior view *(Crown copyright)*

as the engines ran down. Bits of Vulcan flew into the air and lots of coloured wires sagged out of the hole carved by the propellers. I started to go through the after-shutdown checks to make sure everything was turned off. I also got onto the intercom. to tell the guys in the back what had happened, but I was already talking to myself. Obviously the sharp braking and the engines being shut down had convinced them that something was wrong and it was time to get out.

As I made my way down from the cockpit there were already groups of people standing around and there was some laughter. Rather like a cocktail party without the drinks! A black staff car was at the bottom of the steps, and the Superintendent of Flying, a Group Captain, was waiting for me. With him was Nick Bennett. They both climbed up to the cockpit and briefly checked it. On their return the Group Captain asked me what had happened. I told him the left brake had failed.

'Hop in the car and I'll take you back to the squadron', he said.

As we drove off I could see the way he was thinking.

'How many hours have you flown in the Gannet?' he asked.

'Well, I haven't flown this model yet', was my reply, and as I saw him visibly pale added, 'But I do have a number of hours in other models and they're all basically the same.' I explained the complexity of the braking system in the Gannet, and related the sequence of my actions since commencing to taxi. He then told me I had damaged the 'Blue Steel' Vulcan. It had arrived for evaluation the previous day, having spent six months installing the trial's instrumentation. I had damaged both the fuselage and the pressurised cabin, and all the pretty wires were from the instrumentation. It was estimated that the accident had set the test programme back some six to nine months and had done at least £4 million of damage. Had the Gannet had a nose-wheel steering system the accident wouldn't have happened.

It turned out that a new brake unit had been fitted incorrectly to the left wheel prior to me taxiing the Gannet, and that had given normal braking on first application and no braking on the second.

Autumn saw the arrival of the number 12 DB Buccaneer for the start of the weapons release programme. It should have arrived in the spring, but one of the features about the work at Boscombe Down was that few of the trials managed to commence on time. Things seemed to get done when they were ready, and there appeared to be no requirement for the manufacturer to be financially penalised because a programme was running late.

At the end of the year I decided to keep tabs on the number of bombs dropped and missiles fired. The score to date was 17 Bullpups, 10 Sidewinders, 20 1,000 lb bombs and 136 2-inch rockets. As far as flying hours were concerned, I was a little down on 1961, with 135 hours.

Chapter 14

A&AEE Boscombe Down

1963

The year started with the odd little trial. However, my primary task along with Bob Helliwell, the project observer, was to check out the navigation and attack radar systems on the number 12 DB Buccaneer before the main weapon systems trial at West Freugh.

The Buccaneer was equipped with a Doppler navigation system. Along with the radar and attack system, it had been designed to enable it to attack a Russian capital ship with a tactical nuclear bomb. The frequency used for the radar had been selected to enable long-range acquisition on a ship. This enabled the Buccaneer to lock on at a considerable range for the LABS manoeuvre and would provide a radar PUP. However, the radar frequency could only be used in a low-clutter environment. Ships at sea are in a low-clutter radar environment, land targets aren't. So the Buccaneer could only be used in its primary role against ship targets in the open sea. Its secondary, and probably more realistic, role was the ability to deliver up to eight 1,000 lb bombs. To this end, Ferranti, the contractor for the weapon system and radar, had developed a 'dive/toss' mode of delivery where the pilot could dive at a target, initiate the radar ranging and pull out of the dive at a convenient height. The weapon system would do the rest and release the bombs at a suitable point to hit the target. However, there was nothing to prevent you delivering conventional bombs or rockets in a normal dive attack, or using the LABS system if you so wished.

Bob and I flew a few sorties against shipping in the Lyme Bay area. They seemed to work well enough, but the Doppler had problems when flying over a very smooth sea. The system relied on radar returns bouncing back from the terrain over which it was flying, and smooth seas didn't give very good radar returns.

On completion of these initial flights we were ready to take the aircraft to West Freugh and operate with the kine-theodolites on the range. The object of our initial flights was to check the release characteristics of 1,000 lb bombs from the wing pylons and bomb bay at various speeds and dive angles to ensure they left the aircraft cleanly and didn't interfere with each other or the aircraft. The bombs were fired from their stations using ejector release units (ERUs). These ERUs used explosive cartridges to eject the bomb off the station, and each release could be felt as a jolt through the airframe. Cameras were fitted to the Buccaneer to film the bomb releases.

Since we were to spend some time at West Freugh, Bob and I decided to take our families with us and stay at Portpatrick, a charming fishing village on the West Coast of the Mull of Galloway. Anne, Lynne and I were to stay with the Nimmos, two maiden ladies who rented off the ground floor of their house at £2.50 per week, cheap even for the early 1960s. We had a fine view of the harbour. Bob and his family rented a flat next door.

The Buccaneer was delivered to West Freugh airfield, situated at the top of Luce Bay, and Bob and I drove there separately. Portpatrick was marvellous. The weather was super, the people friendly, the scenery magnificent and the flying spasmodic but interesting. We made lots of friends, joined the local water-skiing club and I played a lot of golf. However, back to the trial.

Onboard cameras and the kine-theodolites filmed all of the bomb releases. We carried out conventional dive-bombing against a buoyed target, and the fall of shot was measured for each bomb released. Various combinations of multiple bomb releases were made. After a few flights it was established that there were no problems

We switched to dropping single live bombs to check the fusing. The first two bombs released operated normally and the range controller came up with a fall of shot. On releasing the third bomb I didn't feel the ERU fire the bomb off as normal, and on the pull out called 'No bomb' over the radio to indicate we had a hang up. Some few seconds later the range controller came up with a fall of shot.

I asked Bob if he had felt the bomb go and he agreed with me that he thought the bomb had hung up.

'Neither of us felt the bomb go,' I called over the radio, 'I'm not happy about it and we're going back to land at West Freugh.'

We turned off the range, lined up on the westerly runway and landed straight away. Before shutting down the engines I rotated the bomb bay to the open position. There was a flurry of activity as Bob and I unstrapped and climbed down from the cockpit. As I had rotated the bomb bay, a lethally explosive combination of hydraulic fluid, fuel and liquid oxygen had spilt onto the dispersal. We had not felt the bomb release from the bay because the ERU housing of the third bomb had fired itself up through the fuselage when the cartridge had fired. The bomb had simply just fallen off, and the ERU housing had severed hydraulic and liquid oxygen lines on its way upwards to puncture one of the fuselage fuel tanks. It was thought that had I stayed airborne to complete the bomb releases, I would either have lost control of the aircraft because of a hydraulic failure or the aircraft would have blown up!

The first words of the project engineer on surveying the errant ERU have rung in my ears from that day to this. He looked at it very carefully and said, 'It's impossible for the ERU to have done that.'

The weapon release trial was suspended until it was determined what had happened. This was to take a month, and in that time Bob and I switched to operating dummy attacks using the weapon system to lock onto the Luce Bay target ship. These dummy attacks were in preparation for delivering 1,000 lb bombs in the 'long toss' mode.

The Buccaneer's weapon system was the answer to the guesswork type of long toss attack carried out in the Scimitar. The radar could be locked on well before the PUP, enabling the system to know the range and direction of the target. The Doppler navigation system determined the ground speed and drift of the aircraft and compared it to the aircraft's heading and true air speed to obtain the wind affecting the aircraft on the run-in to the target. This was also assumed to be the wind affecting the bomb during its flight time to the target after release. All this information was fed to the weapon system electronics to enable it to calculate the PUP and release data for the bomb. At the same time relevant information was fed to the strike sight, the forerunner of the head-up-display system used in modern aircraft. The strike sight gave pre-warning of the pull-up, and a display that enabled the pilot to track the correct heading in the loop and pull the correct 'g' required by the attack profile. This was achieved by using an 'aim dot' which the pilot had to keep centred within an 'aim circle'. At the PUP the aim dot would be programmed up the strike sight, and the pilot had to pull the required 'g' to bring it back into the middle of the aim circle. At the same time the aim dot was programmed in azimuth to maintain the correct heading until bomb release, which was signalled by the thump of the ERU firing the bomb and the strike sight display disappearing. You then completed the loop manoeuvre by reverting to the flight instrument panel, rolling out on the

This page and next: The sinking of the target ship, using a 2,000 lb inert nuclear bomb *(Crown copyright)*

reciprocal of the attack heading to make your escape. All this practice was required, not only for the crew, but also for the kine-theodolite operators who would be tracking the aircraft and the bomb. From these practice runs it looked as if we would need about a 7,000-foot cloud base and good visibility.

By mid-June we were back to the weapon system trial. It had been determined what had happened to the ERU, but no one told me what that was! No doubt all would be well. The remainder of the bomb releases were completed and we progressed to deliveries in the dive-toss mode. After three sessions of this it was decided that the dive-toss mode wasn't working well. The bombs weren't dropping near enough to the target, so it was back to the drawing board at Ferranti's.

The rest of June and July saw us dropping umpteen 1,000 lb and 25 lb practice bombs to check release and fusing characteristics. At the same time we started to long-toss 1,000 lb bombs at the target. The accuracy seemed pretty good and the target ship got the odd fright from a near miss. Ferranti were operating out of West Freugh with the sixth DB aircraft to further their own trials tossing the 2,000 lb 'nuclear shape'. This was a dummy bomb with the same weight and aerodynamic characteristics as the real thing. They had been monitoring our results tossing the 1,000 lb bombs, and reckoned we were more accurate than they were.

Ferranti's results long-tossing the shape weren't good. Most of their impacts were long. They asked me if I would fly their aircraft

to see what I thought. One of the test requirements was that the strike sight was filmed on all attacks. I said that I would fly it, but that I would like to see the strike sight films of the last few attacks to see what had happened.

Ferranti had always made a point that the aim dot had to be tracked in azimuth, but didn't need to be tracked so accurately in 'g' since any ranging errors would be compensated by the electronic attack system. All of the attack sight films showed that their test pilot hadn't pulled enough 'g' to maintain the aim dot in the aim circle. I pointed out that his technique could result in over-ranging, but they insisted that this didn't matter. I said I would fly the system as accurately as I could.

On 25 July I flew two sorties in Ferranti's aircraft with Mr Graham, Ferranti's test observer. Both involved dive-toss releases of wing-mounted 1,000 lb bombs, followed by long-toss release of a 2,000 lb shape from the bomb bay. The dive-toss releases were no more successful than those on the twelfth DB aircraft. However, the first long toss was followed by a long silence on the radio, followed by 'You've sunk the bloody target'. The inert shape had hit the forward deck of the vessel and then punched a hole in the waterline.

This posed two problems. Firstly, their electronic ranging seemed to be suspect, and secondly it would take three months to find another target ship. It also meant the termination of the trials until another target could be produced, and our sudden return to Boscombe Down.

I arrived back in time to support the first deck trial of the Buccaneer on board HMS *Victorious* taking place in the Channel. I flew the Sea Balliol on board with spare parts and/or personnel. It was quite fun to be back deck-landing a tail dragger again.

The autumn of my last year at Boscombe Down was full of bits and pieces. More bomb releases were made from the Buccaneer over Larkhill range nearby. I was involved with the Sea Vixen Mk 2 equipped with the Red Top, the latest version of the Firestreak. However, the major trial was the high-weight take-offs in the Buccaneer.

The initial take-offs were at 48,000 lb a.u.w with two final flights at 51,000 lb. Unlike twin engined civil aircraft, there were no criteria laid down on airfield capability for aircraft like the Buccaneer, should one engine fail. If you couldn't get airborne for some reason or other you did your best to stop. At Boscombe Down there was a barrier that could be raised to assist your not going too far off the end of the runway, providing you called the tower early enough and they were quick enough to raise it. Also, an engine failure after take-off was not considered from the point of view of being able to climb away on one engine, although instinctively you knew where you were with some aircraft. The Scimitar and Sea Vixen would probably be able to climb away on one engine. Transport aircraft required to be able to climb away on one. However, it was a necessity to determine the safety speed on one engine. This was the speed at which the aircraft could be controlled directionally when

Brian Davies in the Sea Balliol, aboard HMS *Victorious* in 1963 *(Crown copyright)*

airborne with full power on the good engine. On some aircraft you knew that they wouldn't remain airborne after an engine failure. The Buccaneer was one such aircraft. In the event, you lost an engine just after take-off, you 'banged out'.

The Buccaneer proved very sluggish at 48,000 lb. After an interminable time on the runway during the take-off, I eventually lifted off at 165 knots and the aircraft climbed away very slowly. Directional control was a criterion. However, another criterion was the ability to maintain height on one engine. In the Buccaneer control wasn't a problem since full engine power was so low. By throttling back one engine I determined the safety speed to be 220 knots having raised the undercarriage, flaps and droop.

Two aerodynamic boffins from Performance Division were running the trials. One was a theorist and the other, Dennis, would regularly come up with us on trials if there was a spare seat. The theorist briefed me on the 51,000 lb a.u.w. take-off. I expressed my concern at the aircraft's performance on the previous take-off and wondered whether it would be safe at 51,000 lb. He assured me that it would.

The 51,000 lb take-off took up even more of the long runway at Boscombe Down. Lift-off was at 175 knots with the end of the runway firmly in sight. The safety speed this time was 235 knots.

At the end of 1963 my three-year test-flying stint was up. I had now achieved the rank of Lieutenant-Commander, had the most up-to-date experience of weapon delivery from a Buccaneer, and had passed all my squadron command examinations (these latter were a requirement to become a squadron CO). I thought myself fully qualified to become a Senior Pilot on a front-line Buccaneer squadron. Apart from dropping 136 1,000 lb bombs in 1963, making a grand total of 156 for the three years, I'd fired umpteen Bullpups, Sidewinders, 2-inch and 3-inch rockets. The flying hours weren't all that great though. With 133 in 1963, the grand total for the three years was 430: about fifteen months of normal service flying.

In many ways I was also glad to be leaving the test-flying world. I had found the work relatively frustrating. Continuous delays in the test programmes, along with equipment entering service that had been cleared on a political timescale but wasn't up to the job. I had found it a case of bashing my head against a brick wall most of the time.

Having prepared myself mentally for a nice new flying job, it came as a bit of a shock to find my past catching up with me. Since obtaining a General List commission in 1956, I had still to do my 'fish-heading' time. I had to go to sea to obtain a Bridge

Watchkeeping and Ocean Navigation Certificate, something you normally did as a Sub-Lieutenant or junior Lieutenant. It was going to be a little embarrassing arriving on a ship as a Lieutenant-Commander 'additional for training'. I was to join HMS *Eastbourne*, a Type 12 anti-submarine frigate, which was currently completing a refit at Rosyth Dockyard in Scotland.

Eastbourne would eventually be based at Plymouth, and I applied for married quarter accommodation there – for how long I didn't know. Anne and I had become used to living in one place for the past three years and didn't really want to move. But the exigencies of the service came first and we had to look forward to a period of disruptive separation. I didn't know how long I was to be with *Eastbourne* or where I would go afterwards, so we would definitely have to play it by ear.

Chapter 15

HMS *Eastbourne*

1964

I packed my gear and left Abbotts Ann to travel to Rosyth Dockyard by train. I had no idea when I would next see Anne and Lynne again. I was very sad at leaving them both, particularly since we had recently learned that Anne was pregnant. What a time to pick, but in those days children didn't always come at a convenient time.

Rosyth is located on the Firth of Forth at the northern end of the Forth rail and road bridges. (No road bridge when I was there!) I arrived at the ship in the late afternoon. My first impression was of chaotic activity. The ship was in the last throes of being replenished, so there was a lot of activity across the companionways. The ship wasn't habitable and I was to spend a few nights living on board a submarine depot ship used to provide accommodation for ships, crews under refit.

Still, I had to report to HMS *Eastbourne* and she seemed to be open for business. I marched across the aft gangway to the quartermaster's desk and asked for directions to the captain's accommodation. As it happened that wasn't necessary, since the captain of the ship, Commander Robin Squires, was right there on the quarterdeck. I introduced myself. 'Tubby' Squires knew why I had been appointed to his ship, but seemed not to comprehend how on earth I had reached the rank of Lieutenant-Commander without obtaining a Bridge Watchkeeping Certificate. He was a submariner, and his navy was the real navy. He hadn't really come across 'pure' aviators before. He had always been in submarines, and was of some renown, having served in nuclear boats. He was now a poacher turned gamekeeper as captain of an anti-submarine frigate. His first words to me were, 'I don't know that I really want an aviator on my ship.' I felt like replying 'Well, I don't know that I really want to be here.' I'm sure he didn't mean it in any malicious way. It was rather a question of not knowing what to do with someone of my rank who had arrived to do some basic seaman officer training.

It took another couple of weeks before *Eastbourne* was ready to put to sea. I was made Mate of the Upper Deck, a task normally carried out by the First Lieutenant. It meant I was in charge of painting the ship. I also became the wardroom Wine Caterer. This meant being responsible for ensuring the wardroom cellar was suitably stocked, and that proper accounts were kept. In those days I was a complete wine ignoramus. I managed to stock up on wines that some of the officers considered good, but often these also included wines that wouldn't travel well. Not a good idea in a ship.

We put to sea at last, still with a complement of dockyard workers on board completing the final details. After a few days operating in the Firth of Forth to shake down the ship, we set sail for Portland harbour and the ship's work-up, conducted under the auspices of Flag Officer Sea Training (FOST), who was responsible for running each newly commissioned ship and its complement of officers and ratings through a work-up programme to ensure that every aspect of operating a ship was satisfactory. It wasn't so much the operational side that was scrutinised, but rather whether we were prepared for the unexpected. This ranged from ensuring the emergency organisation and equipment worked under battle conditions, where the ship had to be capable of operating with its hull as watertight as possible and sealed from nuclear and biological attack, to organising relief for Third World hurricane disasters, to defending the ship at anchor against enemy frogmen. If there was an unusual situation, FOST's staff had thought of it, and the watchword was 'be prepared'. That hurdle over with, *Eastbourne* was launched on its commission as a competent anti-submarine frigate.

I had started my bridge watchkeeping duties, and had eventually settled down to what was required of me. I had to learn that I wasn't actually in control of the ship. If the captain was on the bridge, he was in control; if he went down to run the ship from the operations room, he was in control and might ask 'visual' advice relating to radar contacts. And finally, just steaming along at night with the captain asleep in his cabin, he was still in control. 'Tubby' Squires became quite nervous when he realised that, initially, I thought I was in charge when keeping watch, and was responsible for course alterations to avoid other shipping. However, he soon realised I had grasped the essentials of bridge watchkeeping, and would only come up to the bridge if I considered it necessary, or he thought the situation I had reported required clarification. It was also the first time I had realised that the captain of a ship at sea gets very little sleep!

After six weeks or so I was beginning to feel at home as a fish-head. I thought I might soon be back to flying again. My hopes were somewhat dashed when the captain called me to his cabin one day to show me a general signal he had just received from the Admiralty. It said that, in Their Lordships' wisdom, it was now a requirement for all aviation officers who had transferred to the General List to complete a year's training at sea to obtain their watchkeeping certificates. Tubby Squires was sorry this had happened since he considered he would have had no problem awarding me a Watchkeeping and Ocean Navigation Certificate well before then.

We arrived in Plymouth in the spring of 1964. We were to operate a day-running routine, which would mean me being able to get home to see Anne just about every night. She had moved to married quarters in Plymstock, a village just to the east of the city.

Our life took on a semblance of domestic routine for the next few months. Some ship's duties required me to remain on board overnight, but most nights and weekends we were together. It was the first time we had occupied married quarters. All the houses were the same shape externally and internally, and all were equipped with the same furniture, curtains, crockery and linen.

Eastbourne was part of the Dartmouth Training Squadron. This frigate squadron operated to give naval cadets at RNC Dartmouth sea experience. As such we weren't a regular anti-submarine frigate, in that the ship's complement was not complete, so that the cadets could fill in as seamen ratings. Although we operated a day-running routine to do the training, in July it was interrupted by a short trip to Gibraltar, with a stop at Oporto on our way back to Plymouth. Oporto was an unexpected outpost of the British Empire in that it had a very large British community producing port wine. Our arrival was of some consequence, and the normal ship's cocktail party invited many of the British community working in the port houses. As the wardroom wine caterer, I was reminded that sherry, a Spanish aperitif, was not drunk in Oporto, and I had to ensure that we had a sufficient quantity of white port for the cocktail party.

Our cocktail party included many invitations ashore, including an introduction to a couple who had embarked on a mixed marriage. He was Portuguese and she English. Both were from good families but both had been banished from their own communities, since intermarriage of the two nationalities was frowned upon. The swinging sixties hadn't reached as far as Oporto, it would seem.

The day of our departure came around all too quickly, although

I was anxious to get back to Plymouth. Our second baby was due in mid-August, and coincidentally I would have some leave to come. Our son, Paul, arrived on the due date with my help, which was a little unusual in those days. Still, the midwife arrived before I passed out!

I remained with the ship for the autumn cruise to the Mediterranean and another visit to Malta. Before our departure my new appointment had come through. My hoped for job as Senior Pilot of a Buccaneer squadron didn't materialise. I was to join 766 Squadron at RNAS Yeovilton in Somerset for a shortened conversion course to all-weather fighters (AWF) and then to join 892 Squadron operating Sea Vixens as the 'third hand', but eventually to take over as Senior Pilot. Over the years the Fleet Air Arm had become a little top heavy, and now found itself in the position of having three or four Lieutenant-Commanders on any one squadron. Not only were the CO and SP Lieutenant-Commanders, but the Senior Observer (Sobs) was also a Lieutenant-Commander. I was to join as the third hand and the third flight leader.

My year at sea being a fish-head had been very interesting. I had my Bridge Watchkeeping Certificate and had proved that I could navigate a ship using the sun, stars and a sextant to obtain my Ocean Navigation Certificate. I had also passed all my ship command exams, which meant that I could, in theory, now be in command of one of Her Majesty's Ships.

After supervising the painting of the ship in Malta, I flew back to the UK in November on a trooping flight with Air Link, one of the small independents in those days.

Chapter 16

766 & 892 Squadrons

1965

I was sent to RNAS Lossiemouth to complete a short refresher course with 764 Squadron, which was now the Operational Conversion Unit for pilots who had completed their basic flying on the Jet Provost. It used the Hunter T8 as the dual aircraft, and the GA 11 as the single-seat operational training aircraft in which they would learn the basics of air combat and air-to-ground ordnance delivery. Number 764 Squadron was also responsible for chaps like me who hadn't flown for a year or more. We were given a two-week 'up to snuff' course of about 20 hours' flying.

It was noteworthy that no deck-landing training was given on this course for the new aviators. All runway thresholds at Naval Air Stations had been equipped with MLS, and the trainees were expected to use it on every landing. In practice it had been established that all pilots who achieved this late stage of training would have no problem operating jets off aircraft carriers. I suppose the small failure rate that had accrued over the years supported this policy. Without the batsman, deck landing had become a do-it-yourself exercise anyway.

The 20 hours' flying included a new instrument rating. I started on an abbreviated all-weather fighter (AWF) course with 766 in mid-January. Since I had flown the Sea Vixen at Boscombe Down, I think it was assumed that I knew it all, and so was down to do a six-week refresher course. This didn't include any classroom instruction on how the Firestreak missile worked, or what the attack sight presentation consisted of, so a little private homework was required to get up to speed.

The AWF role had originated as that of night-fighters. Whereas aircraft in the past had been designated NF, they now had the designation AWF. I suppose the role was basically the same. Sneaking up on a target and shooting him down visually with guns had been replaced with AI radar and the ability to shoot the target down from further away with a homing missile. With the Airborne Intercept (AI) radar able to see a target thirty miles away, we had an autonomous capability.

These attacks required us to get behind the target to enable the missile to acquire the infra-red radiation from the jet exhaust, and the object of the course was to teach a crew to do this in the most efficient and effective way. This required accurate flying from the pilot under the expert direction of the observer operating the radar to put the aircraft in a position to launch a missile. This introduced a slight problem in that you would not be able to identify the target aircraft. The responsibility for designating the target friend or foe was that of the shipborne or shore-based defence radar agency.

In the Sea Vixen it was only the pilot who could see where he was going. His cockpit canopy was well proud of the fuselage, but offset to the left to enable enough room to provide the observer's cockpit. It was completely contained within the fuselage. The only visual contact the observer had with the outside world was a small window set into the fuselage to his right, and an opening to the left where he got an excellent view of the pilot's right leg and arm. He could also see a little of the flight instruments and was able to pass hand-written messages to the pilot if the intercom. failed!

I was given one familiarisation flight before getting down to work. It was the first time I had operated a two-crew aircraft as an operational team. In the past I had flown the Avenger as a taxi driver, and the development work on the Buccaneer at Boscombe Down had required crew co-operation, but not to the level required by AWF operations. Once the target had been picked up on the AI radar, the observer's job was to get the aircraft into the best attacking position. A formalised conversation between the pilot and observer was used, which indicated where the target was and what manoeuvre was required to optimise the attack.

Since most of the pilots and observers on the course were new to the game, pilots would fly with staff observers and observers with staff pilots to begin with. These initial flights started with simple set-ups which would enable the trainee observer to establish a basis for assessing the tactical situation. We would operate in sections of two aircraft, alternating between fighter and target during the sortie. The standard intercept involved the fighter and target flying towards each other head on and slightly offset at the same altitude, where the observer could be sure in which direction the target was heading. This progressed into non-head-on situations where the target would vary its speed, heading and altitude.

Most of the initial training was done at high altitude under the control of defence radar, since at altitude the AI radar was free of clutter and had its best pick-up range. This progressed to low-altitude intercepts under the control of AEW aircraft, where clutter was high from ground returns and pick-up ranges were much reduced.

Since all RN fixed-wing aircraft had to have a strike capability, the course included air-to-ground bombing and rocketing sorties. It also included a high percentage of night flying, with the emphasis on night circuits and landings using the MLS. The fact that you had used the sight to simulate a night approach had to be noted in your logbook. Night flying had never really featured in my flying career up until now. There had always been a requirement to achieve a certain amount of night flying on an annual basis to remain current, but I had not really considered it as a way of life. In my previous operational squadrons, day flying had been the norm, since the eyeball had been the only way of seeing an enemy, be he on the ground or in the air. The AWF world had changed all that. AI radar was now the eyes of the air-to-air confrontation, and Gloworm rockets fired from a Pathfinder Sea Vixen provided the night illumination for air-to-ground work in the dark. I looked forward to night deck landing on a carrier with mixed emotions. It would be something to achieve as the ultimate piloting experience, but had resulted in a high attrition rate of aircraft and aircrew. Harold Bond and three of my own flying course had been killed in night deck landing accidents, so I can't say I was looking forward to it a great deal.

Number 892 Squadron was half way through its commission as one of the squadrons operating from HMS *Centaur*. I joined it on 1 March at Yeovilton whilst *Centaur* was in Plymouth on a self-maintenance period.

As I was a new boy to AWF, and had not deck landed since 1959, March became a quick get-up-to-speed period for me as third flight leader. Although the squadron was still organised as three flights of four aircraft for formation and strike purposes, in the self-defence role intercepts were now carried out on a one-to-one basis. The necessity to have a wingman following through on an air-to-air attack had disappeared. The main threat was considered to be Russian Navy subsonic bombers attacking singly with conventional or stand-off bombs.

Anyway, there was a good variety of flying in the four weeks before embarkation in *Centaur*. It ranged from high- and low-level intercepts, to photographic reconnaissance, to in-flight refuelling and night dive-bombing attacks against RN ships in the English Channel.

Night dive-bombing was something new to me. You would be

HMS *Centaur* with Sea Vixens in the forward deck park, photographed in 1965
(Crown copyright)

able to identify the target ships with the AI radar whilst running in at low level. The attack would be led by one or two Gloworm-equipped aircraft. They would run in and pull up into a 30 degree-ish climb and fire the Gloworm rockets in a long arc so that the flares would illuminate 1,000 feet over the target, providing enough light long enough for a co-ordinated dive attack with bombs or rockets. A co-ordinated attack meant flying at low level in formation on a pitch-black night over the sea, pulling up to the dive entry height under the guidance of the observer, and ideally having the target illuminated as you turned in for the dive. At the same time another formation would have positioned itself in another part of the sky and would be turning in to attack from a different direction, preferably not exactly at the same time. Since the technology was before close-range SAM missiles had been developed, the target ships would have little chance of seeing us visually or acquiring us on their gunnery radar to be able to shoot at us. But the combination of night flying on instruments or night formation flying until the flares lit, attacking visually, and then reverting to instrument flying to escape at low level proved quite exciting.

We embarked in *Centaur* in the first week of April to deploy to the Mediterranean. *Centaur*'s flight deck had changed little since I had last seen it. Apart from the one time I had landed a Scimitar on it in 1959, the last aircraft I had flown from the ship had been the Sea Hawk in 1955. Making my first approach to the deck in the considerably larger Sea Vixen made me realise that it was even more important to place the aircraft accurately on the centre line of the landing area to avoid hitting the island on one side and the MLS installation on the other. The insufficient drag of the Sea Vixen in the landing configuration meant operating the Avon engines in a very flat part of the power curve. This gave poor power response for small throttle movements, but the audio-airspeed detection device (ADD) that had been installed in the aircraft made speed stability and deck landing a great deal easier.

Like the Scimitar, the Sea Vixen was equipped with an angle of attack indicator (AAI). It was a very useful piece of kit. It short-circuited the need to adjust approach speed for aircraft weight, since the speed at which you flew was only a means of flying at the correct angle of attack. The AAI was very useful. Manoeuvre margins could easily be seen on this gauge and it could be used for flying at optimum range or endurance speeds.

One of the problems confronting naval pilots since the introduction of the MLS was that, unlike in the day of the batsman, where he (the batsman) was responsible for your airspeed, using the MLS required the pilot to be responsible for his own approach speed. The problem with this was that you had to take your eyes off the deck and re-focus them on the airspeed indicator to check your speed, before looking back at the deck again. An improvement had been introduced by mounting a large easily read ASI above the left cockpit coaming. This had eased the problem a little in that it was more or less in the line of sight to the carrier deck, but still required the pilot to re-focus his eyes to see it.

However, the final improvement had been the introduction of the audio ADD. You could listen to how fast you were going on the approach. No, not a sexy voice reading out your airspeed, but a series of high-frequency dots and low-frequency dashes combined with a medium-frequency steady note. The system activated some 20 knots above the datum speed in the landing configuration. The dots told you you were fast. At datum speed plus or minus 2 knots the only thing you could hear was the constant note telling you that you were on speed. If you reduced speed to below the datum bracket a low frequency dash note was introduced. With this system you were able to watch the flight deck and MLS at all times and just listen to your airspeed.

Centaur set sail for the Mediterranean and arrived off Malta ten days later, having completed a period of self-exercises on the way. This included dusk flying in preparation for our first session of night deck landings. 'Duskers' meant you started flying at sunset and finished in the gloom of twilight. We flew visual circuits using a faint horizon, but with only just enough light to see the flight deck with the aid of flight deck approach lighting. We spent a couple of weeks with some aircraft disembarked at RNAS Halfar to enable us to keep our hands in while the ship was in harbour. We then re-embarked for an exercise with HMS *Eagle* and USS *Saratoga* before commencing our progressive return to the UK via a stop at Gibraltar on the way.

The work-up for the exercise gave me the opportunity to practise my night deck-landing skills for real. Because the ability of the ship to offer Duskers was limited, but the requirement to precede night deck landings with dusk flying was mandatory, there would only be a few pilots who could qualify. In general, these were the most experienced pilots, since experience counted for just about everything in this field of operations. Many breathed a sigh of relief that they weren't amongst the select few!

Duskers would be the only occasion when we would carry out a visual circuit of the ship. Deck landings in the darkness of night would be made off a carrier-controlled approach. This form of precision radar approach didn't have glide slope information, so the controller would tell you your range from the ship and, what height you should be at that range. The object of the controller was to talk a pilot down to between half a mile to a mile astern so that he could become visual with the ship. The visual part of the approach was relative. Unlike well-lit civil airfields where the object is to enable the pilot to use the lights to line up on the runway and descend on a normal glide slope, the carrier was supposedly operating under hostile conditions. It didn't want the enemy to see it and therefore displayed as little light as possible. If you were lucky you would just about be able to see the ship well enough to line up on the deck and use the MLS from around a mile or two off the stern.

When you sighted the ship your problems had only just begun. Letting down over the sea at night to a height of some 300 to 500 feet above the waves, in pitch darkness, on instruments and with absolutely no visual reference, can induce a certain amount of anxiety. Your first sight of the faint flight deck lighting eased the situation from the point of view that you were probably where you thought you ought to be, but it was at this point that you really had to start working.

Night-time didn't mean the sea was calm and the ship steady. It was almost certainly pitching slightly, but more to the point it would be wandering slightly in heading. 'Flying Stations' always meant there was an experienced coxswain at the helm of the ship, but even the most experienced helmsman can't keep a ship the size of a carrier on course within one degree. Any slight wandering in ship's heading had an immediate effect on your spatial orientation. Without any visual reference other than the carrier, a heading change meant that you were no longer lined up. The problem then was – had the ship moved or had you lost heading? I found myself in exactly that predicament on my first night approach, and ended up badly over-controlling to get myself lined up. It was only at the last instant that I managed to stabilise the situation. And it was only at the last instant you realised the flight deck was coming at you. Suddenly you were on the deck and thrown forward in your seat as the hook picked up the arrester wire. The flight deck floodlights provided sufficient light for you to be able to see the marshaller signalling to taxi forward to the deck park. There was no rush to clear the flight deck. The next aircraft wouldn't be landing for at least two minutes.

The next thrill was to be launched from the catapult into the void whilst flying on instruments. The Sea Vixen flew away well from the catapult launch, and as the 'g' hit you, your eyes were scanning the flight instruments. For a night launch you concentrated mostly on the artificial horizon to ensure you were flying away with the wings level and the nose of the aircraft slightly above the horizon. But it was a good idea to scan the

HMS *Centaur* at Grand Harbour, Malta, in 1965 *(Crown copyright)*

The view on final approach (by day) *(Crown copyright)*

other instruments as well to ensure the artificial horizon was telling you the truth. Gyro instruments don't really like a lot of acceleration. It induces errors. On the launch the airspeed went from 0 to 130 knots in no time flat, and once you were off the end you double-checked the VSI to ensure you had a positive rate of climb. Over the next couple of months I did a lot of night flying, but I can't say it was my favourite form of flying. Challenging though! Luckily no one was killed during this period.

At the end of the exercise the ship put into Gibraltar. We disembarked some of the aircraft to RAF North Front, the airfield at Gibraltar, to enable us to get some flying practice whilst the ship entered a period of ten days' self-maintenance. Both the captain of *Centaur* and the resident RN establishment at Gibraltar were a little concerned about our extended stay. The long wrangle with the Spanish government about the future of the Rock had just begun, and the frontier between Gibraltar and mainland Spain had been closed. This meant that Jolly Jack wouldn't be able to visit his favourite bars in La Linea, the local border town, and it was feared that, with USN units putting into Gibraltar at the same time, Gibraltar might become a venue for some pretty riotous behaviour. As a result, the authorities at Gibraltar had made available two motor fishing vessels (MFVs) for the use of *Centaur* personnel, to enable them to visit Tangier in North Africa for a few days at a time. The MFVs were normally used to afford mass transport from ships anchored in Algeciras Bay into Gibraltar, and under these conditions could carry a lot of people. In the holiday configuration each one could accommodate 30 or 40 people using hammocks slung in the hold.

Number 892 Squadron and the 849 Flight of AEW Gannets were allocated one of these MFVs for a long weekend in Tangier. The only problem was that whoever went in charge of the 'ship' had to have a Bridge Watchkeeping Certificate! And so it was that I got my first ship command.

It was back to sea for a final exercise after our two-week stay in Gibraltar. After that it would be home to the UK. The exercise involved night flying on Gloworm strikes. It was interesting to carry out these attacks in complete darkness from launch to land-on, where the only thing you could really see properly illuminated was the target!

We disembarked to RNAS Yeovilton on our return to the UK. Came the middle of October and Admiralty appointments branch contacted me. Would I be interested in taking the job of evaluating the British version of the McDonnell Phantom II fighter at the USN Flight Test Center (American spelling!), NAS Patuxent River, Maryland, USA? The RN was buying some fifty aircraft equipped with the reheated version of the Rolls-Royce Spey engine. One of the requirements for the US Government to sell the aircraft to the UK was for it to be evaluated and accepted into service through the auspices of the USN. I was to be 'our man' at Patuxent River, officially to be on a straight exchange appointment, but unofficially to integrate myself into the USN's procurement system on the RN Phantom. The job would take two years. At the end of it I would become the Senior Pilot of 700P Flight at Yeovilton to evaluate the Phantom for service use, and then become the CO of the first Phantom squadron.

I accepted. I left 892 Squadron in the first week of December. That would give me a whole four weeks to organise my life before Anne, the children and I left the UK on a BOAC flight to New York on 3 January 1966.

Chapter 17

US Naval Air Test Center

Patuxent River, Maryland, USA 1966

There were quite a few things to organise in the four weeks before leaving for the USA, not least the fact that Anne and I didn't have passports. These came through in the middle of December, mine with a working visa!

I tried to find out as much as possible about the British Phantom, but not a great deal was forthcoming. The Phantom II had originally been ordered for the USN and had subsequently been taken up by the USAF. The USN was currently operating the F-4B as a fighter-bomber. They were now working on the F-4J to replace the B, and the British Phantom had been designated F-4K. The K was to be built to the same operational standard as the J, except that it was to be equipped with two Rolls-Royce Spey reheated engines, and not the General Electric J-79 after-burning engine which had powered all USN and USAF models to date.

The Spey at that time was one of a new breed of engines using the bypass configuration of compressors and turbines. The Spey had proved itself a reliable engine in the Buccaneer S2, where it provided much more thrust than the Gyron Junior in the S1. However, the version of the Spey engine to be installed in the Phantom was to be another technological step forward in that it would be the first bypass engine to be equipped with reheat. The installation of the Spey engines would require a major change to the Phantom fuselage. It would have to be wider than the American F-4s to take the increased diameter of the engine. The word was that the Spey would produce much more thrust and better fuel consumption than the J-79.

The Sparrow semi-active missile system was to be the primary weapon system, and the Sidewinder infra-red missile the secondary weapon system. Westinghouse had provided the radar in the USN

F-4s, and the common version for the J and K had a new pulse Doppler capability. The whole programme had been classified 'Top Secret – need to know'. Since I hadn't yet arrived in the USA it was considered that I didn't need to know. On the other hand I got the impression that no one else knew a lot about it anyway.

The F-4K was a two-seat aircraft. Since a large proportion of the work would include an evaluation of the weapon systems, Trevor Wilce, an experienced Sea Vixen observer, would be joining me on the project. Trevor and I had met before – on the training carrier as cadets. He had been on the observer course ahead of me.

The third of January 1966 was a long day. We met up with Trevor and Margaret Wilce and their four children at Heathrow airport early in the morning and left for New York, arriving in the afternoon Eastern Standard (local) Time. From there we hopped onto the shuttle to Washington DC. We were met at Dulles airport by Commander Danny Norman of the British Naval Staff, Washington, and escorted to a motel for the night.

By now we were all pretty tired, but Danny had arranged for us to attend a party, having already organised baby sitters for the kids. Danny assured us that the quickest way to get over jet lag was to stay up and adjust to Eastern Standard Time straight away. The guests at the party were a mixture of British and Americans who were on the military diplomatic circuit, and we were introduced as the newcomers to the US. Anne and I were descended on by a very overpowering American lady who gushingly asked how we were enjoying America. We explained that we had only just arrived, but I'm sure that she must have taken this to mean that we had only been in America a week or two, as she went on to ask a quite normal question which initially proved very embarrassing. I should explain that in 1966 the UK didn't have the equivalent of today's supermarkets, and the American chain Safeway had yet to establish itself in Britian. However, the Safeway chain was up and running in the US and there were various standards of store. Most sold purely American goods, but the odd store had been set up in the more cosmopolitan cities to sell food from other countries. These stores were designated as International Safeways and there was one in Washington. Needless to say, Anne and I were not aware of this fact, and were utterly taken aback when the American lady's first question was 'Do you use the International Safeway?' We thought it rather forward for a complete stranger to enquire about our contraceptive preference! Especially as we didn't know which particular system she was talking about! The conversation didn't get much further before the American lady's embarrassed conclusion that we were talking at cross-purposes.

Our stay in Washington DC was comparatively brief – but crammed with action. The domestics of living in the USA took preference. Danny Norman gave us a brief on the F-4K. Danny and I had met before. He had been a qualified test pilot leaving the RN Test Squadron at Boscombe Down as I was joining in 1961. He filled us in on some of the features of the British Phantom.

The Spey engine had been introduced because its extra thrust would be needed to enable the aircraft to be launched from our new carrier, which would be smaller than those used by the Phantom in the USN. Another modification to enhance the catapult performance of the Phantom was the extra extendible nose landing gear. The USN versions of the F-4 used an extension of the nosewheel oleo strut to increase the nose-up attitude of the aircraft on the catapult to enable it to be launched at a slower speed. Our version was to have an additional strut installed within the current strut to double that extension, producing an even higher nose-up attitude and an even slower catapult launch speed. The whole thing looked rather spindly, but McDonnell had assured us it would work.

However, the main piece of information was that, although a case had been made for introducing the Spey to enhance the catapult performance of the Phantom, the main reason for its introduction was political. The then Labour government had sanctioned the go-ahead for the aircraft provided it was modified to include a high proportion of British equipment. The Spey engine was the major modification, both technically and financially.

Trevor and I bought station wagons at a third of the price they would have cost in the UK. After a few days both families set off in their respective new cars for the Naval Air Test Center (NATC), Patuxent River, some 70 miles south of Washington DC in Southern Maryland. We took up residence in a motel in the small town of Lexington Park that had grown alongside NAS Patuxent River. Southern Maryland and Patuxent River seemed the back of beyond. Lexington Park had its own local radio station whose motto was 'WPTX Lexington Park – land of pleasant livin''. Its main newsreader gave the impression of marginal literacy. First impressions were depressing.

Having ensconced the families in the local motel, Trevor and I reported to NATC. The first thing we learnt was that everyone called the place Pax River or just Pax. In a very different way NATC did the same job as Boscombe Down.

Pax (NATC) was part of the USN and was directly responsible to the Naval Air Systems Command (NASC) in Washington DC for the evaluation of new aircraft and equipment. Procurement for the USN was done by NASC under strictly controlled rules established by rigid specification criteria. These rules included agreed timescales, satisfactory operation of the aircraft or equipment, the demonstration of the aircraft's ability to operate within the specified flight envelope and its service suitability. Any shortfalls in these criteria required a specification change by the USN or a financial penalty imposed on the contractor.

Pax wasn't organised in the same way as Boscombe Down. Pilots would qualify at the USN Test Pilots' School based at Pax and then join one of three test organisations in NATC. Each of these organisations looked after a particular facet of the aircraft. 'Flight Test' (FT) tested the aircraft's flying qualities (handling) and its ability to achieve the specified flight envelope. Within FT there was also the 'Carrier Suitability' section, which looked after the qualitative and quantitative aspects of deck operation. 'Service Test' (ST) looked after the engineering aspects, the correct operation of the aircraft's systems and their suitability to operate in a service environment. 'Weapon Systems Test' (WST) evaluated weapon systems and ordnance delivery. Each of these organisations was subdivided into Fighter, Attack and Helicopter sections. A Rear-Admiral headed NATC. He was a qualified test pilot and his staff co-ordinated the various projects in the three organisations. Thus there would be an F-4 desk run by an experienced F-4 pilot of Commander rank who would overview all the F-4 projects in all the test organisations. Since the only part of the F-4J programme then under evaluation was the enhanced Westinghouse radar system, it was decided that Trevor and I would join the Fighter Section of WST.

The continued hunt for accommodation was assisted by the CO of the WST fighter Section, Commander Alexander Graham Bell Grosvenor. He was a well-connected person. A past relation had been *the* Graham Bell, and *the* Grosvenor was the founder of the National Geographic Society. He had a friend in the local area who owned a large estate on which there were two summer cottages that could be made available to us. An American East Coast winter was not the time of year to live in a summer cottage, but Alex assured us that the central heating systems would keep us reasonably snug. The Davies and Wilces moved in on a temporary basis.

Having moved into the cottages we joined the social life of the Fighter Section. The American way of life was far less formal than that in the RN. We invited all the pilots and radar intercept officers (RIOs), the USN equivalent of observers in the AWF world, for Sunday lunchtime drinks with their wives or girlfriends. They arrived at noon and eventually left around 9 p.m. after being fed a number of times and having consumed a fair amount of our duty-free liquor.

The first thing I had to do was familiarise myself with the USN operating procedures. My short time flying A-4s down at NAS Jacksonville in 1961 helped, but in those days I had been shepherded around the skies by other USN pilots. Now I had to get used to operating by myself. The most immediate requirement was to obtain an instrument rating. Unlike the instrument rating in the RN, which concentrated on the pure ability to handle an aircraft on full and partial instruments, the USN required you to be able to fly in controlled airspace, and their instrument rating was more akin to the civil instrument rating requirements.

My initial air traffic familiarisation was conducted in the T2V-1, Lockheed Sea Star, the USN equivalent of the USAF's T-33 Shooting Star, with Harry Blackburn, one of the WST test pilots riding shotgun in the back seat. I also flew the TF-9J Grumman Cougar, the swept-wing fighter of the early 1950s that I had encountered in the Mediterranean as an adversary in the Sea Hawk. Like the Avenger in 751 Squadron in 1956, the Cougar's cockpit was big enough to take John Wayne, and it was built like the proverbial brick chicken house. It had a high subsonic Mach number capability, but was a bit down on the power/weight ratio. It got there eventually.

I moved on to the C 131, a twin-engined piston transport built by Convair, known as the 340 in civil guise, to get used to airways flying. Chief Warrant Officer Tinsley flew with me on these flights.

The winter of '66 was to be one of the worst for some years on the American East Coast. Came the middle of February and we were in severe blizzard conditions, with continuous heavy snowfall for hours

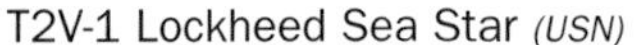

T2V-1 Lockheed Sea Star *(USN)*

TF-9J Grumman Cougar *(USN)*

on end. The summer cottage nearly became untenable. The gaps around the windows and doors let in the cold air, the warm air central heating ran continuously and we had to live in the downwind part of the house to keep warm. The external electric water pump froze up and we had to rely on melted snow. Nevertheless, being well out in the country, the cottage was relatively warm. All the little animals took shelter indoors if they could.

The Americans seem to be organised to cope with this sort of weather. Friends kept in contact by phone. Alex, who lived nearby, would turn up on skis to check that we were OK. After a couple of days, an enormous snowplough arrived and cleared our driveway. The cottages were in a remote area and we could now drive into Lexington Park to get some food. It was necessary for Trevor and me to do an official conversion course to the F-4B. The USN insisted it be a formal course and not a do-it-yourself conversion at Pax. We were both to travel down to NAS Boca Chica, a large airfield next to Key West in Florida. We were to join VF 101, a large training squadron based there. On the one squadron it had 85 Phantoms – more than the total order for the Fleet Air Arm!

The ground school covering the technical aspects of the F-4 was extensive and thorough. By the time I got around to flying the aircraft, it already felt familiar. The USN didn't have a dual-control version of the F-4, so the first flight was made with a VF 101 staff pilot sitting in the back to give advice. American terminology is slightly different from the British in that they call the 'reheat' the 'afterburner' – or 'burner' for short. What is more to the point, they write it as A/B, so I shall use the term A/B from now on, and full basic engine power without A/B was called 'military power', or Mil for short.

C 131 (Convair 340) *(USN)*

The day of my first flight in the F-4B was warm and cloudless. They gave me a 'clean' aircraft and there would be no restriction to the flight envelope. The location of Boca Chica meant that there was unrestricted supersonic flight out over the Gulf of Mexico. The take-off and climb was stupendous. The A/B thrust cut in smoothly on the take-off run, the aircraft leapt into the air and accelerated rapidly to the 450-knot climb speed. We reached 30,000 feet in less than three minutes. At around 40,000 feet we accelerated to supersonic speed with absolutely no indication that we were going supersonic other than a slight twitch in the pressure instruments as we went through Mach 1.

We descended to around 20,000 feet, where the manoeuvre capabilities of the aircraft were astonishing. You could pull 7 'g' continuously with the help of the 'g' suit to keep you conscious. In the F-4 you just used as much A/B as you required to maintain the manoeuvre. It seemed to be the ultimate aircraft. It seemed possible to make it do anything.

The ground school had included a decompression run in an altitude tank to acquaint us with the full pressure suit that could be used in the F-4. The decompression tank could take you to a simulated height of over 100,000 feet. A cockpit pressure failure that could expose you to pressure altitudes of over 45,000 feet would require some form of pressure suit to enable you to breathe. In the UK the services had gone for a pressure jerkin, since nothing much over 50,000 feet was envisaged. The USN had gone the whole hog, since by now a number of aircraft could fly well above 50,000 feet, particularly the SR-71 Blackbird and the U-2 spy planes.

Trevor and I had done our run in the decompression chamber and experienced an inflated pressure suit at 100,000 feet. We were given our certificates to say that since we had flown at over 100,000 feet we were now qualified space men!

I mention this episode because I only used the space suit once. Under normal F-4 conversion an initiation flight would be flown after completing some twenty hours on the aircraft. I wasn't to get that number of hours, so the final flight of the four-flight familiarisation phase was used as an initiation flight. The normal F-4 operational flight envelope didn't go much above 45,000 feet, and it wouldn't be common practice to use the suit under these conditions. However, for me the fourth familiarisation flight was to be solo and wearing a pressure suit. The idea was to take the aircraft out to Mach 2.0 at 45 to 50,000 feet, and maintaining full A/B power haul the aircraft into a 45-degree climb until the airspeed dropped to 200 knots. At this stage you flew at zero 'g' and went ballistic over the top. The airspeed would get down to around 100 knots, but flying at zero 'g' the aircraft couldn't stall, and the airspeed would increase once you had gone over the top and were on your way down. As soon as you got the airspeed up to 200 knots you could start getting the aircraft back to normal flight.

The reason you had to wear the pressure suit was because if the engines flamed out at the height and speeds attained, you would lose cockpit pressurisation. An air accumulator in the aircraft would supply pressure to the suit and keep you alive until you could get the engines restarted. It would be a certainty that the A/Bs would flame out, so you would have to throttle the engines back into the Mil power range.

I set off on the flight well briefed but nervous. Having flown all of two and a half hours on the F-4, I was about to go twice as fast and nearly twice as high as I had ever been in other aircraft. I had already experienced the fact that Americans had a very 'can do' approach to life. A British test pilot with more than four years' test experience could do anything in their eyes, so this run should be a piece of cake (not an expression used in the USA, but they thought it quaintly 'British eccentric'!).

I took off and climbed to 45,000 feet and wound the aircraft up to Mach 2.1. I hauled back on the stick and reached a 45-degree angle of climb. My heart had moved up from my chest and was firmly stuck in my mouth as the altimeter unwound. The sky through the front windscreen changed from dark blue to black, but as the speed dropped my concentration was on the flight instruments. At 200 knots I went to zero 'g' and the nose started to drop. As the speed reached around 100 knots I felt both A/Bs flame out, but the suit didn't inflate so the engines were still running.

I started to relax and enjoy the view as the nose dropped below the horizon. And what a view. Instantaneously I had reached 75,000 feet and the horizon shone in a thick white *curve*. Above this white band the sky was black, and below it the earth was a hazy brown. I was well out over the Gulf of Mexico so I couldn't see what the ground looked like from this altitude. Back in the cockpit the airspeed was increasing and the Machmeter showed that I was already above 1.0 MN. As the air thickened up on the descent I got back to subsonic speed and throttled up the engines to return to Boca Chica. The initiation flight was over and I felt at home in the F-4.

Trevor and I were integrated into the operational training to show us the radar and weapon system capabilities, but with the Vietnam War on and a lot of aircrew to train, we only completed about three flights before returning to Pax. Both families had found permanent accommodation which would be available on our return, and within a short time we had moved to a new three-bedroom bungalow. The bungalow was located in an area to the north of Lexington Park called Hollywood.

Having settled the family in the new house, Trevor and I went to Westinghouse Avionics Division in Baltimore to do a short course on the new pulse doppler radar to be installed in the J, designated the AWG 10, and K designated the AWG 11 (AWG stood for Air Weapons Guided). They were essentially the same radar and missile systems. I found myself between two stools. At Boca Chica I had done a swift conversion onto the F-4, but no ground school on the weapon system, and I had very little experience of actually using it. The radar in the F-4B was a conventional pulsed AI radar, albeit with a better performance than that in the Sea Vixen. It was integrated into the Raytheon Sparrow III semi-active homing system. This meant the missile had a radar antenna in its nose. The missile could pick up returning radar pulses from a target once the AI radar had been locked on. Once Sparrow had acquired these signals it could be launched and would home onto the target providing the AI radar remained locked on. The major advantage of this system over the infra-red missile systems preferred in the UK was that it was 'active'. It had the ability to attack a target from any aspect. Infra-red 'passive' missiles could only be used from the stern quarter. However, the F-4B was also equipped with Sidewinder infra-red missiles as a backup to the Sparrow.

Conventional pulsed radar relies on a transmitted pulse

bouncing back from a target to determine its range, elevation and azimuth. A combination of limited power from an aircraft's electrical systems, a limitation to the size of the radar antenna and the use of a high data-rate frequency, with its associated high attenuation rate, resulted in a restricted target acquisition range capability.

The pulse Doppler breakthrough made by Westinghouse Avionics had vastly increased the target pick-up range. The pulses it transmitted were coherent. This did away with the necessity to wait for a transmitted pulse to return to the aircraft before another was transmitted. The system identified each individual pulse when it was transmitted and received. And each pulse was organised so that it contained a static sine wave format. The receiver had been designed to amplify the returning pulse and to analyse the sine wave characteristic it displayed. It was looking for a frequency shift in the sine wave that would indicate the pulse had returned from a target moving relative to the aircraft. It didn't display ground return clutter, nor did it display targets moving at right angles to the line of sight. The AWG 10/11 used this doppler pulsing mode in addition to the conventional pulsed radar system in the F-4B.

Briefly, the new radar system managed to achieve much greater target detection ranges, but detection was based on the relative speed of the target to the fighter. The advantage of the Doppler radar mode was a target pick-up range of the order of 120 nautical miles. It also provided the ability to have a look-down capability, since ground returns didn't exist and there was no radar clutter.

The course completed, Trevor and I returned to Pax to commence operations with WST, which had an AWG 10 system installed in an F-4B for evaluation. All of the pilots and RIOs in WST Fighter Branch were well versed in the operation of the original pulsed radar and Sparrow missile systems in the F-4B. In fact some of them had used it in anger in the Vietnam War. It was difficult for Trevor and me to horn in on the development and evaluation work with so little experience in the Phantom. Although the evaluation was aimed at proving the radar system against the specification, part of the programme aimed at ensuring the system was useable based on the lessons learnt in combat. The specification might be changed depending on the evaluation. It was notably different from the UK procedure at Boscombe Down.

Simply put, the British military aircraft procurement system was run by the Ministry of Technology (Min Tech), who themselves drew up specifications based on the operational requirements submitted by the RN or RAF. The evaluation of any aircraft or system was the responsibility of Min Tech, using its established Civil

Service procedures and the offices of A&AEE Boscombe Down. The contractor produced his product under a government umbrella on a fixed cost basis, plus any costs needed to modify that product at a later date. No financial penalties were included should the product arrive late or not work. The evaluations of aircraft and equipment I had conducted at Boscombe Down as a military test pilot had never involved me in proving compliance with a specification. If any changes were required they were often made by involving Boscombe Down's know-how. This had two effects. Firstly, any solution to a problem would considerably delay a programme, and the cost would rise. Secondly, a Boscombe Down evaluation would be compromised from the outset.

The USN ran its own procurement system based on an agreed operational requirement, equipment specification and timescale. These three parameters were enshrined in the specification agreed with the contractor. The government would fund any change in the specification. Any shortfall in specification or timescale resulted in a financial penalty on the contractor: an obviously capitalist system aimed at producing the goods on time and to specification. Within this procurement system, Naval Air Systems Command (NASC) in Washington DC established the specification and the contractual requirements. The Naval Air Test Center acted on NASC's orders to evaluate systems and aircraft. If a deficiency in an aircraft was uncovered, the specification could be changed or the contractor had to meet the specification. There was no requirement for NATC to come up with any suggestions as to how a deficiency might be fixed. That could compromise the contract. The contractor had to fix his own equipment if he was responsible for the deficiency, and present it for re-evaluation at a later date. The NATC system also acknowledged that the aircrew evaluating an aircraft or system were probably the best persons to run the programme, since they would have the knowledge of its ultimate requirement. So, unlike Boscombe Down, each project test pilot was responsible for his own programme and would write the final report with the assistance of government technical specialists.

Very experienced aircrews were running the evaluation of the AWG 10 system in WST. Trevor and I weren't in that league yet, and we started off by flying tests that would back up a particular aspect of the trial while we got onto the learning curve. At the same time I converted onto the T-39 Sabreliner, a military version of the executive jet, and the Chance Vought F-8 Crusader. Both of these aircraft were sometimes used as targets for the AWG 10 trial.

The T-39 was a pleasant aircraft. You could fly it in a shirtsleeve environment just like any other civil aircraft. It had quite an agile flight envelope, with a high-indicated airspeed and a fighter-type manoeuvre capability up to around 5 'g'.

The Crusader had been introduced into the USN in the late '50s as a single-seat all-weather fighter. Since then it had been modified to carry out various roles for the USN and USMC. It was one of the most aerodynamically clean aircraft I had come across. At no time had there been a requirement to add drop tanks, and the F-8D's only external appendages were air-to-air weapon pylons either side of the forward fuselage. On its single engine it was capable of reaching 1.8 MN using A/B in level flight. For its size it had a large internal fuel capacity which, combined with a frugal fuel consumption in the Mil power range, gave it an extremely good endurance. It had been designed to remain airborne for a considerable time on combat air patrol, with the ability to markedly increase its performance when going into action using A/B power.

It had an unusual design to enable it to land and take off. The main landing gear used a very short oleo, which retracted into the fuselage. With the gear down, the main wheels didn't lower much below the fuselage line, requiring the fuselage to be kept horizontal to prevent contact with the deck or runway. To achieve this the whole wing was raised by hydraulic rams at the wing leading edge

Chance Vought F-8 Crusader *(USN)*

The Chance Vought F-8 Crusader *(USN)*

to increase the 'rigger's angle', or, if you prefer, the wing angle of attack relative to the fuselage. The act of raising the wing also lowered the landing flap and the leading edge droop. The airspeed had to be below 220 knots to raise or lower the wing. Lowering the wing after take-off didn't prove problematical. Flying the aircraft with the wing raised was a different kettle of fish.

The major problem with this configuration was that the thrust line of the engine didn't have a vertical component. In conventionally configured aircraft, the angle of attack of the fuselage increases with wing angle of attack. This was not so in the F-8. The wing alone generated all vertical speed changes. This gave an entirely different feel to the aircraft. The lever to raise the wing had two positions – UP and DOWN. Putting the lever in the UP position put everything in motion. Over a period of a few seconds you felt the nose of the aircraft lower without any change in height, the drag increased markedly as the flaps and droop extended automatically, and the longitudinal trim changed slightly as the stabilator was automatically adjusted to cope with the changed airflow over the wing. Engine power was quite high to maintain level flight and a three-degree glide slope. Adjustment of speed was difficult since power changes produced no change in overall vertical lift. All glide slope changes had to be made by changing the wing lift alone. Most critical of all was that the aircraft had a very steep back side drag curve. If you got slower than the approach datum speed, the aerodynamic drag increased markedly, requiring a large increase in engine power to recover from the high sink rates induced. As with most aircraft, pilots got used to compensating for any shortcomings, but the F-8 was one aircraft I was glad I didn't have to deck land!

I was involved in the work on the AWG 10 for most of the summer, flying either the F-4 or the target aircraft. Two events of note occurred that summer. The first flight of the F-4K took place at St Louis, and the Labour government cancelled the RN's new aircraft carrier from which it had been intended to operate the Phantom. This had occurred as part of a defence review that also cancelled the American F-111A swing-wing bomber for the RAF. It was replaced with an order for the Spey-powered F-4, designated the M. This aircraft was basically the same as the K but was intended to be used by the RAF as an attack/strike aircraft operating at low altitudes.

The cancelling of the new aircraft carrier resulted in a few senior naval officers tendering their resignations, one of whom was the Captain Air Mediterranean of 1955, Admiral Sir Richard Smeeton. My sympathies were with those who considered the government's decision to phase out the conventional aircraft carrier in the RN unwise. The F-4K programme would continue, with the intention of using a refurbished *Ark Royal* until government policies were firmed up.

There was a long silence from McDonnell after the first flight of the F-4K. Under normal USN procedures a naval test pilot from NATC would be required to fly the aircraft within some thirty days of the first flight to conduct the first Naval Preliminary Evaluation (NPE) to identify deficiencies that would require early rectification. These deficiencies would be classified desirable for rectification or mandatory for rectification. Desirable meant that it would be nice if something could be rectified. Mandatory meant that there would be little chance of the aircraft getting through the service acceptance evaluation without rectification.

The system allowed for three NPEs over a matter of months. The third NPE would establish the suitability of the aircraft to continue on to the service acceptance phase of the evaluation programme. Written reports on the findings of these Preliminary Evaluations would be presented to NASC to enable negotiations with the contractor on the contractual timescale with respect to milestones achieved and financial responsibility. If the aircraft didn't work, who was going to pay, and in the final analysis was the aircraft acceptable for service use?

In the past I had never come across an aircraft or piece of equipment that had ever been cancelled as a result of a Boscombe Down evaluation programme, although I could think of a few that should have been. However, in the few months I had been at NATC, the F-111B, the USN's version of the swing-wing bomber, had been cancelled. It had failed a number of tests at NATC and had been recommended as unsuitable for deck operations. The NATC's evaluations were objective, factual and uncompromising.

NATC were not involved with any problems that might exist prior to the first NPE, since an uncompromising attitude might be biased by involvement. The NASC were our masters and would call us in when they thought it suitable. However, it was part of Danny Norman's job as the Naval Air Attaché to keep abreast of the action on all fronts of the aviation scene. His news from McDonnell was that there were a few problems with the Spey engine.

If I was to be involved in the F-4K evaluation, it was important for me to transfer to a test division that would evaluate the K. I transferred to Service Test (ST) Fighter Branch, since it would be ST who would be most involved with the hardware in the aircraft, evaluating its practical suitability for service use. That summer the word from NASC was that the first NPE on the F-4K would be conducted 'soon'. It was necessary for me to await the call to McDonnell's test facility at Edwards AFB in California, where the F-4K was being test flown. Three flights would be allocated ST to evaluate the engine and any other system we cared to look at. I fitted into other tests being conducted by ST on the F-4. I used some of these flights to establish a flight test programme for the K. It required a certain amount of work study to ensure no time was wasted on the three flights that had been allocated for the NPE. I also arranged a do-it-yourself helicopter course, since the K programme seemed to be indefinitely delayed.

As it happened, the first NPE didn't come up that year. The summer gave way to the autumn and we still had no official news of the K. I spent the rest of the year helping out with various projects at ST, mainly flying the F-4B and F-8D. The F-4K was now very much behind schedule, and the NATC timescale had gone for a bit of a 'ball of chalk'.

We had a very American Christmas with lots of snow. I hoped the F-4K evaluation would get off the ground at last in 1967, a wish that was to come true with a vengeance.

Chapter 18

US Naval Air Test Center

Patuxent River 1967

The New Year saw the arrival at Pax of Lieutenant-Commander Alan Ducker, an RN air engineer officer (AEO) who was to head the maintenance team of the F-4K service acceptance trial. He was soon to realise that the trials programme had slipped somewhat and that his services wouldn't be needed for some time. The F-4K desk at NASC was also manned by Brits. Captain Rennie Cruddas and Commander Colin Little were both RN air engineer specialists, and, along with their own team of technical specialist officers, ran the procurement management programme.

In January NASC informed NATC that the first Naval Preliminary Evaluation (NPE) on the F-4K would be conducted at Edwards AFB in February. Flight and Service Test would conduct the NPE. Lieutenant Ed Clexton Jr, USN, had been assigned as the Flight Test project pilot, and I would fly the Service Test programme. Ed was an experienced F-4 pilot and would verify the contractual points of the F-4K flight envelope and check on the flying qualities of the aircraft.

Ed and I flew to Edwards AFB with an evaluation team. Bud Murray, the McDonnell test pilot assigned to the F-4K test programme, insisted on an extensive briefing on the F-4K before we flew the evaluation, mainly for flight safety considerations.

After five days of flight tests, Ed and I returned to Pax to produce the report on the K's first NPE. It was so utterly damning of the aircraft that the report itself was classified 'SECRET – discrete', which meant only Brits could read it, and 'SECRET – no foreign eyes', which meant only Americans could read it. So in theory no one could read it!

The F-4K had its problems. They were mainly associated with the

First Navy Preliminary Evaluation of the F-4K *(Boeing)*

engine and afterburner, but some were as a result of poor interface design. The cables connecting the throttles in the cockpit to the throttle control on the Spey engine remained the same as those used for the J-79 engines and gave too much play to accurately control the Spey engine. The design of the F-4K cockpit throttle quadrant integrated the HP fuel cock into the first movement of the throttle. Having started the engine the flight idle position was latched beyond the HP fuel cock position. Ed had slammed both throttles closed to the flight idle position during one of his tests. One of the engines had flamed out and run down. The slack throttle cable, along with the high inertia of the throttle cam box on the engine, had allowed the engine fuel control to overshoot the flight idle stop into the HP cock open/shut range before springing back to the flight idle position. This had been enough to interrupt the fuel flow to the engine and had caused it to flame out.

We thought this slack throttle cable system also contributed to the inability to set a constant engine power in the landing configuration. The F-4K required an approach power setting of around 85% high-pressure turbine r.p.m. (HPRPM) to fly on a constant-approach glide path at a constant speed. In the landing configuration we found that it was impossible to set a power setting between 82% and 88% HPRPM. We designated this problem 'uncommanded thrust change'.

The A/B didn't work very well at all. The Spey requirements were that you could select minimum A/B and wait for five seconds before using A/B power, or select maximum A/B power, and have full A/B power cut in three or four seconds later. Selection of any intermediate A/B power would destabilise the engine, resulting in an engine surge. This surge would be demonstrated by a large bang, followed by a recovery of engine power and/or the A/B blowing out and/or the engine flaming out. None of these engine characteristics were acceptable, either for operational or for safety reasons.

At altitudes above 25,000 feet, slamming the throttle to full A/B power when simulating air combat manoeuvres at high angles of attack also induced compressor stalls which could result in engine and A/B flame outs.

We also found that the engines were prone to stagnate at flight idle power. This meant that an engine would either slowly wind down to below flight idle r.p.m. or simply not accelerate when the throttle was opened, requiring you to shut the engine down to prevent turbine over temperature and burn out.

Although the flight envelope of the K took it up to twice the speed of sound and up to 50,000 feet, any of these engine flameouts required you to reduce speed and altitude to less than 250 knots below 25,000 feet before you could expect to restart the engine.

From Ed's experience of the USN F-4 on a carrier, he felt that the K wouldn't rotate quickly enough in the bolter case having missed all the wires, and would not be able to achieve A/B power quickly enough to prevent the aircraft hitting the sea. He also found that the aircraft didn't achieve one or two specification demonstration points as far as speed and Mach number were concerned.

Our overall impression was that the aircraft was a flying engine test bed. Its speed control was inadequate to enable it to land on an aircraft carrier. As a fighter it was pretty useless. Equipped with such unreliable and inadequate engines, who needed enemies!

The five hours I had flown during this first NPE generated enough data to keep months of technical meetings going in Washington and the UK, but some weeks elapsed before the first meeting of NATC, NASC, McDonnell and Rolls-Royce took place to discuss the report. This gave enough time for those involved to respond to our criticisms.

Rolls-Royce admitted they had a problem with the engine throttle system. They were designing a low-inertia cam box to cope with this problem. The inability to set a power setting between 82% and 88% HPRPM was as a result of a compressor bleed valve operating in the range. This would be changed. However, the delay between the selection and operation of the A/B could only be improved slightly. It would appear that the characteristics of a bypass engine were such that an even light-up of the A/B was required to keep the engine stable, and the burner fuel rings had to be fully primed to achieve this. This took five seconds, or thereabouts.

It turned out that the original Min Tech specification for the reheated Spey engine didn't include a time to achieve A/B power. In fact, the only specification points required by Min Tech related to engine thrust. It had been assumed that the engine handling characteristics would be similar to the J-79 and would not require specification.

The engine instability became a bone of contention between Rolls-Royce and McDonnell. McDonnell claimed that it was an engine problem – Rolls-Royce intimated that McDonnell's air intakes weren't providing the specification minimum airflow distortion under 'g'. Whoever was to blame would take the financial rap!

The fact that the aircraft hadn't achieved certain speed demonstration points was also a bone of contention between the two firms. McDonnell claimed the engine wasn't producing specification thrust. Rolls-Royce claimed that the engine was producing specification thrust in their test bed. Perhaps it was the widened fuselage and air intake design producing more drag than McDonnell had planned?

The end result of this first meeting was that we agreed to have another meeting in the near future, having gone away to digest the problems. Meetings would continue for the rest of the F-4K programme.

Ed and I had simply presented the facts of our evaluation. Problem solving was for the contractors. In the true tradition of NATC's impartiality, our response had been that if the contractors would like to present the aircraft for a further evaluation at a future date, we would decide if the various deficiencies had been corrected. The pressure would remain on the contractors to produce their own solutions and on Min Tech in the UK to modify the specification to meet the operational and flight safety criticisms.

It was at this stage that I realised Rolls-Royce had a problem that would be difficult for them to overcome. The British government had initiated the original requirement for the reheated Spey engine to power the Phantom. Min Tech had been the agency for them to work through, as was normal in the UK, and Min Tech had established the original engine specification based on performance alone. However, the production timescale involved meant their development programme for the new engine had to progress with no snags, and time was running out

On our return to Pax I received a letter from BNS. They had received a request from London for an up-to-date personal report,

First Navy Preliminary Evaluation, Edwards AFB, February 1967. Trevor Wilce is on the left and Brian Davies on the right *(Boeing)*

as they hadn't had one for some time. It was unusual for the officer in question to be approached to organise his own report! I talked to the captain in charge of Service Test and asked him to 'write me up'. The British Naval Staff sent down the form and I showed him how it worked.

The commanding officer of the ship or your head of department normally wrote personal reports in the RN. You were always given an idea of what had been written on a slip of paper called a flimsy. This always started with the expression 'This officer has served under my command to my entire satisfaction', and would continue with specific professional and personal comments that would indicate the regard in which you were held. If the word 'entire' was missing, then a comment would follow indicating any shortcomings. The famous comment about an officer who drank too much was '. . . to my satisfaction. I have seen this officer drunk.' When the officer concerned complained that such a comment would be rather damning, the captain concerned had apparently crossed out 'drunk' and written in 'sober'!

The USN captain in charge of Service Test gave me a glowing write-up. However, the use of the word 'outstanding' appeared rather too many times. I was later to discover that the Admiralty didn't seem to take much notice of the USN officer reports since they were all outstandingly similar.

After the NPE I reintegrated myself into the F-4 programmes that were running at ST and WST. By now both these test divisions had their own F-4J to evaluate, and I found it interesting to specifically compare the new version of the J-79, the 'dash' 17, with the Spey. And very smooth it was. It used a different system of engine control from the Spey. It was equipped with a fully variable exhaust nozzle which opened and closed to maintain engine stability according to the thrust demand at any one time, in both the Mil and A/B power range. The A/B operation was smooth and instantaneous and the engine remained stable throughout the whole of the flight envelope. There was no area of the flight envelope where the engine didn't restart, having been shut down, and the A/B operation was stable and reliable in high 'g' manoeuvres at high and low airspeeds up to 55,000 feet.

Shortly after our initial meeting on the results of the first NPE, Min Tech asked if Ed and I could visit London to discuss the implications of our NPE report. We took an overnight flight to London to spend a few days with the various interested parties.

It was to be the first time I was to see the original specification for the reheated Spey. It only defined the performance requirement. There was no requirement for the engine relight envelope to be better than 25,000 feet and 250 knots, and there was no requirement for the A/B to produce a power response equivalent

The Grumman A-6 Intruder *(USN)*

Two Attack Squadron 12 (VA-12) A-7E Corsair IIs

to the J-79. Along with all the deficiencies uncovered in the first NPE, you could say that our London visit had concentrated the minds in Min Tech on what would be operationally required if there was to be any hope of the F-4K passing the USN service acceptance trial at Pax River.

We returned to the USA. I flew two more types of aircraft that summer, the Grumman A-6A Intruder and the Chance Vought A-7A Corsair II. The A-6 was a two-seat attack aircraft similar to the Buccaneer. It was pleasant to fly and had a rationalised cockpit presentation. The flight instruments were much the same as other aircraft, but the ancillary instruments had been arranged so that the pointers were horizontal when operating normally. The idea was that a quick glance would show up any abnormality.

The A-7A looked like a tubby F-8. Luckily, the fuselage design had been arranged in such a way that it didn't have the requirement for the complicated wing mechanism of the F-8. The A-7 was a single-seat aircraft, and, as with the F-8, the pilot operated the radar and weapon systems. It took a bit of time for a two-seat man like me to do both jobs at the same time. Nevertheless, the A-7 was of a new generation of attack aircraft that had reverted to single-crew operation, and from what I could make of it flew and operated extremely well.

Came September, Ed and I conducted the second NPE. Not a great deal of improvement was noted in the operation of the A/B, but the approach speed stability had been improved a little with the introduction of the low-inertia cam box and the adjustment to the bleed valve operation. However, the engine handling in the landing configuration left a lot to be desired.

To try and overcome the problem of nose-up rotation in the bolter case, Rolls-Royce had changed the way the air off-takes were taken from the engine compressor. The flaps of the F-4K were 'blown' to provide slower approach speeds to the deck. To ensure sufficient airflow at approach power settings, the air was bled from the 12th stage of the high-pressure (HP) engine compressors. But bleeding air from the 12th stage of the HP compressor also markedly reduced the engine thrust at Mil power. This was considered to be the main reason why the nose-up rotation was delayed in the bolter case, since the reduced acceleration meant that the stabilator didn't bite quickly enough.

Since high engine power produced more than enough blow over the flaps, the HP compressor bleed changed to the 7th stage with take-off flap selected. More engine thrust could be achieved using 7th stage bleed. If the system could be switched to 7th stage bleed on the bolter, the extra thrust would induce a more rapid aircraft acceleration.

Rolls-Royce had introduced a '12th to 7th bleed change-over switch' activated by selecting full Mil power. It was hoped this would improve the nose-up rotation. Ed noted that some improvement had been made, but since his assessment was purely qualitative, no doubt the carrier trials would prove the system one way or the other! Our subsequent report on the second NPE indicated there was a long way to go.

In late September I visited St Louis, McDonnell's main base, to have a look at the M version for the RAF. The main reason for this evaluation was to check on the cockpit layout related to the different equipment standard.

Rennie Cruddas was also visiting McDonnell to coincide with a visit by the then Minister of Aviation, John Stonehouse. Rennie asked if I could make myself available to talk to the minister about the problems with the Spey engine. I had a word with Rennie before he saw Mr Stonehouse. Rennie would brief him on the overall situation and I was to talk to him about the test programme. After some time in conference Rennie left the office very agitated.

'Shall I go in and see him now, Sir?' I asked.

'Don't bother,' was the reply, 'he doesn't want to know about the bad news. Talking to him is like trying to nail a jelly to the wall.'

The end of my two-year exchange appointment was rapidly approaching, but since the programme was now running very late it was decided to extend it by six months so that I could see the F-4K through the Service Acceptance Trial at Pax.

The problems were beginning to mount at St Louis. The Vietnam

War was in full swing and the F-4 production line was running flat out. The UK Phantoms were programmed into the production line to achieve the contractual date for 'buy off', but there were no Spey engines available that met the specification. Since Rolls-Royce had signed up as a sub-contractor to McDonnell, I understand there were certain financial penalties to honour. McDonnell had lost revenue on other US Phantom models that could have been on the production line in place of the UK Phantoms, and the parking fee

SETP Membership Scroll

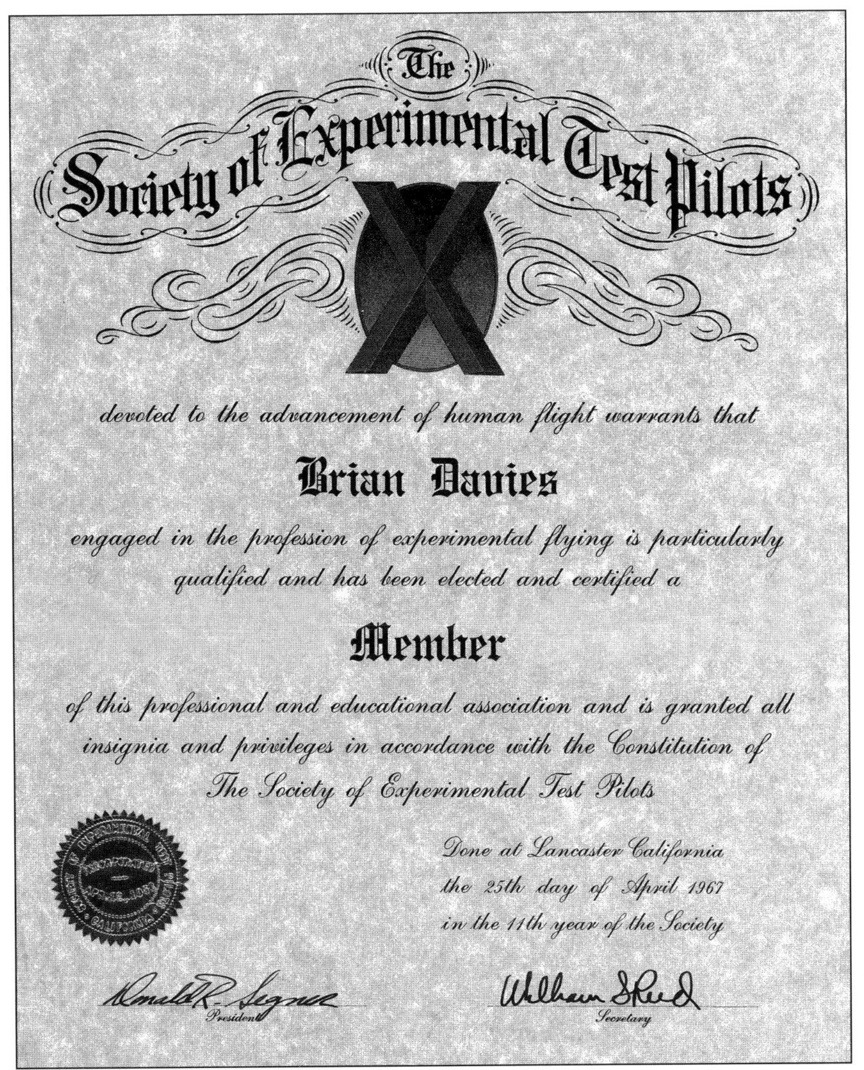

The Society of Experimental Test Pilots

devoted to the advancement of human flight warrants that

Brian Davies

engaged in the profession of experimental flying is particularly qualified and has been elected and certified a

Member

of this professional and educational association and is granted all insignia and privileges in accordance with the Constitution of The Society of Experimental Test Pilots

Done at Lancaster California
the 25th day of April 1967
in the 11th year of the Society

President

Secretary

for engineless UK Phantoms was substantial.

As far as I could make out, the UK weren't too perturbed by a delay in delivery. The change in defence policy to embark the Phantoms in HMS *Ark Royal* meant the whole programme was put back. The problem with the engine was seen as something that would be eventually worked out once the aircraft were delivered to the UK.

I could see the final answer would be a political one. The contractual impasse had to be overcome. Increasingly, NATC appeared to be a stumbling block in the whole process. It was decided that an interim standard of engine would be provided to satisfy the Service Acceptance Trial at NATC. Reliable A/B operating characteristics and safe engine operation would be its main features. A 'Blue' standard of engine would be considered adequate for initial clearance to service. Subsequent work at Rolls-Royce would establish a 'Gold' standard of engine that would be suitable for service use. This would be dealt with through the agencies of Min Tech and Boscombe Down.

Chapter 19

The F-4K Service Acceptance Trial

NATC 1968

I picked up the number 4 production F-4K from St Louis in mid-February and flew it back to Pax. The aircraft was to full production standard, which included the radar and weapon system. During the Service Acceptance Trial Trevor would be flying with me to check out the AWG 11, but on the ferry flight I flew it solo.

Alan Ducker and his team spent the next day going over the aircraft to make sure that it was all there and working correctly. The following day I planned to take it up by myself to have a look around the flight envelope. Alan asked if he could come with me in the back seat. He had covered all the technical ground and saw it as a chance to actually fly in it.

The 14th of February was a fine cold day. We took off and I progressively worked my way up in altitude checking out the engines. I had not been given any indication of the operating characteristics of the standard of engine fitted and therefore restricted myself to checking level flight A/B operation to make sure all was working as expected.

At 39,000 feet I selected both engines to A/B at a slow speed and they lit up evenly. I increased throttle to full power and rapidly accelerated to 0.85 MN. I didn't want to go faster than this and so deselected the A/Bs together. There was the most God Almighty double bang, and looking at the engine gauges I found one engine still running normally, but the other had flamed out and run down. I tried to relight the engine straight away, but to no avail since I was well outside the engine relight envelope. I let Alan know what had happened and that all was under control. We started a descent to 25,000 feet and I reduced speed to less than 250 knots. The engine failed to relight. I tried again at 15,000 feet, 10,000 feet and finally

5,000 feet, where the engine restarted. We returned to Pax and landed. Alan had the engine checked out, but could find nothing specifically wrong with it.

We now had two major problems on our hands. Firstly, both engines had stalled on cancelling the A/B in level flight, with one engine flaming out. Secondly this was the first time I had come across an engine that wouldn't restart in the relight envelope. Under normal conditions, in other aircraft, engine flameouts were rare. In the F-4K they weren't, so it was doubly important that the engine should start within the published relight envelope.

I decided the aircraft should be grounded, and Alan, as the engineer specialist, sent an 'Important Aircraft Defect Signal' to all the agencies concerned with the F-4K. The purpose of this signal was to inform everyone concerned about the failure, that the initial technical investigation had not determined the cause, and could someone please tell us why the engines were behaving so badly. The shit more or less hit the fan!

We had a Rolls-Royce field engineer working with us at Pax who sent his own messages to the parent company in the UK. The reply rapidly focused attention on the fuel we were using. Until now the fuel used in the aircraft had been 'Avtur', a commercial grade of aviation turbine fuel. However, all RN and USN aircraft used 'Avcat', a wider cut fuel with a lower flash point, used for safely reasons onboard all ships operating turbine aircraft. Avcat was in universal use in both navies at sea and ashore.

Rolls-Royce considered that since the burning of Avcat produced more carbon deposits than Avtur, it was coking up the main fuel burners and possibly the A/B fuel burners. It was suggested that we wash them. To do this you had to introduce a commercial agent called LIX into the burners and allow it to soak for some hours to dissolve the carbon build-up.

The F-4K was to remain grounded for a couple of weeks, during which time many meetings were held with everyone who had an interest in the aircraft. On one of these meetings, NATC gave a presentation to NASC and BNS Washington DC to review the state of the British Phantom. We said that the aircraft had severe operational and safety problems, which had by no means been solved, and NATC considered it most unwise to go ahead with deliveries of the aircraft to the UK until some answers to the engine problems had been found. I'm sure that if NATC's criteria had been imposed on the F-4K at this stage, it would have been recommended that the aircraft was completely unsuitable for service use, and it would have gone the way of the ill-fated F-111B.

The two-week grounding had resulted in a thorough check of the engines and the washing of the engine and A/B burners. February in Maryland can be pretty cold. Daytime temperatures of –10°C. began to highlight another problem with the engines. They wouldn't start on the ground! The fuel in the burners would light up OK but the engines would never get to the idle r.p.m. value. As soon as the starter cut out, the r.p.m. would fall and the turbine temperature would increase to the maximum value allowed, necessitating shutting down the engine. It was only by conducting a number of these false starts to warm the engine through that it would finally idle at the correct r.p.m. and turbine temperature.

Of the two engines, one was worse than the other. The Rolls-Royce representative at Pax assured me that everything possible had been done to check the engines. I decided that it was time to get airborne again, but I couldn't find anyone willing to come with me in the back seat!

I conducted six more flights on the aircraft before grounding it again. One engine behaved more or less the same as the engines on the NPEs. The other was far worse. By around the third of the six flights I was handling the engines separately. I would operate one A/B and ensure engine stability before operating the other.

Deliberately shutting an engine down in flight to check the restart characteristics showed a progressive deterioration in the relight capability since the LIX wash. The final straw was a double A/B flameout, with engine surge and an associated flameout of one engine at 33,000 feet. I got the engine going again and landed back at Pax. I decided I didn't want to try for the Phantom gliding record! I grounded the aircraft.

The meetings started again. I had the distinctive impression that some of the combatants in the Phantom programme were beginning to question my integrity. I had been the only pilot to fly the aircraft on the Service Acceptance Trial. Not by choice, I must say. But it had been difficult to persuade other USN pilots to have a go! The Commander running the F-4 desk at NATC was an experienced F-4 pilot. It was decided to let him fly it to check out the problem areas.

I briefed him on the engine characteristics and the areas of the flight envelope that were most problematical. His flight lasted 40 minutes. He came back on one engine a changed man, insisting that the K was far too dangerous an aircraft to put into service use. We checked the failed engine and found the turbine burnt out, with a number of blades missing. Luckily it was the worst engine, which at one stage had been declared a rogue by Rolls-Royce because they didn't know what was wrong with it.

The uncommanded thrust changes in the landing configuration

had reappeared. Alan had a go at adjusting the bleed valve operation. We used the engine thrust pad at Pax to try and quantify the problem and were surprised to find that even running at a constant HPRPM the thrust would vary considerably. We thought this was as a result of an unexplained interaction between the 12th stage bleed and the blown flap. There appeared to be nothing we could do about it.

Things improved a little having got rid of the worst engine. I decided to concentrate on the areas of the flight envelope where the engine seemed to be reliable, since we had now catalogued the areas of engine instability to no mean tune. I flew a few flights in company with the ST F-4J. Qualitatively the J's performance was superior to the K's. If you started out side-by-side and went to full A/B power, the J was streets ahead of the K by the time the K's A/Bs cut in. I took the K supersonic to about 1.8 MN, and apart from the odd 'pop' stall from the engines, they remained stable.

Alan, Trevor and I were due to return to the UK at the same time, and it was necessary for Alan and myself to write some sort of report on the Service Acceptance trials. It was obvious that the F-4K and the Spey engine weren't going to get a clean bill of health from the USN. The aircraft were being delivered to the UK regardless. Min Tech and Boscombe Down would presumably be sorting out the state of the Phantom FG 1(the British designation of the K).

Our recommendations included a ban on the use of reheat above 25,000 feet and at high angles of attack except for take-offs and landings, and rectification of the poor engine start characteristics both on the ground and in the air. It recommended the inclusion of a warning to pilots about the random stagnation of the engine, to be associated with the installation of a turbine over-temperature warning system. Rectification of the uncommanded thrust changes in the landing configuration, which seemed to occur to a greater or lesser extent on individual engines, was also recommended.

From Alan's point of view, he had found it difficult to set up the engines during the post-installation ground runs. There was no form of thrust meter in the cockpit instrument installation, nor were there any LPRPM gauges. Small variations in the A/B nozzle position and the incorrect datuming of the engine inlet guide vanes could result in the engines delivering less than full thrust. The only cockpit engine instrumentation available was the HPRPM and TGT gauges, along with a course nozzle position indicator. The introduction of LPRPM gauges would assist in assessing whether or not the engine had been set up to produce the maximum thrust.

As far as the AWG 11 evaluation went, I flew with Trevor on one flight in April and with a USN Lieutenant on my very last flight at

Pax on 22 May. We had to cut this last flight short due to an engine failure!

So my sojourn in the States finished with my having flown a total of 310 hours in the two and a half years at NATC – barely enough to keep in practice. It would be fair to say that the F-4K had taken over my life for the past year. As a family we hadn't seen as much of the States as I would have liked.

Alan's, Trevor's and my families were due to sail from New York's Pier 92 on RMS *Queen Elizabeth* in early June. I had decided that we would go to New York early and spend a few days in Manhattan. We had said our goodbyes to the Brits we knew in Washington before leaving for New York. But it wasn't until we checked in to the hotel in New York and found congratulatory messages from Sir Patrick Dean, the Ambassador, Admiral Le Bailly, the Chief of the British Navy Staff and Captain Rennie Cruddas that I realised I had been awarded the Air Force Cross in Her Majesty's Birthday Honours List for my work on the Phantom.

It was unusual for a naval officer to be awarded the AFC. It had happened in the past, but only to FAA officers serving under RAF control. I had been a naval officer serving with the USN and as such didn't qualify for the AFC. But it would appear the rules had been changed to accommodate my getting the award. Since that date the AFC has been unrestricted to naval pilots for 'Services to Aviation'. I was very pleased to receive the award, but would rather not have had it if this had meant the F-4K had been a better aircraft. I was on my way back to the UK to become the SP of 700P, the Phantom Intensive Flying Trials Unit (IFTU) at RNAS Yeovilton, and eventually CO of 892, the first Phantom squadron. I had a feeling that I wasn't going to get away from Phantom problems for very long! Number 700P Flight had already formed at the end of April without Alan and myself (Alan was due to be the Air Engineer Officer).

On a day in early June we all turned up at Pier 92, the Cunard pier in Manhattan, boarded RMS *Queen Elizabeth* and set sail for 'Blighty'. The ship was an instant reminder of the British Empire. The décor was very much 1930s, with lots of dark wood veneer walls (they didn't call them bulkheads in Cunard) and Art Deco fitments. Everything on board was very British, including aspidistras in the Palm Court, where you took afternoon tea listening to a string quartet.

I must admit our arrival back in the UK was for me with mixed feelings. I had enjoyed the lifestyle in the USA and the way Americans approached life. Although I can't say that I enjoyed working on the F-4K, I had admired the USN system of logical evaluation of the aircraft from the user's point of view. The British system I had known seemed to be based on what was politically necessary in the military field, and the users would have to make do with what they got!

It wasn't until the beginning of September that I would get myself airborne again in the F-4K. But, being back in the UK, the aircraft would be called the Phantom FG 1, and reheated Spey engines would power it. There would be no more reference to the K and afterburning!

Chapter 20

700P Flight, the Phantom Intensive Flying Trials Unit (IFTU)

RNAS Yeovilton, September 1968 to March 1969

In September of 1968 I took up my appointment as Senior Pilot to the IFTU. Rolls-Royce had managed to improve the Spey in the form of the 'Blue Standard' engine. The reheat was more reliable but lacked the response of the American engine, and the uncommanded thrust changes in the approach configuration had improved.

September was also the time of year for the SBAC show at Farnborough. Rolls-Royce requested the IFTU to provide a Phantom to take part in the flying display on their behalf. Tony Pearson, the CO of the IFTU, had decided that he would fly some of the demonstration flights, but that I would fly them on the Tuesday, Thursday, Saturday and Sunday.

Tony and I worked out a routine that would show off the best features of the Phantom – noise, speed and engine thrust. If we took off with just 5,000 lb of fuel on board we would have considerably more thrust than weight at full reheat power. We would be able to climb vertically directly after take-off and fly a 'square loop'. We would then accelerate at full reheat thrust away from the airfield, turn back and put a pressure wave over the field on our return pass at 0.99 MN. The remainder of the short display would show off the manoeuvrability and slow-flying capability of the aircraft, followed by a landing.

The initial practices for the Farnborough Airshow were done over Yeovilton airfield at the end of a normal operational flight. By this time the fuel state would be down to around 5,000 lb and the aircraft light enough to do the vertical manoeuvres. The final practice flight was conducted at Farnborough without taking off or

Landing at RAE Farnborough during the SBAC display in 1968 *(Crown copyright)*

landing there, so that the airshow committee could vet the routine. It was considered safe and we were given the all-clear.

The first take-off at Farnborough during the display week was on the Tuesday for me. It was the first time I had attempted a take-off at such a light weight. With 40,000+ lb of thrust and a take-off weight of 33,000 lb, the acceleration down the runway was phenomenal. The Phantom leapt into the air and at around 200 knots I pulled it into a vertical climb. We were at 250 knots as I hit the vertical and around 280 knots at 3,000 feet as I eased it over into the horizontal part of the square loop and throttled back to keep the speed down. The rest of the display went as planned. My observer for this initial flight was Ron Coventry, a test observer from Boscombe Down. On all the other display flights during the week my observer was John Ellis, one of the members of the IFTU. On the days we weren't flying in the SBAC display we were shooting down Meteor radio-controlled target aircraft at Aberporth missile range off the Welsh coast. This was to demonstrate the capabilities of the Sparrow missile and the AWG 11 radar system. On the two occasions we fired the missiles we were some miles from the target in cloud. We only determined that the Meteors had been shot down by the Aberporth radar losing radar contact with the target aircraft.

Nothing was filmed. Shooting down another aircraft in this way seemed very unsporting. And should it be required for real, very impersonal I'm glad to say.

Farnborough week went off well for us, but was marred by a Breguet Atlantique, a French twin-engined maritime patrol aircraft, crashing into the Black Sheds. The pilot had been demonstrating the aircraft's single-engine capability but had lost control and stalled. The crew of the aircraft was killed.

On 5 November I went to Buckingham Palace to be invested with the AFC, with Anne and my mother as guests. Her Majesty Queen Elizabeth the Queen Mother was officiating. We were organised as soon as we entered the Palace. My two guests disappeared to sit in the audience and I into the order of presentation by one of the gentlemen ushers.

We had been briefed to walk in from the Queen Mother's right, turn, and walk towards her for the presentation. During the ceremony a string orchestra played light music from the minstrel's gallery at the rear of the room. When my turn came I was impressed to be engaged in a short conversation with the Queen Mother. She seemed to know the salient points of the flight test programme on the Phantom in the States, and we talked about it briefly.

The work of the IFTU was to fly the pants off the Phantom to determine its reliability and at the same time produce an operating data manual (ODM) which would be the bible of how to operate the aircraft. This ranged from fuel consumption data to how to fight the aircraft. Vietnam dominated the military scene, and the most up-to-date tactics related to the conditions in that theatre of war.

Most of the donkeywork of fuel consumption and manoeuvre margin computation had been completed during the first few months of the IFTU. In November we concentrated on air combat manoeuvring (ACM). Unlike WW2 conditions, which required the best man to get on the tail of the adversary and shoot him down with guns, the fighter tactics of the 1960s related to staying far enough away from the adversary to be able to shoot him down with missiles that had a minimum range greater than the maximum range of a gun. There was no sense in hauling 'g' in close combat when you didn't have a gun to shoot the opposition down, having got on his tail. To this end it was important to be able to see your opponent with your AI radar. You then had the choice of using the long-range Sparrow missile at all target aspects or the shorter-range Sidewinder infra-red missile in the stern quarter.

If your adversary was a gun-equipped fighter it was important not to let him get in behind you at close quarters. As far as the Phantom was concerned, the idea was to maintain a high-energy

Outside Buckingham Palace on 5 November 1968. Brian Davies is accompanied by his wife Anne and his mother

regime at all times. You went in fast, and if you missed, you climbed out to convert your kinetic energy to potential energy so that the eventual stall turn would point you back at the enemy to have another go.

There was considerable concern about the reliability of the engines and some of the ancillary equipment. Alan Ducker's job of producing serviceable aircraft was not helped by an engine life of 36 hours! If they got that old you had to change them. The many engine changes required ground runs afterwards to set them up. It was amazing how far away you could hear a Phantom at full reheat power at 5 a.m! However, the main noise complaints came from the residents of Ilchester, located just off the western end of the main runway. Just about all take-offs were made in a westerly direction, and life came to a standstill at 120 decibels!

As a result of the additional maintenance work on the aircraft, radar and weapon systems, which required more man-hours than had been planned, the average flying time per month for each pilot was running-around 15 to 20 hours, considerably lower than the 25 to 30 hours expected.

At the end of the year another project hove into sight. The *Daily Mail* newspaper had announced earlier in 1968 that it intended to commemorate the 50th anniversary of Alcock and Brown's first west-to-east crossing of the Atlantic in the Vickers Vimy in 1919. The race would be from the top of the Empire State Building (ESB) in Manhattan, New York, to the top of the GPO Tower in London. Various categories of entrant were specified, the idea being that the race would be between individual entrants using various forms of air transport – both private and public. The race would take place in both directions over a period of a week in May 1969. It was anticipated that the RAF would enter individual competitors in military aircraft, and Tony Pearson had made a provisional plan should the Admiralty decide to enter a Phantom in the race. Tony's plan was to race from New York to London.

It envisaged taking off from New York, and once clear of the mainland over Boston, Massachusetts, flying five supersonic legs using four subsonic in-flight refuelling rendezvous to arrive over Weston-super-Mare and then fly on at subsonic speed to a selected airfield in the south of England. It didn't go any further than that, and since its presentation nothing had been heard from Their Lordships. Suddenly at the end of the year we were given the go-ahead to refine the plan and look at one or two options that were open to us. Since May 1969 meant that Tony would have left the Phantom scene, I, as the CO-designate of 892 Squadron, would be participating in the race and I would be responsible for the planning of the flights. Their Lordships also set up an overall management team for the race headed by Ray Lygo, the RN Captain who was to be the first Commanding Officer of the refitted HMS *Ark Royal*. Rather true to form, the Ark was behind on its refit and wouldn't be ready to embark her Airgroup until the summer of 1969 at the earliest.

Ray Lygo called the first meeting of the Trans-Atlantic Air Race Team in January 1969. He was an experienced naval aviator and would be the ideal boss to work for. His first question to me was 'Do you want to do the Air Race?' He saw no purpose in continuing with the planning of the exercise if the guy who would be responsible for the flying didn't want to. I assured him that I did. He then assured me that if I needed anything during the preparation phase, or problems came up that were unforeseen, he was there to lend a bit of clout to get them fixed.

The very first problem we had to discuss concerned the in-flight refuelling. At the time there was a certain amount of antagonism between the RAF and the RN. Defence reviews since the cancellation of our new aircraft carrier in 1966 had gradually seen the proposed demise of fixed-wing aviation in the RN. Various RAF staff studies proffered to Dennis Healey, the then Secretary of State for Defence, indicated that since the only future area of hostilities related to the European theatre, indigenous naval air power was surplus to requirements. RAF fighter aircraft maintained on station with the use of airborne tanker aircraft could provide protection of the fleet.

The RN's contention was that indigenous naval air power was essential for the defence of the fleet and that the strike capability of the Buccaneer gave the ability to attack enemy naval forces. The defence of the fleet by the RAF would be too rigid. Any tactical situation that might develop at sea would happen too quickly to enable the RAF to deploy sufficient of the correct air power in time.

HMS *Ark Royal* would be the last fixed-wing aircraft carrier to operate in the RN, and would decommission in 1971. At that time all RN fixed-wing aircraft would be handed over to the RAF. None of us were very happy about that prospect. It was felt that if the RN Phantoms could win the Trans-Atlantic Air race it might give a boost to Fleet Air Arm morale. Apart from that it would be one in the eye for the RAF, since they wouldn't have their Phantoms operational in time to take part in the race!

It was decided to use our own resources if possible to prevent going cap in hand to the RAF to request the use of their Victor tankers. We looked at providing the in flight refuelling requirements using Sea Vixen and Buccaneer aircraft equipped with flight refuelling pods. The answer was that we couldn't. To be able to refuel the Phantoms in mid-Atlantic, an aircraft carrier would have to be stationed there to enable the tankers to operate. You would also need two carriers at each of the mid-Atlantic refuelling rendezvous, since the spare-deck principle would apply. Politically and operationally this would be out of the question. The RN didn't have four aircraft carriers they could deploy in mid-Atlantic anyway!

It became apparent that one of the Atlantic refuellings would have to be scrapped and the race profile revised. It was decided to retain the first two in-flight refuellings at Nova Scotia and east of Newfoundland. Aircraft based in Canada or the USA could provide these. A third in-flight refuelling was planned about 300 miles west of Shannon in Ireland. This could be provided by aircraft based in the UK, or, at a push, from the American side of the Atlantic.

The final race plan looked completely different from the original.

It was modified to three in-flight refuellings instead of four, with the necessity for the Phantom to leave the second in-flight refuelling with enough fuel to reach Shannon in the event the third in-flight refuelling was unsuccessful.

The departure airfield would be NAS Floyd Bennett, the USN's reserve airfield south of Manhattan Island – the original departure airfield for Alcock and Brown. Instead of taking off with a clean aircraft, we would now have to carry a centreline and two wing external fuel tanks. The first leg would be flown at subsonic speed to Nantucket Island off the coast of New England near Boston. As we cleared the coast, the external wing tanks, which would provide the fuel to get this far, would be jettisoned, allowing the Phantom to go supersonic with a maximum speed of 1.6 MN (the Mach limit for the centreline tank). The first refuelling rendezvous would be made off Nova Scotia, with the ability to land at Halifax should anything go wrong. The second leg would be flown at 1.6 MN to a rendezvous to the east of Newfoundland, with the ability to land at Argentia AFB should it prove unsuccessful. The third leg would have to be flown at subsonic speed to be able to reach the refuelling rendezvous 300 miles west of Shannon with enough fuel to continue to Shannon should it be unsuccessful. Having completed the third rendezvous, we would accelerate to 1.6 MN and fly around the south of Ireland, decelerating to subsonic speed prior to crossing the coast at Weston-super-Mare. From there we would fly to our destination, the British Aircraft Corporation airfield at Wisley in Surrey.

In February some of the team visited the USN headquarters in the Pentagon in Washington DC to see if they could help us with the flight refuelling problem. Although the USN was dead keen to get in on the act, they also had a political problem. It would be difficult to justify any large-scale involvement of men and material in such a project with the Vietnam War going on. At the same time the massive organisation required to fly their aircraft from mainland USA to provide fuel for us off Nova Scotia, Newfoundland and 300 miles west of Shannon was phenomenal. They were talking about using KC 130s to refuel KC 130s that would refuel A-3 jet tankers that would eventually refuel us at the three rendezvous. Any hiccup in the chain would mean disaster! At the same time they wouldn't be able to practise any of this before the day. I had to recommend to Ray Lygo that to use the USN facilities wouldn't be a good idea, even if they were offered.

The revised flight profile meant that the original flight time of around three and three-quarter hours had to be changed to five hours. We had entered the Phantoms in the supersonic class of aircraft. We had to consider if there would be other supersonic aircraft in our category that might do it faster. The only challenge that could come was from the Americans. However, having talked to the Pentagon it was very apparent that the US military were not considering entering the race.

The next problem was – who was going to provide the in-flight refuelling? There seemed to be only one option – the RAF. I went ahead and had the whole thing planned based on our fuel requirements for the revised profile. The first priority was to try and establish some sort of fuel consumption figures when operating in reheat at 1.6 MN at around 40 to 50,000 feet carrying a centreline external tank. Although the Phantom was fitted with fuel flowmeters, they only related to basic engine operation. There had never been a requirement to determine the fuel consumption using reheat power. Reheat was only used in combat, and you weren't thinking of m.p.g. under combat conditions. The only way to determine the fuel consumption at 1.6 MN was to time the rate at which you could see the fuel tanks emptying and relate it to a true air speed. Quite a few flights were required out over the western approaches to tie down the fuel consumption. We soon came up with our fuel requirements at each rendezvous.

At the same time we formulated a rendezvous procedure. The RAF Victor tankers would refuel us at around 30,000 feet with a refuelling speed of 0.80 to 0.85 MN. It was assumed we would use AI radar to acquire the tanker and that the tanker would be flying towards us as we approached it. We would be flying at 40 to 50,000 feet at 1.6 MN on the supersonic legs, and at 39,000 feet and 0.97 MN on the subsonic leg. The idea was to calculate the optimum point at which to turn the tanker through 180 degrees so that as it rolled out on our heading, we would be as close as possible behind it. As a back-up, in case the radar wasn't working for some reason or other, we had a DF system in the Phantom which would give us a relative bearing on a UHF transmission on the frequency in use, and also air-to-air DME. If a suitable channel difference was selected on the TACAN beacons between the aircraft, a read-out of the distance between them could be obtained.

As I recall, the distance at which we would start our deceleration and commence turning the tanker on the supersonic rendezvous was 27 miles. If we selected flight idle at this range and turned the tanker at the same time, we would decelerate to subsonic speed at height and then descend to the refuelling altitude, reducing speed to 0.82 MN. In just about every case we found ourselves 6 to 800 yards astern of the tanker as it rolled out ahead of us. On the subsonic rendezvous we turned the tanker at 16 miles. We formulated the technique with two Phantoms.

The one last external arrangement to be made related to the ground radar control of the aircraft during flight refuelling. In the late 1960s civil traffic cruised at altitudes of up to 35,000 feet on the Trans-Atlantic routes between London and New York. These routes were designated controlled airspace. In general we were going to cruise well above 35,000 feet, but the Victor tankers were limited to a maximum refuelling altitude of 33,000 feet. With the concurrence of US and Canadian civil air traffic control authorities, arrangements were made to use military radar control centres at Nova Scotia and Newfoundland to give us separation from civil air traffic on the American side of the Atlantic when we had to descend below 35,000 feet for the first two refuellings.

The third refuelling was the problem. There was no air traffic control radar in the middle of the Atlantic. After some considerable negotiations with the civil air traffic authorities, it was agreed that the RN could set up its own military air traffic control area around the third refuelling point. We would station HMS *Nubian*, an Air Defence Frigate, in the Eastern Atlantic to control the Victors and Phantoms whilst they were in the altitude band used by the airliners.

Meanwhile, Ray Lygo had been dealing with the politics and planning the terminal arrangements. His approach to the RAF to ask for Victor tanker support had met with some resistance. Their rules implied that the timing of the race was now too close for them to supply Victor tankers at such a late date, and if the Victors were

HMS *Nubian* (*Crown copyright*)

used the planning had to be done by the 'Tanker Cell' at Strike Command HQ. Ray Lygo's response had been that the RN were going to do the planning and all we wanted was for the Victor tankers to turn up at the refuelling points at the time we specified with the fuel we specified. As far as timescale was concerned, it was mooted that it might be a bit embarrassing if it was made public that the RN wouldn't be able to enter the race because the RAF couldn't provide tanker facilities at less than three months' notice. It was agreed the RAF would provide the tankers.

The 'Moss Site' jump *(Crown copyright)*

The terminal arrangements related to getting the race entrant from the top of the ESB to Floyd Bennett and from Wisley to the top of the GPO Tower. Having clocked out from the top of the ESB and taken a lift to the bottom, it was intended to use a BSA motor cycle team, who would be doing promotional work in New York, to transport the race entrant to the 30th Street West Heliport on Manhattan Island, where he could be flown by RAF Wessex helicopter to Floyd Bennett. On arrival at Wisley, an RN Wessex helicopter would take the race entrant to a point as close as possible to the GPO Tower, where he would be transported to the base of the GPO Tower. From there he would hop on a lift and clock in at the top of the Tower.

There were no problems about the New York arrangements, but the then Board of Trade were not happy about helicopters landing at random sites in central London. At this stage the RAF and RN combined forces to explore the possible sites that could be used, since the RAF were also entering a competitor, flying in a Victor reconnaissance bomber to Wisley. Both services would require a helicopter landing site near to the GPO Tower. As it happened, the area to the north and west of the GPO Tower was being redeveloped by William Moss Ltd. This construction firm would be only too glad to let helicopters use it. They would clear the site and provide a small landing pad if necessary. The Board of Trade wouldn't hear of it, but eventually came to the compromise of allowing the helicopters to hover over the site area without actually touching the ground. The idea was the Wessex could hover close enough to the ground to allow the race entrants to jump the last couple of feet without the helicopter landing. Thus a landing site didn't have to be authorised. The race entrant then ran to the GPO Tower!

Between January and March ninety per cent of my flying was related to the Trans-Atlantic Race profile. Although we had come up with fuel consumption figures at 1.6 MN, it was important to fly each supersonic leg in its entirety to determine the distance covered and the fuel burnt for the attained speed. This we did out over the Atlantic to the south of Ireland. We practised rendezvous and refuelling techniques over the North Sea with 55 Squadron out of RAF Marham, and the Victor tankers managed to fit in with our plans. We also found the air-to-air DF and DME worked a treat.

The main feature of the Victor tanker was that it had a high-speed refuelling hose extending from the fuselage. The high-speed hose related to the rate at which it could pump fuel. These aircraft also carried wing-mounted refuelling pods as a back-up and to give them the ability to refuel three aircraft at the same time. From our point of view, the centreline high-speed refuelling facility would be the only viable way of refuelling the Phantoms in the race. As I recall, the pumping rate of the high-speed hose was around 4,000 lb/min.

We hit a snag with respect to our using the high-speed hose. Although the Phantoms had been proved against other tanker aircraft, it had yet to be used with the Victor's equipment. The clearance to do so had to be issued by Min Tech through A&AEE Boscombe Down, and that wasn't going to happen quickly enough. I decided to take things into my own hands and clear the system myself, since we couldn't afford to wait for Boscombe to do its bit. I arranged a little unofficial trial with the CO of the tanker squadron. I did some 'dry' contacts with the drogue to ensure there were no mechanical problems with physical contact. I then had the Victor progressively increase the fuel pressure in the refuelling system up to the limiting value, and conducted a complete refuelling of the sort of quantities we would need during the race. This trial ran over three or four flights, with suitable checking of the Phantom's fuel system in between to make sure all was well. I then wrote my own report and sent it to Boscombe Down. They weren't very happy about it, but did issue a clearance for the period of the race practice and the race itself.

During the latter part of March we refined the arrival procedure at Wisley using Yeovilton airfield. The final run into Wisley would be at 20 to 25,000 feet, and we had to determine the optimum distance at which to slow down and descend to make a safe but expeditious arrival. At the same time, when making the final landing on these practices, the Wessex helicopter pilots who would be picking up the observers (the race entrants) practised arriving as close as possible alongside the Phantoms on their landing rolls.

By the end of March we had addressed all the problems, and were reasonably confident that we would be able to slot together all the various facets of the race profile and get from New York to London in the fastest time. Up to this point we hadn't experienced any problems with the engine operating at continuous reheat power. If you treated it gently, and kept the aircraft straight and level at high speed, the Spey seemed a reliable piece of kit and would, hopefully, last the five-hour flight time.

At the end of March the IFTU disbanded, and on the 31st of the month 892 Squadron commissioned at Yeovilton.

Chapter 21

892 Squadron, the Daily Mail Trans-Atlantic Air Race – and Aftermath

Spring and Summer 1969

Number 892 Squadron, equipped with thirteen Phantom FG1s, commissioned on 31 March 1969. As the CO of the squadron, I was given complete freedom to paint whatever I liked on the aircraft – within reason. Each squadron had its own heraldic coat of arms in the squadron crest, and in the past this had in general been the only concession to any decoration of the aircraft. One of the exceptions had been the Sea Hawks of 806 Squadron in the '50s, when they had used the Ace of Diamonds motif to enhance their formation aerobatic status. We were to be the last fighter squadron in the RN. Since we were shortly to take part in the biggest public relations exercise the RN had ever been involved with, I thought it appropriate that we pick a very visible motif to plaster all over the fin of the Phantom. I eventually came up with a geometric

Brian and Anne Davies on the day 892 Squadron commissioned

arrow design. This incorporated a very prominent letter 'Omega' in black on a white background to remind everyone that this was the end of the Fleet Air Arm as we knew it.

The squadron aircrew were a combination of the experienced and the recently qualified. Number 767 Squadron had formed in January as the training squadron to convert aircrew to the Phantom, for both the RN and RAF. The crews that were to make up the majority of the squadron had all completed just three months' flying on the aircraft. In 892 Doug Borrowman was the Senior Pilot, Pete Goddard the Senior Observer and Alan Hickling the Air Weapons Instructor (AWI). In total some three complete crews from the IFTU formed the experienced part of the squadron.

An aid to the PR scene was the operational numbering of the squadron aircraft. Each front-line squadron had an allocation of three-digit numbers. The new carrier that had been cancelled in 1966 had been designated CVA 01. The aircraft side numbers for the *Ark Royal*'s Airgroup had been maintained from CVA 01. The numbers for 892 Squadron ran from 001 to 013. We were the squadron 'licensed to kill'.

Ray Lygo was putting the finishing touches to the arrangements for the official announcement of the FAA's entry for the Trans-Atlantic Air Race. The *Daily Mail* had been pressing the RN and RAF over the past couple of months to confirm that they were going

The route and the team *(Crown copyright)*

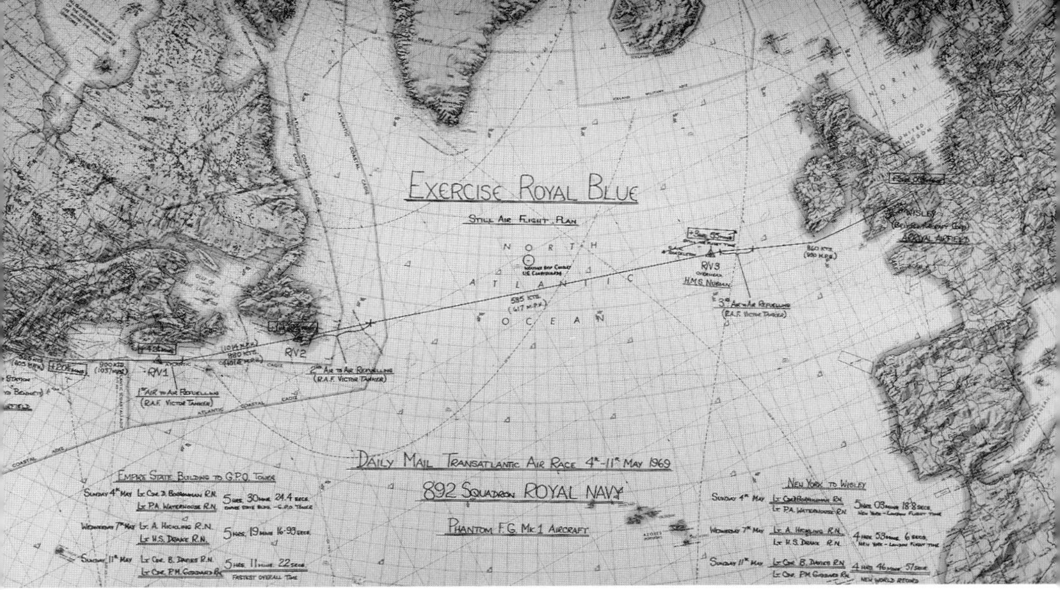

The race route *(Crown copyright)*

to enter the race, but neither organisation was in a position to announce anything until the political and financial authorisations had been made. Even then Ray Lygo wasn't one to jump the gun.

The final strategy was to enter three Phantoms in the race, partly to ensure that at least one made it across the Atlantic, and partly to keep the interest in the RN entry alive in the UK during the eight days of the race. When I say that we wanted to make sure that at least one Phantom crossed the Atlantic, it was not intended to imply that someone might end up in the drink, but rather that we could probably ensure that at least one of the three aircraft would be serviceable to do the trip!

The race order envisaged one aircraft flying the race on Sunday 4 May, one around Wednesday and the final aircraft on the Saturday or Sunday at the end of the race week. It was decided that Doug Borrowman and his observer Paul Waterhouse would fly the first aircraft, 002, Alan Hickling and his observer Hugh Drake the second, 003, and myself and Peter Goddard the third, 001. We had no direct opposition from other supersonic aircraft, but the RAF planned to fly competitors in a Harrier and a Victor Reconnaissance aircraft from New York to London. The Victor could fly direct, and the Harrier intended to fly in company with a number of Victor tanker aircraft to enable it periodically to top with fuel *en route*.

Although we were confident that we could beat the flight times of these aircraft, our route profile relied on meeting up with tankers at the planned refuelling points. Any errors in that area could add many minutes to the flight time. Additionally, the Harrier planned to carry out a vertical take-off from the United Nations heliport in New York, and arrive in a disused coal yard not far from the GPO tower in London. How on earth the authorities authorised a single-engined aircraft to fly over London and conduct a vertical landing in a disused coal yard after all the 'argy bargy' about restricting helicopters, I don't know. Since the Harrier would not need to use helicopters at either end, its terminal times would be considerably shorter than ours. If we were to win, it would be by a matter of minutes rather than hours.

On 10 April the RN made the official announcement that they would be entering three Phantoms of 892 Squadron in the Trans-Atlantic Air Race. The PR side of things rolled into action and we found ourselves the object of media attention. We also found ourselves doing the occasional flypast at various venues, plugged into a Victor tanker hose to show how the services were co-operating on the project. However, most of the serious work went towards tuning up the three Phantoms to make sure they were on top line for the flight out to Floyd Bennett.

Alan Ducker and I had decided to keep the Floyd Bennett detachment as small as possible. We would need a maintenance team, but could afford to keep the numbers below 20, with a stores back-up of the most likely things to go wrong. We had a total of three aircraft, so there were bound to be some spares available on the other two to ensure the third could get across the pond! As the CO I had insisted that I would fly the last serviceable aircraft out of Floyd Bennett should one or two of the aircraft suffer any permanent unserviceability!

On 24 April the three Phantoms took off from Yeovilton, each carrying a centreline and two wing external fuel tanks. We met up with a Victor tanker off the western coast of Ireland, topped up with fuel and set off for the flight to Argentia AFB in Newfoundland, where we would land and refuel for the onward flight to Floyd Bennett. It was the first experience for all three crews to be flying the Atlantic. Even with the other two aircraft in company it seemed a very lonely flight, since, once out of UHF radio contact with the Victor, we were on our own. Commercial aircraft kept in touch with Air Traffic Control using long-range HF voice radios, but the Phantoms didn't have this equipment. We had a limited VHF radio capability and it was thought that we would be able to contact the odd weather ship *en route*, but nobody responded to our calls on the published frequencies. It was obvious that if some major failure occurred in any of the aircraft, requiring the crew to bale out, it would take some time for rescuers to find them.

The observers conversed with each other during the flight to come to some agreement as to where we were. They had obviously got it right when we came into range of the TACAN beacons in

Arriving at NAS Floyd Bennett. 'Pete' Goddard is on the far left, Brian Davies in the centre and Captain Frank Steele, USN on the right *(USN)*

Newfoundland and we found ourselves on track and on time.

We refuelled at Argentia and flew on to New York, arriving at Floyd Bennett to a PR welcome from Captain Frank Steel, USN, the base Commanding Officer.

We had ten days before 4 May, and we had a lot to organise. The arrival profile had been practised endlessly in the UK, but we had obviously not been in a position to refine the departure procedures from Floyd Bennett.

One of the first requirements was to determine the time it would take for a competitor to go from the top of the ESB to the Phantom waiting on the runway at Floyd Bennett. The times to get down to the bottom of the ESB and to be taken by motor cycle to the 30th Street West Heliport were practised, but we still had to await the arrival of the RAF Wessex helicopter to do the flight from the heliport to Floyd Bennett. In the end it didn't arrive until a few days before the race started.

The RAF had the Victor and the Harrier in the race. From the RAF PR point of view, it would be a good idea if the Harrier could beat the Victor. The Harrier was shortly to go into service with the RAF, and a victory in the subsonic class of the race could enhance its reputation and might positively affect the foreign sales of the aircraft. If the Wessex arrived late at Floyd Bennett, there would be less time for it to practise with the Victor and ourselves, which might affect the outcome. I'm sure this wasn't the case, but there was this sneaking suspicion!

To this end the USN came to our rescue. I had mentioned the lack of helicopter support to Frank Steel, who immediately offered the services of the reserve Sea King helicopter squadron based at

The Trans-Atlantic Air Race crews. From left to right: Doug Borrowman, Alan Hickling, Brian Davies, Paul Waterhouse, Hugh Drake and 'Pete' Goddard *(Crown copyright)*

Floyd Bennett. These weekend warriors knew the area like the back of their hands. The CO of the squadron was the chief pilot of New York Airways, a civil airline operating helicopters in the New York area. The executive officer (Senior Pilot), whose name happened to be Ed Sikorsky (no relation to THE Ed Sikorsky of helicopter fame), was an ordinary traffic cop in the NYPD. The CO would be only too happy to fly us on the practice runs, and Ed would see what he could do about the traffic from the ESB to the heliport!

Another requirement was to go and talk to the civil Air Traffic Control authorities in the New York area. Our departure from Floyd Bennett would take us north-east towards Boston. We intended to clock out of the top of the ESB at 08:00 local time, and our estimates put the take-off from Floyd Bennett at around 08:10 to 08:15. This just about coincided with the rush hour, both on the ground and in the air. New York Air Traffic Control Centre was concerned about the timing, since their traffic would probably be arriving to land towards the south-west at JFK, and we would have to climb through the approach pattern on our departure. I asked what sort of upper limit would be on the approach pattern. Around 12,000 feet was the reply. I told them we could be at 12,000 feet within two minutes after take-off. There was an incredulous silence, followed by eagerness on their part to see a Phantom actually perform that way on their radar screens. We would be able to climb unrestricted if we could achieve that sort of climb performance.

After a couple of days at Floyd Bennett Alan Ducker had a bit of a shock. One of the more unreliable pieces of kit on the Phantom was the constant speed drive unit (CSDU). This provided a constant speed to run the AC generator on each engine. The CSDUs had failed on a regular basis, and one of the ways of determining its imminent demise was to sample the oil being used in the unit. If the oil contained minute metal chips the CSDU was on its way out. Oil samples from all six CSDUs had been sent back to the UK for analysis, and the message came back that four of them needed to be changed! Within a very short time new CSDUs had arrived from the UK. Nevertheless, the aircraft would be out of service for a few days whilst the work to replace them was carried out.

Frank Steel was having an accommodation problem. With three Phantoms, their maintenance crews, the aircrew and one or two members of the Race Planning Team, we made up around thirty officers and men. To give us flexibility of transport we had hired three rental cars and had them authorised to operate within the base. To operate a Victor, a Harrier and a Wessex, the RAF had requested accommodation for 180 officers and men and a large amount of stores and equipment. This request included a detachment commander and his organisation, including three service Land Rovers. As it turned out, the Land Rovers couldn't operate off the base since they were not insured. The first RAF transport to arrive, which we hoped would be carrying the Wessex, so that it could be put together and used, had a large consignment of tents, stores and the Land Rovers. The tents were required to provide accommodation for most of the RAF personnel and their stores. The RAF detachment commander came to us to find out how we organised things. He was very much operating under the diktat from Strike Command HQ in the UK, who didn't appear to be aware of the local conditions.

To some extent this microcosm of organisational priorities reflected the attitude of the two Services. The RN had always worked from the bottom upwards and the RAF from the top downwards. Historically, because of the far-flung nature of the RN operations, and the fact that the man on the spot normally knew best, junior and middle-ranking naval officers knew that they would have a senior officer's backing if their decisions were logical and within the political and operational yardsticks of the occasion. At the same time many things were organised on an informal basis.

Although Ray Lygo was in overall charge of the RN race organisation, he and I had come to an agreement on how it would be run. His priorities would be based on any political or PR gains that could be made without prejudicing the operational and safety requirements of the flights. However, there were certain criteria that had to be established to trigger the launch of an aircraft. We had to have a serviceable aircraft. The weather at Goose Bay in Canada and RAF Marham had to be suitable to allow the tankers of 55 Squadron to operate. Weather criteria at Wisley, Halifax, Argentia and Shannon had to be above a certain minimum. He would determine that information before ringing us the night before to set up a provisional 'GO'. The 'GO' would be verified at around 4 a.m. New York time, and the race details would be planned by us with the up-to-date wind and weather information. As far as I could make out from the RAF aircrews taking part in the race, none of them had a say in when they would be racing. They would just do as they were told. Theirs was not to reason why.

The Services in the late 1960s were not used to PR. Service exposure in the media was done on a very conservative basis. At all times there had to be the stiff upper lip, and the 'Official Secrets Act' governed everything you would discuss. The possibility of Service personnel taking part in TV programmes like 'The Generation Game', as is the norm today, would have been very much discouraged. In general the RN PR organisation had done a good job. We had presented an image of relaxed professionalism. In the UK, TV programmes on which we appeared had been restricted to those of a news or current affairs nature. I think the PR team thought the American TV would have the same attitude. CBS and NBC didn't seem to be interested. However, a local New York TV programme was.

It was arranged that Peter Goddard and I appear on a programme that I think was called 'Mothers and Daughters'. We were to report to the studio in the Rockefeller Center and do whatever the programme producer required. As this would be official PR exposure we were to appear in uniform. I had my suspicions. 'Mothers and Daughters' did not sound like a current affairs programme to me. Peter and I arrived at the studio and were met by the production team. There wasn't an RN PR representative in sight, so it looked like the tactical situation was up to me. The audience was gathering in the studio and – guess what – they were all mothers and daughters. Not a man in sight. Well there was the odd male in trousers around, but no men.

The format seemed to be that the guy who was the star of the programme was a well-known fortune teller and he would take various questions from the audience about forecasting the future. All the questions seemed to be from mothers who wanted the fortune teller to forecast various events on their daughters' behalf. The vast majority related to when these daughters were going to meet 'Mr Right' and get married. The odd question asked him to forecast who would win the Trans-Atlantic Air Race!

I decided that official exposure on a programme like this wouldn't do us much good, so Peter and I were not going to appear in uniform. We sat ourselves in the audience incognito, keeping our heads down until he got around to us. 'Ladies and gentlemen,' the host announced, 'we have two British Navy fighter pilots with us tonight. Would they make themselves known?' Peter and I stood up. Mothers' and daughters' heads turned for the appraisal. We both felt rather embarrassed. 'Are you two gentlemen British Navy pilots?' asked the host in a voice which was tempered to include the unsaid query 'Where are the damn uniforms? These women want fighter pilots and uniforms.' We said we were. Now was not the time to try and explain the difference between pilots and observers, or why we weren't in uniform.

'Ladies and gentlemen, these two British pilots will be flying in the Trans-Atlantic Air Race which will be run from 4–11 May between New York and London, England. I have been asked to predict how they will do.' I have no doubt the PR men had assumed that the guy would rightly predict that we would win. We had the fastest aircraft, and if anyone was going to win it would be us. If he wanted to enhance his reputation with a correct prediction, all he had to say was that we would come first. It was obvious that the PR men did not understand Americans. He wasn't going to say we would win. New York mothers and daughters didn't want to hear unpatriotic predictions about foreigners winning races. Americans always won. I don't suppose the host knew anything about the race, but there was bound to be an American in it. 'Well, ladies and gentleman, we wish these two British fighter pilots well, but I predict that an American will win the Trans-Atlantic Air Race.' And he added, to get his own back on us for not wearing uniform, 'I predict an American will come second. I'd put these gentlemen a close third.'

Having planned and practised the transition from the ESB to Floyd Bennett, it was necessary for each crew to fly a dummy run as far as Boston to check out departure procedures and the aircraft equipment, including the new CSDUs. Apart from this one flight, I hadn't considered it a good idea to fly the aircraft, since it could tempt providence to induce other mechanical failures on us.

The flights went well and we calculated that the wing external tanks would be empty by the time we were ready to jettison them off the coast of Boston. However, from 30,000 feet or so it looked as if it was breeding time for small boats. Hundreds of white lines curled back and forth across the blue waters below us as speedboats, fishing boats and motor cruisers left their foaming wakes. There was a chance of our drop tanks hitting one of these boats, or at least frightening the occupants. One evening in the Floyd Bennett Officers' Club, Frank Steel came up and asked me how things were going. I mentioned my concern about our drop tanks hitting a boat.

The observer's ramp at Floyd Bennett *(Crown copyright)*

Frank thought for a moment and then said, 'Don't worry, Brian, I'll send my Paint Shop Chief over tomorrow and he'll fix it for you.'

'What's he going to do?' I asked.

'He's going to paint your tanks in US Marine Corps colours and serial numbers', was the reply. 'If anyone gets hit by a tank, it'll be a Marine Corps tank.'

'Won't that cause the Marines a problem?' I asked.

'No', said Frank. 'The American public have a soft spot for the Marines. They're the original 'Gung Hos'. If someone gets hit by a Marine Corps tank they'll keep it as a souvenir and boast about it to their friends.'

The final adjustments to the departure routine related to saving the odd second. We devised and built a shallow ramp, which we placed alongside the Phantom's fuselage to enable the observers to run up it and jump into the cockpit. With the agreement of Frank Steel and under the supervision of the station fire department, we also planned to have the Phantoms sit on the end of the duty runway with their engines running and a fuel bowser plugged in to keep us topped up to the very last minute.

Just prior to this, the US Mail would deliver 100 first-day covers suitably stamped with the date and departure time of the aircraft involved at Floyd Bennett's official post office. These would be rushed to the top of the GPO Tower on arrival to be stamped with the date and time of arrival. These covers would be the first to be carried at supersonic speed.

The week of the race arrived, and the decision to 'GO' on Sunday 4 May was made on the Saturday evening. At 4 a.m. on Sunday the 'GO' was confirmed and the planning for departure went ahead. Although there was a slack weather system on the route, giving a mean tail wind of only 9 knots, the excellent weather conditions at all the airfields involved could not be ignored. Doug Borrowman and Paul Waterhouse made their preparations to depart. Their main objective was to get to Wisley adhering to the flight plan, but also to determine where we might save time on the subsequent flights.

Paul clocked out at 08:00 from the top of the ESB. Unluckily the motorcyclist hit just about every red light on the way to the heliport. Paul leapt into the cockpit of Phantom 002 at 08:15 and closed the canopy. Doug roared down the runway, turned left towards Boston and rapidly disappeared. The BBC was on hand to film every thrilling moment, and I had to say my little piece.

The climb-out went well, and the first leg to Nantucket Island was uneventful. They jettisoned the external wing tanks over the sea and accelerated to 1.6 MN heading for the first rendezvous off

Nova Scotia. The first refuelling didn't go to plan. The DME didn't lock up between themselves and the tanker, and Paul had problems picking up the tanker with his AI radar. However, using bearings and help from the ground radar they completed the first refuelling.

The supersonic leg to Newfoundland went well and they picked up two minutes on the planned flight time. However, they had the same problem with the DME, which hampered the rendezvous with the second tanker. On the subsonic leg to the third rendezvous some time was lost due to colder than average air temperatures at 39,000 feet, resulting in an inability to maintain the planned TAS. Remarkably they were able to speak to the Victor tanker using UHF radio from around 350 miles away, and HMS *Nubian* was able to give them bearings from 300 miles out. Their final rendezvous went well.

It wasn't until they set out on the last supersonic leg that they hit real problems. The ambient air temperature at 40 to 50,000 feet was considerably warmer than standard, resulting in the inability of the Phantom to reach 1.6 MN due to the reduction in thrust because of the warmer air.

The run into Wisley went as planned, but the landing became a bit of a spectacular for the press and TV when Doug was a little over-enthusiastic with the brakes and burst both main wheel tyres

Paul Waterhouse clocks in *(Crown copyright)*

on the landing roll. Subsequently it turned out that the Phantom's anti-skid unit was unserviceable. Their flight time of five hours and three minutes beat the existing record from New York to London by 26 minutes, and Paul Waterhouse's 'Top to Top' time of five hours 30 minutes and 24.43 seconds wasn't going to be easy for the opposition to better.

We learnt a lot from this flight. In particular it showed us that to better the time we would have to look for warmer temperatures on the long subsonic leg across the Atlantic to improve the TAS, and colder temperatures on the last leg to achieve a better supersonic performance. Apart from the DME and radar problems they hadn't experienced any technical failures. The weather conditions were due to remain the same for the next two days, so we definitely decided to hold fire until Tuesday evening for the second flight.

On Tuesday the American Global Weather system was forecasting improved tail winds and temperatures, but also a progressive deterioration in weather conditions at the *en route* diversion airfields. This tied in with Ray Lygo's information at Strike Command HQ, and it was decided to launch the second Phantom on Wednesday morning with a forecast mean tailwind of 19 knots.

Hugh Drake managed to knock one minute off Paul's time from the ESB to Floyd Bennett, and Alan Hickling roared off down the runway at 08:14. At the first rendezvous 003 was having radio problems. Difficulties arose on the handover from Boston ATC to Monckton Military Radar in Canada. This, combined with no DME range, resulted in the refuelling being conducted some four minutes late after a somewhat hectic manoeuvre when Alan spotted the tanker coming towards him head on. The second rendezvous was also hampered by lack of DME, and was made slightly prematurely by not turning the tanker early enough. The third leg went well and 003 was able to maintain a high TAS over the pond. The third rendezvous proved no problem, and a high TAS was maintained at well over 1,000 mph to Weston-super-Mare. Touchdown at Wisley was some four hours 53 minutes after take-off, and Hugh's 'Top to Top' time was five hours 19 minutes and 16.93 seconds.

Meanwhile, back at Floyd Bennett, Peter and I were looking rather anxiously at the forecast weather for Thursday and Friday. A frontal system was approaching New York from the south-west, and was forecast to continue up the East Coast of the USA and Canada, progressively blotting out Nova Scotia and Newfoundland. The forecast for Saturday indicated that 200 feet cloudbase and a half-mile visibility would be the order of the day as far as Nova Scotia and Newfoundland were concerned. The weather wasn't much better at Wisley. With an Aircraft Approach Limitation (AAL) of 300 feet on the Phantom, we wouldn't be able to leave New York.

Friday was the day that Graham Williams, the race entrant in the Harrier, was told to 'GO'. The weather that day hadn't yet deteriorated to below Harrier limits *en route*, and the weather at the London coal yard was just about good enough for him to make a visual approach. In New York it was sheeting down with rain. Graham was thoroughly soaked by the time he had had his motor cycle ride from the ESB to the UN heliport. Being a single-seat aircraft, he was the race entrant as well as the pilot. Vertical take-offs in the Harrier were meant to be conducted under visual weather conditions, but by the time he had lifted off to just a few feet above the ground, he was flying on instruments. He managed to meet up with the tanker, and flew in formation with it all the way to London.

As our main competitor, we were interested in what sort of race time the Harrier would establish. The RAF had kept us on tenterhooks all week long wondering whether our previous Phantom times had been fast enough. As it happened, Graham's time was 20 minutes longer than Hugh Drake's, so it looked as if we were home and dry.

The only other threat would come from the Reconnaissance Victor. However, it looked as if the RAF 'Brass' were doing their best to make sure the Harrier won the subsonic class of the New York to London race. They had apparently ordered the Victor to do its run on the Saturday, when the weather would be so bad at Wisley and in the south of England that the Victor would have to arrive with enough fuel to divert to Scotland. This would mean

001 refuelling from a Victor tanker *(Crown copyright)*

001 landing at Wisley *(Crown copyright)*

slowing the *en route* cruise speed to save fuel. The CO of the Victor squadron, who would be piloting the aircraft, wasn't a happy man. He had seen how the RN worked the race, and he didn't want to fly on Saturday. I understand he said so. The response came that his station commander and the AOC expected him to race on Saturday, but it was his decision. He said he'd fly on Sunday. Apparently that wasn't the answer the AOC was expecting, so he in the Victor and Peter and I in the Phantom would be racing on the last day.

Peter and I digested the information on Alan and Hugh's flight. They had found they had been 'making' fuel on the flight. It looked as if we could adjust some of the numbers to give us a faster time by pulling the last rendezvous further west. This would give us a longer supersonic leg into Weston-super-Mare.

Needless to say, we were given a 'GO' for the flight on Sunday 11 May. Weather conditions at Wisley were looking reasonable, but we would be a little short of the 1,000 feet cloud base and one-mile visibility criteria at Halifax and Argentia. Shannon weather would be 'adequate'. The only really depressing forecasts were for the first and second refuelling rendezvous. Layered cloud up to 36,000 feet with moderate turbulence didn't augur well for a successful refuelling. We planned to make the first two rendezvous with a little extra fuel on board in case we ended up on approach to Halifax or Argentia in bad weather conditions. Our mean tailwind for the flight was forecast at 23 knots.

The New York terminal procedures went well and Peter managed to clip two minutes off Hugh's time. The climb-out and first leg went well, with wing tank jettison one minute ahead of planned time. The first refuelling went well, as this time the DME and DF worked and ATC helped. We completed the refuelling with

'Pete' Goddard leaves Wisley by 'chopper' *(Crown copyright)*

distance and time in hand and without cloud and turbulence. The second leg went well, although we had a bit of a hiccup when the primary tanker's high-speed hose and drogue failed to stream (there were two tankers at each rendezvous). We took fuel from the secondary tanker. On the third leg we lost two minutes on the planned time. However, the adjustment to the third rendezvous position improved the situation on the last leg. We really made up time by staying low (40,000 feet) at 1.6 MN, with just the occasional pull-up to 45,000 feet to stay abreast of the fuel consumption. On deceleration to subsonic speed by Weston-super-Mare we had a lot of extra fuel on board, so we flew the last leg lower than planned, picking up an extra 50 knots or so of TAS. I nearly screwed up the approach by seeming to be too high and too fast, but managed the optimum arrival by closing the throttles and gliding in. I touched down well down the runway with the braking chute deployed. I didn't burst any tyres! The RN helicopter was waiting alongside as Peter leapt down and dashed off to complete the last leg to the GPO Tower.

I taxied into the dispersal at Wisley feeling absolutely knackered. Little sleep, and having to get up at 04:00 meant that it had already been a long day. As I climbed down from the cockpit I learnt that we had established the fastest flight time of the week and that I now held the World Airspeed Record from New York to London in the time of 4 hours 46 minutes.

The helicopter returned to Wisley some twenty minutes later and took me to the GPO Tower. Anne and Peter's wife, Colleen, were there. They had left Yeovilton about the same time as Peter and I had taken off from New York, and hadn't beaten us to the tower by much! Peter had already been interviewed by Cliff Michelmore for BBC TV, and I had had a quick word with Brian Johnson who was there for BBC Radio. The First Sea Lord, Admiral Le Fanu, and celebrities of the era were there to greet us. The champagne flowed. Incidentally, the CO of the Victor reconnaissance squadron had managed to get the last laugh on the Harrier. His crewmember, Derek Aldous, had beaten Graham Williams's time by 20 seconds!

I wasn't prepared for the publicity that was to come. The Monday newspapers were full of the last day of the air race. The front page of the *Daily Mail* had a picture of Peter, Colleen, Anne and me at the GPO Tower. The headline said, 'Greatest air race ever ends in a blaze of glory. WORLD BEATER BY THE NAVY!' Most of the other popular newspapers had us on the front page with similar accolades. Rolls-Royce, who had kept their heads down since the inception of the race for fear the reheated Spey's relative unreliability might prove a factor in our losing the race or worse, took out an advert congratulating us on winning the race using their engines.

Once back at Yeovilton all I wanted to do was get on with the job of running a squadron. But it wasn't to be as simple as that. The PR people took over, and Peter and I became minor celebrities. What I hadn't realised was the amount of exposure the Phantoms had

After the race. Cliff Michelmore is on the left and 'Pete' Goddard on the right *(Crown copyright)*

generated during the week of the race. The BBC, as well as the Press, had taken it up as an event of some moment. Doug and Paul had initiated it on the first day by establishing the fastest time and arriving so sensationally at Wisley. Alan and Hugh had kept the interest alive by flying even faster on the Wednesday. The suspense had been kept going by speculation as to whether Peter and I would fly even faster on the last day. Small scenes at Floyd Bennett had been filmed by the BBC and flown to London (no satellites in those days) to be shown on the update for the race the next day. My face, it would appear, had become quite well known to the general public.

Peter was the overall winner of the race from New York to London. But there had been many other winners in all the different categories, so loads of people had won the race. Our PR pushed the fact that the RN was the winner. The RAF pushed the fact that they were the winners, and even managed to convince a lot of people that the Harrier had won the race. In fact the Harrier had won the race from London to New York (piloted by Sqn Ldr Tom Lecky-Thompson) in just under six hours and twelve minutes. However, the Phantom stuck in the public's mind because we had also broken the old airspeed record from New York to London.

The New York to London Airspeed Record Diploma

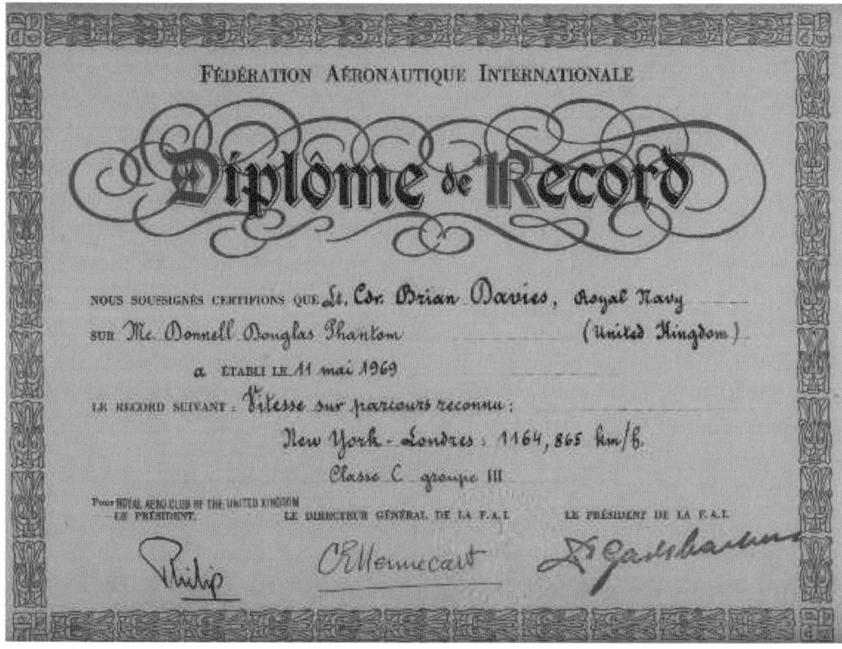

FÉDÉRATION AÉRONAUTIQUE INTERNATIONALE

Diplôme de Record

NOUS SOUSSIGNÉS CERTIFIONS QUE Lt. Cdr. Brian Davies, Royal Navy

SUR Mc Donnell Douglas Phantom (United Kingdom)

a ÉTABLI LE 11 mai 1969

LE RECORD SUIVANT : Vitesse sur parcours reconnu :

New York - Londres : 1164,865 km/h.

Classe C groupe III

Pour ROYAL AERO CLUB OF THE UNITED KINGDOM — LE PRÉSIDENT | LE DIRECTEUR GÉNÉRAL DE LA F.A.I. | LE PRÉSIDENT DE LA F.A.I.

The RN PR machine rolled into action. I found myself giving lectures on the race to schools, giving presentations to Sea Cadets, doing fly-pasts at various venues and attending dinners to give the after-dinner speech. Peter and I were guests at various functions, which used celebrities of 'the stage, screen and radio', as the saying used to go. We were the 'nouveau' celebrities alongside old hands like boxer Henry Cooper.

Four particular functions stuck in my mind during the round of social occasions that would continue for some months. The first was the *Daily Mail* Trans-Atlantic Air Race Winner's Dinner and Prize Giving at the Royal Garden Hotel, Kensington. In memory of the Alcock and Brown flight in 1919, Vickers Ltd, who had originally designed and built the Vimy aircraft in which they flew, had sponsored the Alcock and Brown Trophy to be presented to the competitor who had achieved the fastest time between New York and London, along with a prize of £1,000. The *Daily Mail* had also sponsored the winner to the tune of £5,000. Peter Goddard was the winner of these prizes, and I would attend the dinner with him. Needless to say, Peter didn't keep the money but handed it over to his sponsor – the RN.

The RN PR intended to wring the most publicity possible out of the occasion. The dinner coincided with the RN's preparation for the Royal Tournament. It was decided to feature the Fleet Air Arm's Field Gun Crew in our arrival at the Royal Garden Hotel. The plan was for Peter and me to travel to London by train and be met at the railway station by service transport. It would take us to a hotel where we would stay overnight. Here we would change into mess undress, the term used for the Royal Naval officers' formal evening uniform consisting of monkey jacket, stiff shirt, black bow tie and medals. A car would pick us up and take us to a fire station some 200 yards from the Royal Garden Hotel. There we would mount and sit on the FAA's gun carriage and be towed down Kensington High Street to the Royal Garden Hotel by the field gun crew. Here we would dismount from the gun carriage and join Vice-Admiral Sir Richard Janvrin, Flag Officer Naval Air Command (FONAC), on the steps of the hotel, standing either side of the Admiral whilst the field gun crew marched off.

It didn't quite go like that. Peter and I boarded the train for London in civilian clothes. Due to the train arriving late in London and the evening rush hour, the RN captain who met us at the station in a staff car decided that we were running out of time. We would have to go directly to the fire station. In a small back room of the fire station we hurriedly changed into mess undress without the opportunity of a bath or shower. We walked out to the waiting field gun and climbed up to sit on the ammunition box. Ahead of us stretched the sailors of the field gun crew, and, a little to our surprise, ahead of them was a Royal Marine band! We set off down Kensington High Street, and the band struck up with 'Those magnificent men in their flying machines'. I felt very embarrassed, as if we should be in a middle European operatic setting rather than Kensington High Street. As Anne said later, having seen it on the 6 o'clock TV news, my face looked like thunder. We jumped off the field gun at the hotel and ranged ourselves either side of the Admiral. The band and field gun crew marched off back to the fire station. The rest of the evening was quite enjoyable.

The next episode involved us both going up to Blackpool, at the request of the organisers, to officially start the 'Top of Blackpool Tower to the Top of Snaefell, Isle of Man Race', which hoped to emulate the Trans-Atlantic Air Race on a smaller scale. This was quite a good jaunt and also involved us in judging a heat of the Miss Great Britain beauty contest at a local swimming pool. We had some fifteen very attractive girls parade past us, and we had to pick first, second and third. We picked the winner, who was promptly disqualified for wearing pants and bra instead of a regulation two-piece bathing suit. Apparently there were very strict rules determining what constituted a bathing suit. Had she got her bra and pants wet, she would have contravened the rules of decency existing at the time.

'Pete' Goddard and Brian Davies on the Fleet Air Arm field gun in Kensington High Street

(Crown copyright)

The record-breaking aircraft *(Crown copyright)*

Rolls-Royce's gratitude at the successful image of the Reheated Spey generated by the race included the offer to loan a Silver Shadow as a squadron car on an indefinite basis. Their thoughts on the matter followed the lines of my sending three of the squadron's engineering Petty Officers to the Rolls-Royce car division. There they would be instructed on the servicing, maintenance and driving of the car. The car would then come under my control to be used on suitable official occasions. The offer had come through the offices of Admiral Janvrin, who had authorised me to accept.

I replied to Rolls-Royce, through the Admiral's auspices, thanking them for their offer, but regretfully declining it. I could see the Petty Officers in question could be very put upon. However, if Rolls-Royce could see their way to offer the use of the car to all squadron personnel over the age of 25, and support the cost of insurance, servicing and maintenance, I would be only too glad to accept it. Much to my surprise they agreed to these terms, and on 4 September the centre page of the *Daily Mirror* featured pictures of the handover of the car in front of a line of Phantoms. The car would eventually go to sea in *Ark Royal*, and I could see Ray Lygo asking me to borrow it for use on official business in foreign ports.

The fourth event was the making of a TV documentary of the squadron. PR said the BBC was coming to do a programme on us. I asked what exactly the BBC wanted to do. They didn't really know, but they were sure that everything would be all right. Any publicity would be good publicity.

The BBC arrived and went about its business. They gathered a lot of information and filmed all the various aspects of squadron life, did a lot of air-to-air filming and interviewed me and other members of the squadron. They asked to follow a pilot and observer in their day-to-day lives. This involved visiting their

The day Ray Lygo (left) flew the Phantom.
He is pictured with Brian Davies (right) *(Crown copyright)*

homes and talking to their wives. After a few days they went off to sort out the various sequences into a programme.

It went out on BBC 1 South and West in early September, and I suppose made some sort of case for the retention of the conventional carriers. Its main point covered the gradual reduction of the FAA over the next two years. It concentrated on the interview data relating to how the aircrew officers were going to cope with forced redundancy and what their wives would miss in service life. In this respect one of the young wives had been persuaded to use a script, since what she was saying 'wasn't quite what we're looking for'. Poor Jenny, who had been interviewed in her own home, got stick from the rest of the wives for saying that she would miss 'the cocktail parties, lunches and wearing her Jaeger clothes'. That is apparently what the production team wanted to hear. They obviously had their own ideas about the upper class background of naval officers! The programme ended with a long shot of Yeovilton village church and a close up of the gravestones of aircrew who had been killed in flying accidents. I suppose it made a political point, but it didn't do much for squadron morale.

That summer Ray Lygo completed a ground school course to fly the Phantom. On his first flight I rode 'shotgun' in the observer's seat in case he needed some help. He didn't.

Chapter 22

892 Squadron Aboard USS *Saratoga*

17 to 23 October 1969

Because of the delayed refit, HMS *Ark Royal* would not now be ready to embark her squadrons until mid-1970. A proposal was mooted just before partaking in the Air Race, that a detachment of Phantoms be made aboard the USS *Saratoga* of the American Sixth Fleet in the Mediterranean in the autumn of 1969.

Commander Danny Norman and I flew to Malta in early summer. Danny had returned from his appointment in Washington DC and was now, I think, on the staff of FONAC. The object of our visit was to go aboard USS *Saratoga* off Malta to discuss detailed arrangements for the embarkation of four of 892's

USS *Saratoga*, Mediterranean 1969 *(USN)*

Catapult loading aboard USS *Saratoga* *(USN)*

Phantoms in the autumn. The *Saratoga* was one of the large class of carriers built in the post-WW2 period. It was due to make a short visit to Malta before returning to the Sixth Fleet's Mediterranean base at Naples.

There seemed to be little problem with accommodating the extra aircraft and squadron personnel. By our standards the *Saratoga* was vast and had a complement of some 90 aircraft and 4,000 officers and men. We were to operate under the wing of VF 103, one of the two Phantom squadrons on board. The remainder of the air group consisted of A-7 Corsair IIs, A-6 Intruders, A-5 Vigilante supersonic reconnaissance/attack bombers, E-2 Hawkeye aircraft, and a flight of A-3 tankers. The A-3 had been a medium bomber in the USN in the '50s, but now, like the Victors in the RAF, had been converted for use as an airborne tanker.

We talked details with the ship's personnel. All seemed well except that the ship's air department indicated that they would like to have a British Phantom on board prior to the detachment to satisfy themselves that it would be compatible with their catapult hardware and procedures.

We finalised on the period of 17 to 23 October as the detachment dates. This was a shorter period than would have been ideal from the operational viewpoint, but the equipment reliability of the British Phantom was such that any longer detachment could have aircraft left on board awaiting spare parts. To ensure we disembarked on the 23rd, we planned to establish a maintenance unit at the US Facility at Sigonella Air Base in Sicily. We could fly an aircraft to this airfield if, during a flight from *Saratoga*, an aircraft suffered an equipment failure that we knew couldn't be rectified on board in time or through lack of spares. To satisfy *Saratoga*'s request for a Phantom to play with before the detachment, it was planned to fly one on board on 12 October.

That summer, 'C' Squadron, Boscombe Down, conducted the deck trial of the Phantom in HMS *Eagle*, the sister ship of *Ark Royal*, and cleared it for carrier operations with various modifications and recommendations. The aircraft they used had been considerably modified compared with the aircraft I had been flying in the States and in 700P. The cockpit instrumentation now included LPRPM gauges and a 'simple' method of calculating whether or not you were getting full engine thrust prior to launch by comparing LP and HPRPM with TGT and reheat nozzle position. Because the Phantom was also a bit touchy longitudinally on catapult launch, they had devised a modification to ensure a smooth catapult launch.

The Buccaneer had been the last aircraft cleared for carrier operations. Its longitudinal control system had been dynamically balanced during catapult launch, and pilots had been able to do a hands-off launch, providing the tailplane trim had been set correctly. However, the Phantom didn't have a dynamically balanced longitudinal control system. The test pilots had considered the best way to prevent any backward movement of the stick was to simulate the Buccaneer system. A stick positioning device (SPD) was installed. This consisted of a reel of flexible wire encased in housing mounted at the bottom of the instrument panel. One end of

The Saratoga detachment. *From left to right:* CPO Stringer, Alex Stuart, Roger Pinhey (ALO), Mike Maddox, Pip Coombes, John Leng, John Love, Hugh Drake, Brian Davies, Pat Knox, John Spencer, Rod O'Connor, Gene Carolan, Alan Hickling and Doug Mitchell (AEO) *(USN)*

On the catapult aboard USS *Saratoga* in 1969 *(USN)*

the wire protruded from the housing and could be pulled out by releasing a clutch. The loop on the end of this wire was placed over a hook on the forward face of the stick. The idea was that the Phantom stabilator could be set to the optimum position for the launch, the wire placed over the hook and tensioned against the clutch. The break-out force of the clutch was set to hold the stick in place during the launch. Thus, you would be able to fly away from the deck virtually hands-off. After launch the wire could be unhooked from the stick. The break-out force on the clutch was around 30 lb. So you could pull back on the stick with the wire attached, but it would need one hell of a pull so to do. Associated with this device was a table of various centre of gravity (CG) positions and the stabilator position for various aircraft configurations.

The summer passed with some six crews on a separate programme of catapult launches, MADDLs and deck landing practice (DLP) in preparation for the *Saratoga* detachment. The catapult at RAE Bedford was used to practise the launches using the SPD, and HMS *Eagle* was made available on occasions to practise some touch and goes.

It was around September when I was told I had been selected as the Royal Navy's 'Man of the Year'. The British Council for the Rehabilitation of the Disabled had established this annual award to around fifteen men who were nominated by various agencies as having achieved something of note during the year in question. It had started in 1960, and past nominees had included Sir Bernard Lovell, Sir Francis Chichester, Roland Beamont and Sir Alex Rose. The year 1969 would include members of the British Antarctic Expedition, John Fairfax and Tom McLean the Atlantic rowers and Jackie Stewart who had won the World Racing Drivers' Championship. I assumed my nomination was for the Trans-Atlantic Air Race. The dispositions were to be presented at a lunch at the Savoy Hotel on 13 November. I felt rather overwhelmed.

The *Saratoga* deployment really started on 9 October, when Alan Hickling and I flew two Phantoms to Malta in preparation to land one on board on 12 October. We had taken two Phantoms to guarantee one would be serviceable to take aboard. We had already deployed a maintenance team to Luqa, so if any problems arose there was a fighting chance they would be fixed.

Alan and I took off from Luqa on the 12th and made our way out to *Saratoga* operating to the south of Sicily. She made herself available for both of us to conduct some touch and goes. I eventually landed on and Alan returned to Luqa.

The list of recipients

MEN OF THE YEAR 1969

Selected by The British Council for Rehabilitation of the Disabled, from nominations submitted by the Home Office, the Services and the Press

Capt. J. R. Chapman, M.B.E., 1st Battalion Green Howards.
Sqd/Leader F. Church, R.A.F., Radio Operator, British Transarctic Expedition.
Lt./Commander B. Davies, A.F.C., Royal Navy.
Flt/Sgt. F. S. Ditchfield, B.E.M., Royal Air Force.
Sub. Officer J. Docherty, B.E.M., London Fire Brigade.
John Fairfax Esq., Atlantic Rower, Westbound.
Robert D. Hearn Esq., M.A., Dip.Ed., English Rugger Cap.
Major K. Hedges, M.B., Ch.B., R.A.M.C., Medical Officer, British Transarctic Expedition.
W. Herbert Esq., Leader, British Transarctic Expedition.
Trooper Tom McClean, Atlantic Rower, Eastbound,
Coxswain/Mechanic Eric Offer, Royal National Lifeboat Institution.
David Ryder Esq. Polio walker from John O'Groats to Lands End.
Jackie Stewart Esq., World Champion Racing Driver.
M. B. S. Tulloh Esq., Ran from West to East America.
Det. Sgt. John S. N. Wharton, G.M., Metropolitan Police.
Det. Constable Philip J. D. Williams, G.M., Metropolitan Police.

24

THE CHEQUE OR COVENANT ENCLOSED WILL HELP THE BRITISH COUNCIL FOR REHABILITATION OF THE DISABLED IN THEIR WORK OF RESTORATION OF THOSE WHO THROUGH PHYSICAL OR MENTAL DISABILITY ARE UNABLE TO LEAD A NORMAL LIFE

To save you posting it please hand the form to the young ladies at the door on your way out

REHAB
Tavistock House (South)
London, W.C.1

Men of the Year Luncheon

This disposition records that

Lt Commander B. Davies,
A.F.C.

was elected a

Man of the Year

by the British Council
for Rehabilitation of
the Disabled

Signed

Chairman

Dated this Thirteenth
Day of November 1969
Savoy Hotel, London.

The Man of the Year Disposition

The *Saratoga* was enormous. It was at least a third larger than *Ark Royal* and had a fully angled deck. By the time you got over the round-down, it looked as if you could pick and choose where you landed.

I remained on board *Saratoga* with our advanced maintenance party for the four days she spent in Naples. They got used to the differences between our Phantom and theirs. On 17 October the *Saratoga* put to sea and I was the first aircraft to be launched from the port bow catapult to meet up with the three other Phantoms of 892, which had flown directly from UK to land on the ship. The launch itself was very smooth, and the aircraft flew away very well from the deck using the SPD. The *Saratoga* gave the four of us some touch and go practice before the final hook-on.

The first launch of two FG 1s on 19 October resulted in the splitting of welded seams on the starboard bow catapult deck-cooling panel. The increased attitude of the FG 1 on the catapult put the bottom of the engine exhaust pipes only inches above the deck. The intense heat generated by the engine reheats at full power proved too much for the deck cooling system. Subsequent launches during the detachment were made without using the reheat and were therefore at a reduced weight. So, the FG 1s weren't able to integrate into the deck cycle of 1 hour 45 minutes, due to lack of fuel. The programme was re-adjusted to a short-cycle operation for us of just 20 to 30 minutes. *Saratoga* would launch the FG 1s first and we would tag on the end of the landing cycle to at least experience the recovery control system on a US carrier and to get in some DLP. We managed to get some operational experience with the aid of the ship's A-3 tankers. Two aircraft per day were launched and then immediately topped up by an A-3 so that they could complete the 1 hour 45 minutes operational rotation.

The five-day operation was soon over, and on 23 October we flew the four aircraft off *Saratoga* directly to Yeovilton with the assistance of a couple of A-3 tankers. Those of us on the detachment came away very impressed by the way *Saratoga* had operated. The first impression of the ship was one of capability. It was big enough and

Landing on the USS *Saratoga* *(USN)*

Topping up from the A-3 tanker *(USN)*

had the hardware to do more or less anything. The specialist A-3 tankers made life much easier and safer for the overall carrier operation. A tanker would be launched at the beginning of a deck cycle to provide fuel to those aircraft that might be a bit short. The RN depended on a spare deck or being in range of a shore diversion airfield.

However, modern warfare demanded the ability to know what the electronic environment was. To this end, the FG 1 fell well short of current tactical thinking. At Patuxent River I had pointed out that no provision had been made for any passive electronic countermeasures equipment in the FG 1. The response had been that this sort of equipment wouldn't be necessary for RN operations. In fact, we were now sadly disadvantaged compared with VF 103. All their F-4Js were equipped with passive warning of S, X and C band radar transmissions, enabling their crews to know what sort of radar was scanning them or what sort of missile system was scanning them. Finally, they were able to know if a missile system had locked onto them so that they could take avoiding action. In the FG 1 we knew nothing.

From the deck operation point of view, the *Saratoga* had been pure luxury. The ship was equipped with four catapults – two on the bow and two waist catapults located on the angled deck.

The detachment also highlighted many problems with the FG 1. The extra extensible NLG seemed to work well enough, and luckily we had only had to change one of them, but it turned out to be a two-day job. The use of the SPD proved very cumbersome and took up a lot of time on the catapult

We also found that setting the SPD to the correct angle for launch was a bit dodgy. As it happened, I was the one to find out about it. Although the tables relating to stabilator angle versus CG gave an angle at which to set the stabilator, there was no stabilator angle indicator in the cockpit. Having decided on the angle to be used, it was up to a member of the catapult team to give you the 'thumbs up' when you had set the required angle. On the launch in question he got it wrong. I was fired off with the stabilator very much out of trim, nose down. Apparently the aircraft sank out of sight of the catapult crew as it went off the bow. From my point of view I realised I was heading for the sea. I just pulled through the breakout force to around 35 lb. The aircraft pitched up and climbed without stalling. It was subsequently estimated that I had dropped about 60 feet off the bow. All subsequent launches were made over trimmed nose-up, and once some experience had been gained of the post-launch handling characteristics, all the pilots considered that the SPD wasn't really necessary.

On the deck operating side of things, the FG 1 proved to be a more unstable aircraft to deck land than the F-4J. The bolter situation proved satisfactory. The '7th at Mil Power' switch worked because you could feel the extra power come in as you hit the Mil

The forward deck park on board the USS *Saratoga*, 1969 *(USN)*

An elongated Phantom. The length of the aircraft accurately measured its speed just before deck arrest *(Crown copyright)*

stop. The one thing that concerned me was the day this switch failed!

All the other problems related to the reliability of the Spey engine and ancillary equipment. Nothing major had gone wrong, but any extended embarkation would have seen the necessity to change the engines on a regular basis. The engine starter systems were unreliable. Luckily we didn't have any failures, but the time taken to change the left one was four hours and the right one twelve. The CSDUs were still lifed on engine oil analysis. We had sent specimens off to the UK on 20 October. They had shown the requirement to change one of the CSDUs. However, we hadn't received this information, and the aircraft in question had flown another nine hours without the CSDU failing. All in all we had some way to go.

During November I attended the 'Men of the Year' luncheon at the Savoy Hotel, London. However, I was now beginning to feel a bit of a fraud in having been nominated for the honour. With the demise of the conventional aircraft carrier within eighteen months, I was seriously considering whether my future lay in the Royal Navy.

Chapter 23

December 1969

In December 1969 I had to make a decision. I think most of us at the sharp end of the RN and RAF knew the staff proposals relating to the RAF providing air cover for the fleet within the NATO area were pipe dreams. There was no doubt that on paper there was a plausible argument to be considered, but the reality was that 24-hour air cover would be very thin on the ground and very inflexible. However, there was no refuting the fact that getting rid of aircraft carriers would save a lot of government money!

The first big defence review had come in 1957 with the 'Sandys Axe', when the Army and RAF had been hardest hit. Mr Sandys, the then Secretary of State for Defence, had been persuaded that the era of the missile had arrived and that manned fighters would not be needed in future. Enemy bombers would be shot down by surface-to-air missiles. The RAF's roles would be to provide a strategic bombing capability and air transport for our smaller Army. The latest defence review would remove the fixed-wing element of the FAA, leaving the RN without any viable air defence and with no Airborne Early Warning for the fleet.

I was beginning to wonder where I might fit into this new RN. The officer structure has its *raison d'être* based on promotion. Unless you can find a niche you enjoy, the pressure is ever upwards. Lack of promotion implies failure. Within the RN promotion to the rank of Lieutenant-Commander on the General List was automatic. It became selective to the rank of Commander within a zone of two to seven years' seniority as a Lieutenant-Commander. Promotion selections were made every six months in June and December within the zone. Obviously my name had been through the mill a few times without being selected for promotion. I had six years' seniority as a Lieutenant-Commander and only had two shots at promotion left.

There was a Prussian general of the 19th century who had assessed all officers as having two of four possible qualities. They were intelligent or stupid, industrious or lazy. He considered the stupid lazy officer would do as he was told. The stupid industrious officer was an absolute menace. The intelligent industrious officer would make a good staff officer and the intelligent lazy officer would always get to the top. On a very simplistic basis it was a good evaluation. Other than industry occasionally being mistaken for intelligence it probably worked well.

It would be fair to say I was lazy. The simple, honest solution would always be the best in my book. It was really a question of whether I was intelligent enough for senior rank.

Intelligence in the sense of IQ wasn't the issue. Intelligence in the RN related to convincing the chap who was going to write your report that you had done a good job. It was also necessary to make sure that you managed to manoeuvre yourself into the sort of job that attracted the best reports. The best jobs in which to do this were in the mainstream RN.

I was beginning to realise that I hadn't been very intelligent. Over the years I had managed to get the jobs that I had wanted, but these related to getting the jobs I wanted to do and not the jobs that were best for my naval career. From the promotion point of view, you were pushing your luck to become a test pilot, since it involved some four years out of the mainstream RN. Ironically, I was also CO of a squadron that was operating an aircraft that I had been instrumental in not accepting into service. As a result of the Air Race a lot of senior naval officers now knew who I was, but whether it would do me any good in the promotional stakes was debatable.

In any case, if I were promoted what on earth would I do? I couldn't continue my career as a very specialised fixed-wing aviator in a navy with only helicopters. I could possibly do a staff course, which would set me up to fly a desk. But even if it happened it wasn't me. To be honest with myself, the only course of action was to leave the Service and pursue a career in civil aviation. From a domestic point of view the family had become nomadic. Anne and I had now been married for ten years and had lived together and apart in nine different houses. With two children we felt we should be establishing ourselves somewhere, but with the decimation of Naval Aviation where would that somewhere be? We discussed the situation, and Anne said she was happy with whatever I wanted to do.

December 1969 was the crunch point for me in that the RN had established a financially attractive voluntary redundancy scheme for officers in the more senior bracket in the ranks of Lieutenant-Commander, Commander and Captain. The deadline for applications ran out on 31 December 1969. In my own mind I had determined that I was more an aviator than a naval officer. In the words of Thomas Carlisle, 'There is an endless merit for a man to know when to have done.' I applied for redundancy.

Chapter 24

892 Squadron Aboard HMS *Ark Royal*

January to September 1970

We were ready to embark in *Ark Royal*. It was just a matter of waiting for the ship to get to sea. Our only problems related to the poor aircraft availability as a result of the unreliability of the engines, ancillary equipment and radar. Outside that, everything was 'hunky dory'.

Ark Royal commissioned on 24 February 1970. I attended the ceremony with Anne and was presented to Her Majesty Queen Elizabeth the Queen Mother, who was to commission the ship, for the second time.

In March I was informed that my application for redundancy had been successful. In some ways it came as a shock to think that I would have to start again in another career in my late thirties. However, I managed to talk myself into membership of the British Institute of Management through the auspices of Sir Leslie Rowan, the then chairman of Vickers, and attended the odd redundancy course.

I would not be leaving soon. The RN wanted me to remain as CO of 892 until the Phantoms had become established in *Ark Royal*. I was the guy who knew all the problems and could possibly help sort them out.

At the end of April we embarked three Phantoms in the Ark to conduct a deck trial to prove the arrester gear and catapults. Having just come out of refit, it was necessary to find out if the ship's major equipment worked OK. Things seemed to go reasonably well, and, unlike *Saratoga*, no problems were experienced with the deck cooling systems behind the catapults at full reheat power. From the qualitative point of view we found the ship had a bit of a 'hole' just short of the stern where, if you didn't apply a bit of power, the Phantom sank below the glide path just prior to deck arrest. We

HMS *Ark Royal*'s commissioning on 24 February 1970. Brian Davies is presented to Her Majesty Queen Elizabeth the Queen Mother by Captain Lygo RN (far left) while his wife Anne looks on (far right) *(Crown copyright)*

would become proficient at anticipating this characteristic in the future.

On 12 June *Ark Royal* embarked all her squadrons for the final eighteen-month commission. They consisted of 892 Phantoms, 809 Buccaneers, 824 Sea Kings and 849B Flight of AEW Gannets. We remained in the English Channel to shake down the ship into an operational unit. It was during this period that we lost the first Phantom, killing the crew. It was a mystery as to what happened. The aircraft was flying unmonitored by ship's radar and just disappeared. It never came back to land on. The aircraft had obviously crashed into the sea without the crew ejecting, and after an extensive search of the area no wreckage was found. It was assumed that the accident was as a result of pilot error, since no radio transmissions were received to indicate that the aircraft had mechanical trouble. Anne and the wife of the Captain of Yeovilton visited the widows.

Night flying was commenced in the middle of July, using a few of the more experienced and capable pilots. We still had problems with the speed stability of the aircraft in the landing configuration, but had managed to cope with it during day operations. I still remember my first night arrested landing in a Phantom. It was one of my more dodgy arrivals on the deck of a ship. Night deck landing didn't give you a very good aspect of where you were on the approach until you were in amongst the arrester wires. And my hook bounced on the deck before number 1 wire!

The month of August saw us disembarked back at Yeovilton. We re-embarked at the beginning of September to take part in the autumn exercises off Norway. A significant incident that month was when John Leng, luckily one of the best of the inexperienced pilots, launched from the catapult and subsequently couldn't retract the landing gear because the extra extensible NLG didn't shrink after launch. In this event the book recommended ejection, since it would be too dangerous to recover the aircraft aboard, or land it at an airfield, with the rigid nose strut. The only way the NLG could be shrunk was through the automatic switchery (there was no manual override), and I think this failure had originally come under the 'it can't happen' school of thought, but if it did, we weren't likely to lose that many aircraft!

However, having already lost one Phantom, I think the political situation wouldn't allow us to lose two in such a short period of time. This could be considered carelessness! It was decided to go against the book and attempt to land the Phantom at RNAS Lossiemouth nearby.

To attempt to land a Phantom on a runway with the NLG extended and rigid was rather dangerous and would require skill from the pilot. Unless flown very delicately onto the ground, the strut could sheer. If you managed to get it on the ground in one piece the nose-wheel steering would be inoperative, and differential braking would strain the NLG even more.

I talked to John on the radio and told him what had been decided. I briefed him on the pitfalls we could think of and mentioned that the very last thing not to do was land too fast, contacting the runway nose-wheel first! The ejector seat envelope for the Phantom had been improved to be able to eject at ground level above 100 knots. If he wasn't happy about things above this speed he was to bang out. The weather at Lossie was fine with little surface wind. I wished him luck. Fifteen minutes later we heard that John had made a successful landing without mishap.

I handed over the squadron to my Senior Pilot, Nick Kerr, and flew off the ship for the last time on 26 September. Nick had taken over from Doug Borrowman earlier in the year. Doug had moved on to take command of 767 Squadron.

I was leaving 892 to join 781 Squadron at Lee-on-Solent. It was a communications squadron operating Sea Heron and Sea Devon light transport aircraft. I would be able to obtain my civil flying licences through their auspices. I had arranged for Service married quarter accommodation at Seafield Park nearby, and in October the family moved down to the coast for my final year in the RN.

Chapter 25

781 Squadron, RNAS Lee-on-Solent

October 1970 to February 1972

I moved straight down to Lee-on-Solent as soon as I left 892. Anne and the family followed as soon as the married quarter was finalised. It felt a little strange having responsibility for nothing apart for myself. However, the level of work soon put Phantom flying firmly in the past. I spent the first two weeks converting to the Devon and Heron. I obtained an instrument rating and got used to flying in UK controlled airspace.

The aircraft were equipped with a single VOR VHF navigation beacon, an associated instrument landing system (ILS), a short-range medium-frequency non-directional beacon (NDB) and a Decca area navigation system. The Decca could give your position accurately anywhere in the UK, Europe and the Mediterranean. Both the Heron and Devon were unpressurised and had to be flown below 10,000 feet. The official crew comprised a pilot and a Petty Officer crewman who flew with you to assist in the operation of the Decca and with two-way VHF communications in controlled

The de Havilland Sea Heron *(Crown copyright)*

airspace. However, all the pilots were capable of coping with the aircraft and systems when flying solo. There was one WREN who flew with us as a stewardess if the passengers were very VIP, but otherwise the passengers just sat in the back and did as they were told from instructions shouted from the flight deck. The Devon carried eight passengers and the Heron fourteen.

The flying was a mixture of one-off VIP flights and a scheduled service up and down the country connecting all the airstations and outstations in the UK. The longest regular run we did was from Lee-on-Solent to Lossiemouth via Yeovilton, Belfast Harbour, Glasgow/Prestwick and Edinburgh. We would night stop at Lossie and do the reverse run the next day: two quite busy days when flown at 150 knots.

From the test-flying days of getting 15 hours per month, I was now clocking up some 60 hours a month of quite exhausting flying. I was beginning to realise what an easy time I had had swanning around in the stratosphere, clear of all the weather, or stacking for the day if the weather at the home base became unflyable. Flogging up and down the airways at low level in the UK in winter, in a relatively unheated aircraft, coping with turbulence from the occasional shower cloud, of which you had no pre-warning, airframe and engine icing became quite a challenge.

The flying qualities of the Heron left a little to be desired under these conditions. I think it must have been designed to fly in the warmer climes of the British Empire. By modern standards it had a very large wing for the size of aircraft, and in extreme turbulence its handling qualities could only be described as akin to a leaf. On one occasion I recall having to abandon an approach to Belfast Harbour when the turbulence became so severe on the approach that I virtually lost lateral control of the aircraft. I had to fly back to Liverpool airport to find suitable landing conditions.

There were many occasions during my time on the squadron where bad weather conditions proved challenging, but it would take too long, and be too boring, to recount them all. However, it was a period in my naval career when the elements re-established themselves as something very much to be contended with in the flying world.

To be able to get a flying job in civil aviation I had to get a pilot's licence. There were a number of tests and examinations I had to pass to enable the Board of Trade (Civil Aviation Division) to issue me with a licence, and the RN was not averse to me using 781 Squadron aircraft for this purpose. In fact 781 Squadron had built up a large file on how it was all done, and what tests and examinations had to be passed.

The main hurdle to jump was the written examination. If you wanted to eventually command a large civil airliner it was necessary for you to pass the examination for the Airline Transport Pilot's Licence. I had more than enough flying experience to qualify for the licence, so it was a question of studying for the ATPL written examination. These examinations were held periodically during the year at a number of locations throughout the country.

I eventually managed to pass the written exam in the summer of 1971. However, the licensing authorities insisted that all of the licence requirements be completed within a comparatively short time. That summer I used the Devon to fly out of Stansted airport on my civil instrument rating test, flew a type rating on the Devon and obtained my RT licence. On 8 October the Board of Trade issued me with an ATPL. It had taken a little longer than I thought.

Meanwhile back in the mainstream of the RN, *Ark Royal* had been reprieved from the scrapyard. The Tories had won the election of 1970 and the Heath government reversed the decision of the outgoing Labour government. The 'Ark' would now remain in service indefinitely. That meant the personnel who had been made redundant were now no longer surplus to requirements. Suddenly there was a shortage of Lieutenant-Commanders.

However, unless a new carrier-building programme was established, the shortfall would be temporary. The programme to build the 'through deck cruiser' was established, which would eventually result in the building of our present-day aircraft carriers. However, these ships were not intended to replace the multi-role aircraft carrier like the *Ark Royal*, but rather to retain a restricted fixed-wing capability in the form of the Sea Harrier.

I eventually established a release date around January 1972, thus enabling me to apply for flying positions during the winter months. Although I was an experienced pilot, there would be no question of my leaping straight into a modern airline as an aircraft commander (Captain). I would have to spend some time as a co-pilot to obtain sufficient experience.

The alternative to joining an airline was to take a job in general aviation operating in command of a private aircraft, but at the beck and call of the owner. On my initiation into airways flying with 781, I completed a link trainer course at Gatwick airport with an outfit called Air London owned by a guy called Tony Mack. As a finale to the course I had flown in a twin-jet executive aircraft with a crew who were renewing their civil instrument rating. They had flown in from Athens for the tests. They flew as captain and co-pilot for Stavros Niarchos, the Greek shipping magnate, and I asked what their routine was like. They implied that it wasn't too demanding.

Apart from grouse shooting in Scotland and going on Safari in Africa, where they would be away from home and on call, life was very nice thank you. They had the use of the aircraft most weekends and could take their wives shopping anywhere in Europe. The Captain was on £10,000 a year, quite a tidy sum in 1970. I began to wonder whether I could find myself a similar job!

At the other extreme, I had contacted an ex-RAF Squadron Leader called Stew Mead who was the chief pilot of a one-horse outfit called JF Airways operating out of Portsmouth's grass airfield using Twin Pioneers. The 'Twin Pins' operated a service to the Channel Islands. A local car dealer owned the airline. Stew took me on a flight to Guernsey. I hadn't flown a Twin Pin before, but it seemed quite fun. I could have a job with JF as a Captain and there was some thought about them buying Yak 40s, a twin-engined small Russian airliner being offered to the West through an Italian agency. The one aircraft we had seen had the registration I-JAKA! The idea was that the Yak 40 would operate from Shoreham airport along the coast near Worthing. After a couple of months Stew seemed to think the business side of the airline wasn't doing too well and didn't see the outfit lasting very long. Stew and I were to meet up in the future, flying for Dan Air Services out of Gatwick.

I made up a CV and went to interview with various airlines. The CV had been constructed to cover everything I had done over the past 20 years. It was not well received by a chief pilot of a well-known airline. Having called me for interview he harangued me about my intentions. With all my experience and management qualifications, did I think I would be joining to get his job? He considered me far too qualified to join his organisation as a junior First Officer.

In the end I accepted a job with a new airline. Courtline Aviation flew holidaymakers out of Luton Airport using BAC 1-11s. The two main reasons I had for joining Courtline were that there was a high proportion of ex-FAA pilots with them, and Peter Dibley, the Chief Pilot, seemed quite the nicest man I had met in civil aviation to date. Also, at the time of my interview, Peter Dibley had implied that I would probably get a command in a year or so.

Anne and I started to look for a house in the late autumn of 1971, and eventually bought a three-bedroom property on half an acre in the village of Aspley Guise near Woburn on the Berks./Bedford border. It was the time of gazumping. House prices were rising rapidly, and we ended up in a bidding race for the house, eventually buying it at the inflated price of £13,700!

My final month in the RN related to sorting out my finances. I was entitled to a small pension, and as far as the Service was concerned I was now a pensioner. I left the RN on 3 February 1972. As a junior First Officer with Courtline I would start on a salary of £3,500 a year. My salary as a senior Lieutenant-Commander was £3,700 a year, and my pension more than made up the difference. Everything in the garden looked rosy.

But that's another story.

Glossary

A&AEE	Aeroplane and Armament Experimental Establishment
AAI	Angle of Attack Indicator
AAL	Aircraft Approach Limitation
A/B	Afterburner
ACR	Aircraft Control Room. Where the location and designation of all aircraft on board a carrier is kept
ACM	Air Combat Manoeuvring
ACRO	Aircraft Control Room Officer. The officer who runs the ACR
ADDL	Assimilated Dummy Deck Landing. Practice deck landing at an airfield in association with a Batsman and the old straight deck-landing configuration of aircraft carriers
Audio ADD	Airspeed Detection Device. An audio system that indicates to the pilot the speed of an aircraft in the landing configuration
AEO	Air Engineer Officer
AEW	Airborne Early Warning
AI	Airborne Intercept radar
ALO	Air Electrical Officer
ASI	Air Speed Indicator
ATC	Air Traffic Control
ATPL	Airline Transport Pilot's Licence
auw	all up weight
AWACS	Airborne Warning And Control System
AWF	All-Weather Fighter
AWG	Air Weapon Guided
AWI	Air Weapons Instructor
Batsman	Landing Signals Officer qualified to land aircraft on a carrier using 'bats'. Associated with straight deck landing
blc	Boundary layer control. Air from the compressor of a jet engine 'blown' over the flaps and/or ailerons to reduce approach speed
BNS	British Naval Staff, Washington DC
Bolter	A failure to hook an arrester wire when attempting to land on a carrier's flight deck
BPC	Barometric Pressure Control
CCA	Carrier Controlled Approach. Same as a GCA at an airfield, but without glidepath information
CG	Centre of Gravity
CPO	Chief Petty Officer
CRDF	Cathode Ray Direction Finder. Used in Air Traffic Control to obtain a bearing of an aircraft's radio transmission

CSDU	Constant Speed Drive Unit
CTFI	Chief Test Flying Instructor
'Cut'	Mandatory signal from a Batsman to cut engine power
DB	Development Batch. Pre-production aircraft built to conduct trial flights
DLP	Deck Landing Practice. Those arrested and 'touch and go' landings conducted on a carrier's deck during a session of deck landing practice
DF	Direction Finder
DME	Distance Measuring Equipment. Associated with a TACAN beacon
DR	Ded(uced) Reckoning
ECM	Electronic Counter Measures. *Passive* relates to listening to radio and radar transmissions to determine their nature. *Active* relates to jamming radio and radar transmissions. Active ECM is also known as Electronic Warfare
Elint	Electronic intelligence. Relates to Russian spy ships that would shadow NATO forces in particular in the '50s, '60s and '70s to obtain intelligence on frequencies used and NATO techniques
ERU	Ejector Release Unit. A 'gun' which fired bombs off aircraft wing and bomb bay stations. Also used to release external fuel tanks
ESB	Empire State Building
ETPS	Empire Test Pilots' School
FAA	Fleet Air Arm
FDO	Flight Deck Officer
FDEO	Flight Deck Engineer Officer
FLYCO	Flying Control. Controls all operations on the flight deck
FOAC	Flag Officer Aircraft Carriers
FONAC	Flag Officer Naval Air Command
FOST	Flag Officer Sea Training
FTS	Flying Training School
'g'	Units of Gravity
GCA	Ground-Controlled Approach
Gloworm	A 3-inch rocket flare used to illuminate a target
Go around	Abandoning an approach to land on a carrier or airfield
HP	High Pressure
HPRPM	High Pressure Turbine RPM
IAS	Indicated Air Speed

IFTU	Intensive Flying Trials Unit
IGV	inlet guide vane
ILS	Instrument Landing System
IP	Initial Point. A navigation position used in a LABS Long Toss manoeuvre
IRE	Instrument Rating Examiner
LABS	Low Altitude Bombing System
Long Toss	A LABS bombing manoeuvre which 'throws' a bomb forward from the bombing aircraft. The bomb release occurs at around 45 degrees on a pull-up into a loop manoeuvre
LPRPM	Low-Pressure Turbine RPM
LSO	Landing Signals Officer
MADDL	Mirror Assimilated Dummy Deck Landings. To practise carrier approaches at an airfield using a Mirror Landing Sight
Manoeuvre Margin	a term used to generally describe the ability to manoeuvre an aircraft between the stall speed and maximum speed or MN. It relates to the amount of 'g' available to manoeuvre and depends on speed, altitude, MN and the 'g' limit of the aircraft. For example, at the straight and level stall speed there is no manoeuvre margin. The 'g' limit is only available within a certain speed/MN range.
MFV	Motor Fishing Vessel
Min Tech	Ministry of Technology
MLS	Mirror Landing Sight
MN	Mach number
NAS	Naval Air Station (US)
NASC	Naval Air Systems Command. A USN equipment procuring agency based in Washington DC, USA
NATC	Naval Air Test Center. A USN agency that tests aircraft and equipment against specification for introduction into service use. Based at NAS Patuxent River, Maryland, USA
NDB	Non-Directional Beacon
NLG	Nose Landing Gear
NPE	Naval Preliminary Evaluation. A system of equipment evaluation used at NATC
ODM	Operating Data Manual
OFS	Operational Flying School
OR	Operational Requirement
OTS	Over the Shoulder. A LABS manoeuvre that uses the target as a pull-up point

PIO	Pilot-Induced Oscillation
PR	Public Relations or Photo-Reconnaissance
PRF	Pulse Repetition Frequency
PUP	Pull-up Point. The position in a LABS attack at which the aircraft is 'pulled up' into the bomb delivery manoeuvre
QFI	Qualified Flying Instructor
RAE	Royal Aircraft Establishment
RIO	Radar Intercept Officer. The USN's equivalent of the RN observer in two-seat All-Weather Fighter aircraft
RNC	Royal Naval College
SAM	Surface-to-Air Missile
SObs	Senior Observer. Second-in-command of an RN aircraft squadron or the most senior observer
SP	Senior Pilot. Second-in-Command of an RN aircraft squadron or the most senior pilot
SPD	Stick Positioning Device
ST	Service Test
TACAN	Tactical Air Navigation beacon
TAS	True Air Speed
TGT	Turbine Gas Temperature. The temperature at the turbine in a jet engine
Touch and go	The term used to describe a 'hook up' practice deck landing
VSI	Vertical Speed Indicator
Wave off	A mandatory command to abandon a deck landing and 'go around'

Index

The index is arranged alphabetically, except for entries under Brian Davies, which are in chronological order. Page numbers in italics refer to illustrations.

Index

Index